# Rethinking Consumer Protection

# Rethinking Consumer Protection

## Escaping Death by Regulation

Thomas Tacker

LEXINGTON BOOKS
*Lanham • Boulder • New York • London*

Published by Lexington Books
An imprint of The Rowman & Littlefield Publishing Group, Inc.
4501 Forbes Boulevard, Suite 200, Lanham, Maryland 20706
www.rowman.com

6 Tinworth Street, London SE11 5AL, United Kingdom

British Library Cataloguing in Publication Information Available

**Library of Congress Cataloging-in-Publication Data Available**

ISBN 978-1-4985-7741-0 (cloth : alk. paper)
ISBN 978-1-4985-7743-4 (pbk : alk. paper)
ISBN 978-1-4985-7742-7 (electronic)

∞™ The paper used in this publication meets the minimum requirements of American National Standard for Information Sciences—Permanence of Paper for Printed Library Materials, ANSI/NISO Z39.48-1992.

Printed in the United States of America

# Contents

# Introduction

This book is designed to appeal to anyone who is at all interested in topics related to making life better and safer—for all us consumers. Our current approach to consumer protection is extremely flawed; sometimes costing lives rather than saving them. There are better ways to protect ourselves and the people we love.

Whether you are a beginner or an experienced practitioner or scholar, there will be some relevant content for you here. However, scholars and other experts would likely be most interested in the case studies in chapters 2, 3, 4, and 6. These studies are not overly technical, easily comprehensible without prior study, but they do thoroughly cover existing scholarship along with some practical extensions. Chapters 1 and 5 are primarily targeted toward readers who are not experts on economics and consumer protection or for professors and instructors looking for some teaching ideas on these topics. The material in these chapters has been shaped by hundreds of class discussions with thousands of students over my teaching career. That teaching experience is mostly with college students, but I've also taught a fair amount in high schools, Elder hostels, and on-site to industry practitioners since I began teaching these topics in the 1980s. (Let's assume I was a child prodigy economist, starting my teaching career at age 7!) Hopefully, all this varied experience and feedback has helped to make this material more stimulating and easier to understand.

Chapter 1 covers some foundational economic and moral issues, beginning with regulatory concerns and problems inherent in attempting to protect consumers from high prices. Chapter 2 details unintended dangers created by our current regulatory approach regarding the approval of new medicines, while chapter 3 explains how we can dramatically reduce the cost of those medicines while also saving many thousands of lives every year. The

study of consumer protection regulation, much as the study of most anything involving politics, can be a bit depressing. Politicians so commonly disappoint; so much harm continues to be needlessly inflicted on consumers by the corruption and ineptness of the political process. But once in a while, reason prevails, harmful policies are reformed, and we actually have a mostly happy ending. We see this in chapter 4 for the case of taxi regulation reform. Moreover, the rise of Uber and other rideshare services demonstrates how the modern technology used to make both passengers and drivers safer might be applied more broadly to better protect consumers everywhere.

Chapter 5 addresses various issues that people tend to raise when first exposed to some of the surprising implications of the economics of regulation. The discussion there is eclectic not intended to be comprehensive. Instead, the idea of chapter 5 is to briefly address some worries that occur to people as they begin to contemplate leaving consumers more free to make their own choices. Hopefully, it will help readers begin to reconcile common preconceptions with some unexpected implications of economic analysis. Chapter 6 details the fatal flaws inherent in our approach to airport security screening and explains both ideal reform and a feasible beginning. Chapter 7 wraps things up with a short discussion of lessons learned and practical steps we can take on the road to ideal reform. The essential idea is to more or less keep the regulations that mostly work while replacing ineffective, sometimes even harmful, command and control regulations with systems that advise consumers rather than rigidly limit their choices. Government becomes less a dictator and more an advisor. This is how we can escape death by regulation. If this book is half as interesting to read as it was to research and write, then you're going to love it.

# Chapter 1

# Economic Foundations of Morality and Consumer Well-Being

## MORAL JUDGMENTS AND KNOWLEDGE

Is it immoral to saw off someone's arm? Not if the arm is so seriously infected that it is impossible to save, and amputating it is the only way to save the patient's life. In this dismal scenario, morality requires amputation. Even so, a young child informed that a doctor plans to amputate the limb of someone they love might well believe that such an action is just inherently wrong. A lack of knowledge and understanding can sometimes sabotage one's moral compass. Our society's lack of knowledge in the area of economics often renders most of us confused about the workings and morality of an economy with substantial elements of free enterprise. We sometimes condemn certain behavior in business, falsely seeing immorality when, if we were better informed, we would see things in an entirely different light. In short, if one lacks a working understanding of economics—and most people do—then reasonable moral judgment involving economic issues is sometimes difficult if not impossible.

Consider, for instance, the issue of "price gouging," defined loosely as firms charging an "unfairly" high price. Notice, for starters, that there is no term in our language, or it seems any language, for unfairly low prices. Rock bottom, going out of business sale prices might well reflect tremendous suffering of a firm's owners and employees, soon to be unemployed. Nevertheless, consumers think of these prices as being simply "good deals!" So, we have a theory of morality where we consumers have a firm moral "right" to a "fair" price yet sellers have no rights at all. A moral theory with only self-serving rights and zero responsibility is clearly suspect; however, this is just the tip of the iceberg regarding flaws in this view.

3

## PRICE GOUGING CONFUSION

Price gouging often emerges as an issue in the aftermath of hurricanes and other natural disasters. Let us delve into a representative example—the price of a bag of ice in Charleston, South Carolina, after the devastation from hurricane Hugo back in late summer of 1989. In that year, under normal circumstances, a bag of ice cost around 80 cents. In the immediate aftermath of the hurricane the price shot up to a staggering $20 (Laband, 1989)! The vast majority of people, including me before I got into economics, would naturally assume that such a price was a prime illustration of immoral price gouging, sellers ripping off consumers because they could. But, in reality, that $20 price was the best possible price for consumers in the awful circumstances created by the hurricane.

Most surprisingly, even the poor are best served by channeling aid through the extraordinarily high price. If you are like most people you're probably thinking, "Economists must be crazy; the poor will just suffer and be forced to do without if that price is $20." Well, first keep in mind there are two possible main strategies to help the poor, somehow force the price lower or give them money so they can afford to buy at that high price. Forcing the price lower seems like a simple, expedient solution, one that allows us to help the poor (and ourselves if we are ice buyers in this case) without any actual sacrifice on our part—as long as we aren't the ones selling the ice. But, as we'll soon see in some detail, the expedient solution, as is often the case, is no solution at all and would make things much, much worse. The high price is analogous to the amputation example, a harsh treatment but still the only viable treatment. One problem with forcing price lower is that it will discourage some potential ice sellers from bringing ice in, especially if they live far away and will incur high costs to get to Charleston.

Economists virtually unanimously support giving the poor money rather than attempting to manipulate price in their favor. (If one counts only honest, drug-free economists this support is probably exactly unanimous, as we will see!) Actual government policy, to understate, does not always follow economic logic and consensus but in this regard it usually does. Let us leave the post-hurricane scenario for a moment, and consider the various standing government programs we have to help provide low-income people with enough food. These agencies may not be perfect but, thankfully, not a single one of them is so foolishly structured that it mandates that grocers must sell to the poor at below market prices. Main federal programs include Temporary Assistance for Needy Families, the Supplemental Security Program, the Supplemental Nutrition Assistance Program (food stamps), the Special Supplemental Food Program for Women, Infants, and Children (WIC), and the Supplemental Security Program (Jones and MaCurdy, 2018). These programs give either cash or vouchers, such as food stamps, to people with lower income so as to increase their buying power. There is controversy in the details, but increasing someone's buying power is a sensible way to try to aid them. Price control regulations requiring merchants to sell food to the poor at super low prices do not exist in these programs because such regulation would discourage sales to the poor and be far less effective than income supplements. Some might find a legal loophole to avoid selling to the poor altogether. Failing that, grocers might locate far from poor neighborhoods and convenient bus lines, or manage to be rude and offer poor quality and service to the poor as firms perversely compete to drive them away rather than attract them. Price controls are more likely to starve people than feed them. There are no circumstances, including hurricanes, which can alter this logical law of supply, suppressing price will suppress supply. To best aid the poor we need to increase their income, rather than sabotaging the pricing system we need to work within it.

## THE REAL CONFLICT: URGENT MEDICAL NEEDS VERSUS THE MASSES WITH SPOILING FOOD

Returning to post-hurricane Charleston, there was a crisis, due mainly to virtually all electrical power being knocked out, that created an ocean of need for ice (enormous demand) while simultaneously wiping out almost all available ice, leaving only a few bits of supply. In other words, it was quite impossible to get ice to everyone who needed it. In such a case, it is vital to conserve the ice mainly for those who need it most. Consider, for example, someone with lifesaving medicine that must be refrigerated, and if it is not refrigerated that person will die. In addition to preserving some vital medications ice can also be crucial in treating certain injuries and high fevers. But, if the price stays at a low, "fair" level, then most people, without urgent needs, will not stop to think that they should leave the tiny amount of available ice for those who really need it. Instead, most of us will grab any ice we can find to preserve food or chill down some cokes. (Or, perhaps chill something stronger to ease the pain imposed by the giant storm.)

The key struggle here is not between rich and poor but between those who need ice for urgent health needs and those who do not, those who will suffer and even die without ice versus those who might see some food items spoil. Furthermore, those with desperate medical needs are always vastly outnumbered in these situations; at a normal price these hordes of typical consumers will swarm everywhere, gobbling up every cube of ice they can find. The only feasible way to keep ice available for the greatest needs is to let the price rise so high that most people conclude purchase is uneconomical;

they would generally spend more on ice than their spoiling food is worth. This "exorbitant" price firmly drives us to conserve ice. Granted, a few will splurge and spend $20 just to cool down drinks but most will not. The soaring price happens naturally, virtually instantaneously and is the only practicable way to make sure the meager amount of available ice is used primarily to treat human health problems rather than preserving food or chilling drinks.

So, step one, making sure scant ice supplies are held back for urgent needs, is achieved. The vast majority of people with health needs for ice will be able to come up with the cash on their own or through family and friends, though not always without some hardship. Major hurricanes truly are disasters. But what about those people with urgent health needs who are destitute? Those who don't have $20, have nothing to sell for $20, and have no capacity to earn $20. The high price works wonders to screen out most (relatively) casual demand for ice but it doesn't, by itself, solve this problem. We, as a society unquestionably need to assist such people in need. But the only way to effectively help them is to buy the ice for them or give them the cash to buy it themselves. Happily, ours is an often generous society, and it is far easier to transfer purchasing power to the desperately needy than it is to transport ice. Charities such as the Salvation Army are quickly on the scene; FEMA may also be helpful, though perhaps not quite as quickly. The point is that these organizations have plenty of resources to buy ice for the destitute with health needs but, like all of our society, they aren't able to readily transport massive amounts of ice quickly. The hard part is finding those few bags of ice amidst an ocean of need; financing is comparatively easy. The high price makes sure ice is available to meet health needs, whether paid for by consumers, a charity, or government agency.

To drive this point home, consider a philanthropist with a truckload of ice anxious to help. Suppose this humanitarian has only two options to distribute ice: (1) give it away to whoever shows up in time to claim it, or (2) sell it for the going rate of $20. Giving it away, a natural impulse, would result in more people having ice to preserve that food or icing down those drinks, but very few, if any, of those with critical health needs would happen to show up just as the ice was being given away. Alternatively, charging $20, aka price gouging, would result in most of that ice being used for important health needs. The ice would not be quickly snatched up, providing high priority buyers time to find and buy the ice or arrange for someone to buy it for them. So, an enlightened philanthropist would wisely target her aid by "price gouging," then maybe giving the profits to the Salvation Army, as opposed to freely (randomly) distributing this suddenly rare, potentially lifesaving commodity to whoever happens to be around with a hankering for something cold to drink. Of course, our society praises the person giving ice away and vilifies the seller charging $20. We'll discuss just why there is pervasive economic confusion in our culture, and elsewhere, shortly.

## LAW OF SUPPLY: TO GET MUCH MORE ICE
## WITH FAST DELIVERY, PAY A HIGHER PRICE

Just as the high price sorts out priorities on the demand side, it works a similar magic regarding supply. To minimize suffering, in these situations, we need everyone who possibly can to drop whatever they're doing and rush into town with as much ice as they can handle, then leave and hurry back with more ice, and repeat. At the time of Hugo I was teaching at Embry-Riddle Aeronautical University in Daytona Beach. A number of our students who were young pilots were happy to fly ice into Charleston and, thanks to the price soaring to $20 a bag, they could afford (barely) to do so. Likewise, for other people, perhaps not quite so far from Charleston, taking time off work and renting a refrigerated truck became financially viable. This is the law of supply—an "unfairly" high price enables many more people to supply much more ice than does a normal, low "fair" price.

Even so, one can imagine that some suppliers were getting a much higher price than needed to motivate them. Perhaps, some teenagers living just out of the hurricane zone would willingly bring ice in for just $2; instead, they greedily enjoy "excessive" profits at $20. However, even "excessive" profits can sometimes be socially useful. For instance, these suppliers may rush back and forth frantically several times a day for $20 per bag versus a trip once a day for $2 bags. The higher price empowers them to buy more ice chests or use larger capacity, gas-guzzling vehicles, and it creates a lot of excitement and publicity that will help entice other people to join supply efforts. Still, there are likely to be some suppliers who in some sense are overpaid. Sellers, for example, who bring in no more ice at $20 than they would have brought at, say, $18, just as a few buyers will splurge and buy ice just to chill their beer a few sellers may earn "excessive" profits. But such imperfections are impossible to eliminate and relatively unimportant in the scheme of things. Amidst all the post-hurricane chaos the price, rather miraculously but also naturally, immediately leaps to $20 and thereby coordinates a disparate society, motivating appropriate conservation and supply efforts by the selfish and kind-hearted alike, and by those who can barely cover the cost of bringing in ice as well as those of great wealth. Moreover, this super-high price will last only exactly as long as it is needed. As power is restored demand for ice will decrease while supply simultaneously increases, the forces combining to bring price relentlessly lower until power is generally restored and price returns to its normal "fair," pre-hurricane level.


## PRICE CONTROL PROBLEMS

Unfortunately, the above scenario was not allowed to progress in this fashion at that fateful time in Charleston. Instead, politicians stepped in and set a legal maximum price of $2 per bag in order to prevent "price gouging" and ensure that the price was "fair." Law enforcers became "ice police," and a hotline was established so consumers could readily report "price gougers" and have them arrested and fined (Laband, 1989). This regulation was extremely popular and, as is not uncommon with popular regulations, disastrously harmful. Our Embry-Riddle students immediately stopped flying ice in since they could no longer cover the cost of the aircraft and fuel. Likewise, almost no one could afford to rent a refrigerated truck or even drive in with a bunch of filled ice chests. Only well-heeled or at least well-funded humanitarians, along with people barely outside the hurricane zone making a few sporadic trips, continued to bring in ice. The flow of ice, which had already been so small compared with the tremendous need, now slowed to a tiny trickle. In attempting to justify price controls, politicians will often cite "concern for the poor." But this is of no help to the poor. A low hypothetical price is useless when there is nothing to buy.

Even worse, perhaps, than the suppressed supply effects, the artificially low $2 price brought virtually all consumers back into the market, looking for ice to chill food and beverages. The extreme conservation practiced when the price was $20 gave way to virtually no conservation as an avalanche of demand was unleashed. The hordes of $2 consumers, or, more accurately, would-be consumers were like locusts frantically scouring the area and stripping away the last remaining morsels of food in an already barren land. Most of this swarm would end up with no ice but what little ice there was ended up mainly being devoured by some random few in their group. Thus, that tiny trickle of ice supplied was mainly snatched up by comparatively casual users. The low price helped essentially no one, least of all those with urgent medical needs, rich or poor. It merely unleashed a costly but mainly fruitless ice quest by the horde of consumers-cum-locusts who did not have urgent needs.

Figure 1.1 summarizes the harm done by the government price control. Initially, the $20 price motivated substantial, though still far from adequate, quantity supplied while simultaneously restraining quantity demanded, motivating the extreme conservation needed. Moreover, as market prices do, the price coordinated the actions of buyers and sellers so that ice, though expensive, was relatively easy to find since quantity demanded equaled quantity supplied, at Q*. Then, government forces the price down to $2, quantity supplied collapses to QS2 and quantity demanded explodes to QD2 as virtually all conservation efforts cease. Note, these results are a certainty, as inevitable as gravity; there is no competing economic theory that people might somehow conserve more when prices are lower or that suppliers will want to sell more when price is forcibly reduced to 1/10 of market value. There is no way that having far less ice and using it far less wisely can benefit society.

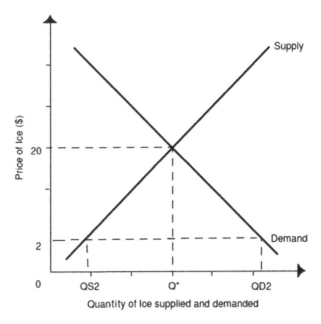

**Figure 1.1    Figure One.** *Source*: Author.

Also, since QD2 is huge, likely hundreds, even thousands of times greater than the measly QS2, ice sellers will quickly run out, finding ice becomes difficult, often impossible. This massive imbalance between supply and demand lead to a brutal, first come first served, competition as consumers fought over the few morsels of ice available. Long lines quickly formed whenever a rare chance to buy ice presented itself. Next, fights broke out and expanded into riots as people fought for position in line, realizing the ice would be grabbed up long before people at the end of the line would have a chance at it. The National Guard was called out to keep peace and order in these ridiculous lines that shouldn't even have existed (Laband, 1989). Most observers probably assumed that the massive lines, riots, and commonly fruitless treasure hunts for ice were all a product of the deadly hurricane and its aftermath. In reality, these particular disasters were unrelated to Hugo, a product of corrupt politics, though politicians gave us exactly the "fair price" most of us would demand.

Beginner students often suggest that maybe there could be some sort of compromise between the efficient price of $20 and a "moral" price. Economists maintain that efficiency and morality are synonymous in this example, as is often the case generally. Part of the students' confusion relates to our opening analogy of amputation. If the patient will die unless the whole arm is amputated, there is nothing moral about compromising by just cutting off a few fingers. What moral good is achieved by suppressing supplies of ice and encouraging casual consumption that denies ice to people with urgent needs? Furthermore, that $20 price was already a compromise; this is the direct implication of the facts as depicted in figure 1.1. For consumers, the lower the price the better; a zero price would be optimal from our viewpoint, or maybe even a negative price. Oh my, wouldn't it be great if the law required producers to just give us $20 and a free bag of ice! For producers, on the other hand, the higher the price the better. If the law required ice to be priced at $40 a bag, there likely would have been plenty of ice supplied. Many pilots could afford to fly ice in from all over the country!

We would never think of imposing a $40 legal price floor to make sure producers could afford to bring plenty of ice so that, "hypothetically," consumers could buy all the ice they wanted. We know better than to focus on producer affordability exclusively, ignoring affordability for consumers. But what we actually did with the price control was exactly equally foolish, as we myopically focused on only the consumer half of affordability. In our self-centered, foolhardy quest for a normal price in the midst of completely abnormal, massive disaster, we end up with no ice for most people. A unilateral approach to affordability only made things far worse. Only mutual affordability is worthwhile.

The price that maximizes mutual affordability, maximizes the amount of ice that consumers actually get, is the price where supply and demand intersect, the equilibrium price, in this case $20. A lower price increases quantity demanded by consumers but simultaneously depresses quantity supplied. Any price below $20 means fewer people, not more, actually get ice. People would be willing to buy more ice if only they could find it but it is certain that they won't be able to find it. Of course, imposing a $19 price would not have harmed consumers nearly as much as the $2 price control did but the general result is the same—less ice not as well conserved for the most crucial uses. Similarly, any price above $20 will depress quantity demanded, trumping the increase in quantity supplied, and also resulting in fewer people actually getting ice. We get ice to the most people with the most crucial needs at $20; there's no better compromise. It is actually amazing how prices naturally tend to move to this optimal level as sellers, through trial and error, rush to find the price the market will bear, the highest price that enables them to sell their full inventory.

Of course, pricing logic applies to all goods. In disastrous situations, with government imposed "fair prices" gas stations quickly run out of fuel as those consumers who get there first fill up every vehicle they own as well as every gasoline container. Many evacuees who can't find fuel anywhere run out of gas, further clogging roads and delaying evacuations. With "price gouging" motorists will conserve fuel, sometimes cramming into a single vehicle rather than driving multiple cars, and filling the tank only half full—reasoning, correctly, that prices will moderate as they drive out of the hurricane zone. Likewise, hotels quickly fill up and turn numerous evacuee families away when prices are "fair." "Price gouging" drives large families to cram into a single room, and sometimes motivates acquaintances, or even strangers, to share a room to offset expenses. Of course, this pricing also increases supplies, leading affected businesses to hold greater inventories in hurricane season, and opening new supplies of rooms, including spare bedrooms via services like Airbnb. Regarding the latter, some people might offer a spare room for free just to be nice to evacuees. On the other hand, sharing one's house with a stranger can be an awkward hassle; the compensation of a high price would bring much more total supply into the market.

Yet, despite all this, we can generally count on politicians to use brute force to depress prices. We can count on government to make any future disaster far more disastrous by discouraging conservation and depressing crucial supplies, even lifesaving supplies—all in the name of protecting consumers from price gouging.

## ECONOMICALLY SPEAKING, VOTERS STILL BELIEVE THE EARTH IS THE CENTER OF THE UNIVERSE

How is it possible that governments across the United States and around the world can continue to make such a tragic, fundamental policy error again and again? A simple answer is that politicians are more followers than leaders; if a huge majority of people want something then politicians generally give people what they want, and we the people want price controls in emergencies. So, next then, how is it that most otherwise reasonably educated people want price controls? Economists, liberal, and conservative alike, have understood, and frequently taught, this pricing logic for more than a century. The folly of price controls is covered in some form in virtually every basic economic textbook; it's a staple in ECON101 classes everywhere. Yet, what is common knowledge to people well versed in economic principles remains completely unknown to the vast majority of people. Why? Sure, it's a little counterintuitive that high prices can benefit consumers, but grasping the fact that a surging price motivates conservation and massive supply efforts is hardly quantum physics.

The physical sciences seem not to have this problem at all. Few of us know all the details, but any reasonably well-educated person accepts that, despite all appearances, it is the earth revolving around the sun, not vice versa. Matter appearing to be solid is actually full of space, electrons orbiting a nucleus and all that. Even the freakishly strange theory of relativity is commonly accepted—time slows as speed vastly increases. Wow! How is it physicists have convinced us to drop our mistaken preconceptions and believe all these weird, very counterintuitive ideas yet economists have had virtually no success in eliminating common misperceptions in our field? Of course, the physical sciences had some rough patches earlier in history—after astronomers figured out the sun was the true center of the universe it was several centuries before they were able to spread that knowledge through society broadly. Scientists had trouble getting ideas through an education system where leaders feared, perhaps needlessly, that learning the earth wasn't the center of the universe would trigger a crisis in faith.

It seems that acceptance by the education establishment is the key factor in the dissemination of counterintuitive knowledge. Obviously, children and young adults more readily accept teaching that contradicts their preconceptions. I didn't fully appreciate this until, as a young professor, I attempted to teach the logic of pricing and illogic of price controls to a group of senior citizens attending an Elderhostel, using the same approach I used in my undergraduate classes. I got through to some of them but many angrily dismissed pricing logic out of hand. It's a cliché but for good reason: Adults tend to assume they already know the important stuff and the longer people have believed a myth the more difficult it is for them to learn and accept the truth.

Economists have the same problem today that astronomers had back in the day—the education establishment does not teach economic principles well. Public schools dominate education, with 90% of all K-12 students (U.S. Department of Education, 2016). Every book and all aspects of curriculum in these schools are controlled by politicians. Unsurprisingly, politicians are universally reluctant to approve curriculum and books that would make them look bad. It's not exactly a conspiracy; essentially government blundered into price controls and other bad but very popular policies first. Then, as teaching some form of economics became common, politicians just made sure material that would expose their poor policies was never included. From the politicians' viewpoint, the beauty of suppressing and censoring counterintuitive ideas is that one generally doesn't have to lie. If we want children to ignorantly believe the sun orbits the earth we don't have to even address the subject, they will naturally believe what their senses seem to tell them. Likewise, if one wants people to believe price gouging is harmful and evil, and that we should all be thankful for noble politicians saving us with price controls the topic need never be addressed. And it isn't. I've been teaching freshmen economic classes since the 1980s. High school economics classes in public schools have become the norm but, based on my own in-class surveys, only about one public school student in a thousand is taught these pricing principles, no doubt by a rogue teacher who happened to know economics and didn't follow the state dictated curriculum.

Private schools are only slightly better on average, probably because many private school teachers went to public schools, or if not, perhaps their teachers' teachers went to public schools. As long as public schools dominate education, entrenched economic myths are likely to persist. Even in the college setting, where outright censorship is rare, I have known colleagues who avoided thoroughly debunking price controls, often just to avoid controversy, particularly in this politically correct age. In extreme cases I've known economics professors who taught economics so abstractly and theoretically that students gained virtually no insight about price controls or any other misguided policy. In other words, even though college economics course generally expose the myth of price controls, this is sometimes too subtle or abstract to penetrate entrenched preconceptions. Of course, many students never even take a single economics course. Bottom line: as long as incoming college students have no clue that obvious errors in standard economic policy exist, there won't be enough students learning enough economics to change much.

Still, anyone at all curious can google "economic impact of price controls" and learn the truth with an hour or so of reading with an open mind. But such curiosity and open-mindedness are not common. In fairness, people have no reason to believe the topic is worth investigating since there seems to be such a solid political consensus; Republicans and Democrats alike virtually unanimously continue to perpetuate the myth of virtue in price controls. No doubt politicians have heard from economic advisors and, hopefully, understand the truth but if so they remain afraid to challenge public misconceptions. Similarly, economists in key government positions play politics with the issue as well. Most are reluctant to lie in their writings (again, just google the issue) but a fib or carefully worded evasion works well with television reporters and audiences. Harsh to say but it seems many economists outside of government are also willing to sacrifice integrity on this and other issues, perhaps because they hope to work for government one day or to obtain a key government grant. In this age of universal politicization even economists who seek no personal gain sometimes seem willing to fib just to protect a favored politician.

All of this is compounded by the problem economists have termed "rational political ignorance." Voters the world over tend to not be well informed because the chance of one person changing the outcome of an election is typically about zero. Obviously, a majority of voters can impact elections, but there is no way to harness that group impact to individual incentives. The motivation for an individual to become informed is mainly intangible; the only reliable benefit is gaining a sense of fulfilling one's civic duty. In contrast, the cost of becoming well informed is enormous in terms of the time it would take to research each issue. Morally, we all have a duty to be well-informed voters. Alas, when moral duty entails high personal cost but no tangible benefit to anyone we tend to neglect moral duty. So, while it is probably immoral for a voter to be uninformed it is logically consistent with our preferences—we prefer to spend our precious time on activities that generate tangible benefits. In this sense, we say it is rational, though certainly not good or desirable, for voters to remain uninformed. Of course, voters have no idea that a knowledge of economics would radically change their view of price controls and other policies. How can anyone judge the value of knowledge they don't have? News media personalities apparently are generally no better informed than the public so news reports primarily reinforce beliefs in mythical benefits of price controls and other confused policies. Although some reporters must know the truth, and for others it wouldn't take much investigative reporting to find it, the truth remains buried.

Thus, we have a sort of perfect storm of ignorance in this area. Politicians continuously fail to deliver the right policy, public education failure perpetually covers up the error, some economists participate in the cover-up—especially those economists working for politicians, and most of the media fails to unearth the truth or, seemingly, to even look for it. While politicians and the media may deserve our scorn, we the people may not be blameless. Perhaps politicians and media have little interest in finding and fighting for the truth because many of us voters prefer politicians and media personalities who confirm our own biases rather than pursuing truth, challenging our misconceptions.


## WHAT GOVERNMENT GOT RIGHT

Despite the fundamental problems, it's worth mentioning that government did some important good things in the aftermath of Hugo. The post-hurricane ice market was left wide open; government wisely did not insist that sellers obtain an ice license or work through time-consuming inspections and paperwork to assure that proper water quality was used in making the ice. Anyone was free to come in and sell ice to a population in desperate need. This sensible lack of explicit regulation was feasible in part because of government implicit regulation through laws regarding liability. Sellers who sold ice made of seriously contaminated water would have been held financially liable, perhaps could even have faced criminal charges. There is room for improvement in liability (tort) law but most economists agree this is probably the most useful thing government can do for consumers.[1] Basically, consumer protection via tort law can help assure that a voluntary trade is truly voluntary, that the consumer is not surprised by some shocking quality problem that really wasn't part of the deal. This can greatly increase the scope and power of voluntary trade; we can, to some degree, trust strangers enough to trade with them. Thus, when they could actually find it, people were comfortable buying ice from strangers, often quite young, with no brand name to protect; strangers who would likely soon be gone never to be seen again. No small achievement.

## IT'S MUCH HARDER TO IMPLEMENT BENEFICIAL REGULATION THAN IT WOULD SEEM

While the government response to the disaster of Hugo wasn't irrational in every regard, there is no denying the colossal failure of their price controls. Politicians that can't get emergency pricing right, can't successfully get a very basic supply and demand issue right, are politicians that cannot be relied upon to necessarily get any consumer protection policy right. A social-political system that can't reach the economically clear conclusion that suppressing price will depress supplies and lead to wasteful, inefficient consumption is a completely unreliable, untrustworthy social-political system. While not all policies are this bad, neither is this, as we will see, a rare case. We cannot automatically assume that any existing government consumer protection policy makes any sense whatsoever, or that it will naturally evolve in a sensible manner, even over a century or so. We can't even assume that an economic policy enjoying virtually unanimous bipartisan support, a policy that the media and "everyone knows" is right, is in fact a good policy. It is worth reexamining our entire approach to consumer protection regulation.

## NARROW SELF-INTEREST CAN BE CHANNELED TO BENEFIT SOCIETY

Just as this ice example exposes government failure it also reveals how the dynamic rough and tumble of free enterprise is not always the disaster many imagine. Self-interested economic behavior by sellers is not automatically harmful to consumers. Adam Smith, often regarded as the father of economics, spoke of how people acting in their own interest are sometimes guided, "as if by an invisible hand," to also act in the interest of society. The person who spends a week-end delivering ice into the hurricane zone, in the worst case, may be completely selfish, thinking only of selling ice bags for $20 a pop. Even so, the ice he provides will reduce human suffering, quite possibly even save lives. Noble results can ensue from ignoble motives; this is essentially how free enterprise, though imperfect, works as well as it does in such a flawed world. By definition, a voluntary purchase only occurs because both trading partners see themselves benefited. Any government regulation may risk preventing that beneficial trade, stifling crucial cooperation, as we have seen. On the other hand, it is possible for some government policies, such as efficient tort law, to augment and reinforce the invisible hand.

We have all had some bad experiences with private businesses; the invisible hand is hardly perfect. Of course, bad experiences also occur with government and every other human institution, nothing involving humans is perfect. We often fail to behave honorably even with loving spouses, children, and parents. Even in a great marriage or loving family, we let each other down at times. Given our nature, it is hardly surprising that economic cooperation between strangers sometimes breaks down badly. Perhaps it is more surprising how well things work out in the vast majority of our trades with people we hardly know or don't know at all. For many of us the day begins with the alarm on our smart phone rousting us out of bed. It's easy to love these phones; it's hard to think of a product that better epitomizes the triumph of entrepreneurship in a free enterprise system.

I'm old enough to truly marvel at all the everyday miracles delivered via that phone. Just being able to hear virtually any recorded song in existence at any time is well worth the cost of the service. Anyway, once up, one might toss some frozen breakfast into the trusty microwave and gulp down some food. Start the car up, Bluetooth audio hooks up, and away we go. Whoops, the car is almost out of gas. No worries, quickly fuel up, pay right at the pump, and easily make it in time to for work or the day's first class. Throughout the day, we use a myriad of products bought from businesses—teams of complete strangers, often massive teams, likely focused more directly on benefiting themselves and their families than on benefiting strangers (customers), and these products typically work exactly as they should. My daily consumer experience is not constant perfection, but it is generally positive, though we often take the successes for granted and notice the occasional glitches more. Are your consumer days so different?

Compared to other places and other times, there is little doubt that we live in a sort of consumer paradise today. But, since we have substantial elements of both free enterprise and government command and control, it isn't always clear who to credit for our success, or even who to blame for the failures. Culturally, we have some tendency to have faith that government regulation generally works reasonably well to make things better. We've seen a case where that faith is not at all justified, and we'll get to some others. On the other hand, economists generally believe government has some useful role to play, such as in establishing appropriate tort law. Sometimes government makes things worse, sometimes better. But, is there a way to judge the impact more generally? There's no precise measurement but we can get some insight through international comparisons. Countries vary substantially in the degree of government control of the economy; we can see how government intervention correlates with income, real GDP, our approximate barometer of economic well-being. To show this most concisely we can group countries by degree of free enterprise, commonly referred to in the literature as degree of "economic freedom."

In figure 1.2 countries are divided into quartiles based on their degree of economic freedom in 2014, the latest available data; the countries with the comparatively lowest levels of regulation, taxes, and government spending are in the top quarter and have average income of $41,228 per person. It is clear that as government intervention increases (defined here as economic freedom declining), income (adjusted for purchasing power) plunges dramatically, to the point where countries in the quarter with the most government intervention have a meager income of only $5,471 (Gwartney et al., 2016).

There are limitations to studies of this sort. For instance, only the level of government regulation is measured, since there is no distinction between productive and harmful regulation, it may still be true that there are many useful regulations; these statistics provide no specific guidance concerning a particular existing or proposed regulation. It could be possible that a high level of *ideal* regulation would be helpful. Still, this data strongly indicates that *actual* government intervention is often harmful.

In fact, the clear implication is that at least three-fourths of the world's governments intervene in such a manner that, in practice, they make their economies worse, harming consumers rather than protecting them. The United States incidentally is nowhere near the top, we are ranked 16th in economic freedom in this study, but we are squarely in the top quarter. With only fifteen countries ranked higher there, perhaps, is not enough in this particular

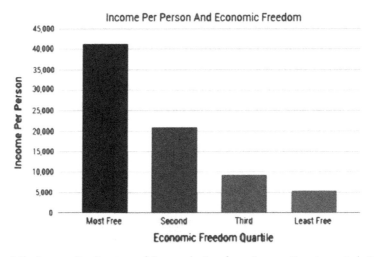

Figure 1.2   Income Per Person and Economic Freedom. *Source*: Gwartney et al. (2016, p. 25).

data to necessarily have clear implications for us. Still, given the frequency of harmful regulation in the world, these statistics provide added reason to closely scrutinize regulation in the United States.

## HELPFUL PRO-CONSUMER REGULATION MUST TAKE PRODUCER PREFERENCES INTO ACCOUNT

When government attempts to force sellers to give consumers a better deal than the one that emerged through competition and voluntary trade, the results can easily backfire, harm consumers because the option imposed by government isn't worth making. Short of totalitarianism, we can't really regulate young pilots such that we force them to fly ice in for $2 bag. The regulation can only stipulate, "*IF* you fly ice in. the price can be no greater than $2." The response from 100% of the pilots I knew was simply, "Okay then, can't afford that, no more flying ice in." This point is worth emphasizing: Producers can always just take their ball and go home. If sellers don't have enough to gain they will not show up. If regulators hassle them too much about a given product they are likely to simply stop making it. Being too tough on sellers is automatically harmful to consumers.

Consumers clamored for regulation, a price ceiling, largely because they naively assumed sellers were generally earning "excessive" profits and that they would offer about the same amount of ice for $2 as they would for $20. It is generally ridiculous to assume that forcing a price 90% lower will leave supply unchanged, as we've seen in this example. Yet, society frequently makes this sort of mistake; we wildly overestimate sellers' profit. For example, when the price of gasoline peaked in 2011 at over $4 per gallon, Exxon famously earned annual profits that set an all-time record. However, the profit was only about 7 cents per gallon, about 1.5% of the selling price (Bradley, 2011). More generally, surveys show consumers wildly overestimate profit rates. In a recent Roper Poll the average consumer estimated the profit rate was 36%, about seven times the actual rate (Perry, 2015). So, with such a thin profit margin most any regulation runs some risk of harming consumers by driving producers out of the market.

## SOME NOTES ON SAFETY

Firms are naturally very interested in improving safety, primarily because consumers value it and are more likely to buy safer products and be willing to pay more for them. The auto industry illustrates how the invisible hand drives profit seekers to make products safer and safer. Innovations such as seatbelts, safety glass, airbags, antilock brakes, and, now, anti-collision technology and automatic driving may ultimately end traffic fatalities altogether. All of these were created or are being developed by profit-seeking entrepreneurs. Sometimes these safety features naturally become standard, while at other times government eventually mandates that safety innovations be universally adopted rather than continuing as options left to consumers to choose or decline. Producers likely have some natural preference for making safety innovations standard since there are economies of scale involved; it is typically much cheaper per car to make safety innovations standard rather than optional. Product standardization is almost always cheaper than product differentiation. Improving standard safety also generates good publicity and is likely to win brownie points with politicians and regulators. There is really only one reason to not make a safety feature standard, many consumers don't want it, or more precisely, they don't value the added safety enough to pay for it.

We often assume that people who value a given safety feature substantially less than we do are simply mistaken, perhaps they haven't thought it through, are not very bright, or maybe are mentally ill. This is not such a reasonable assumption when dealing with adults who are not obviously incompetent generally. Safety is valuable but it is not sacred, even if we completely accept as a given that human life is sacred. We all routinely sacrifice some degree of safety in a trade-off to save money or have more fun. None of us attempt to be as safe as we can possibly afford to be. As you read this, are you wearing a helmet? Any true safety maximizer who could afford a helmet would, by definition, wear that helmet all the time, since one never knows when a possible head injury might occur, perhaps from a plane or meteor crashing onto your roof. In addition to the helmet, the safety maximizer would wear body armor, a mask to inhibit germs and would avoid most human contact since people spread disease and occasionally attack other people. Beyond that, a society that wanted to maximize safety would, for starters, ban swimming, skiing, any other sport, flying, driving faster than 15 miles per hour, and having babies, not to mention even having sex! Some reduction in safety is well worth the risk inherent in many enjoyable activities. Again, this is not saying that human life is not sacred. It's saying that living an enjoyable, meaningful life entails accepting at least some slight physical risks.

How much risk should we accept? This is somewhat like asking, "What's the most attractive color to paint a house?" The answer is subjective; it depends on your unique personality and subjective preferences. Hang gliding is inherently fairly risky but can also be thrilling fun. Some people do it all the time, while others think it's too risky to ever do once. No one has to be wrong. So, consumers are not wrong to buy, say, a standard sedan when they could afford to buy a far safer vehicle, such as an optic yellow dump truck. Consumers are not necessarily idiots even if they buy motorcycles, death traps compared to that dump truck. So, it is not so certain that the consumer who didn't want to pay for ant-lock brakes or airbags is less intelligent than you and me. Even if they buy that motorcycle we still can't confidently throw stones, especially if we aren't driving that optic yellow dump truck ourselves. Given the complexities of life, it is even possible that a motorcycle allows the purchaser to improve her safety overall by, say, saving enough on transportation to be able to afford a home in a much safer neighborhood or obtaining better health care.

In a business, it may be occasionally true that a manager who resists improving safety is just stupid but it is probably more likely that the manager is actually fighting for the right of adult consumers to make their own choices in the pursuit of their own overall happiness. Remember, profit-maximizing firms are always willing to improve safety if consumers are willing to pay for it. In fact, there are few things firms won't sell to satisfy paying customers; safety is probably their favorite thing to hawk given the inherent good publicity and politics. When businesses oppose proposed safety regulations it is often said that "these companies are putting profits ahead of their customers' safety." This is at best a misleading half-truth since safety improvements only depress profits if consumers don't value the safety feature enough to pay for its cost. Firms that don't fulfill their customers' wishes risk their very existence, given the thin profit margins already discussed.

Even though, usually, firms are merely reflecting their consumers' wishes when they oppose safety improvements, there are some complications. Some paternalistic regulation may reasonably override consumer freedom. The obvious examples involve children and clearly incompetent adults but a case might be made for other occasional exceptions. Also, when safety concerns spill over to people other than the consumers themselves, there can be good reason to restrict consumer freedom, the justification for pollution controls. Pollution produced by one driver spills over to others so pollution is clearly more than an individual choice.

However, the broader, key point here is that firms are, contrary to common myths of our culture, generally trying to benefit their customers, since that is how they benefit themselves. But we can only get these benefits if we are willing to fully pay for the production costs entailed. When these costs are unusually high, we tend to leap to the often erroneous conclusion that profits must be extraordinarily high. In disastrous emergencies we even unthinkingly assume that using brute command and control to force price radically lower will have no impact on supply and demand. Regarding safety, we have some tendency to see villainy in any resistance to improved safety when firms are typically just reflecting customer reluctance to pay the cost of a given safety feature, reluctance that every human exhibits in one situation or other.

In summary, if we consumers aggressively use politicians to fire regulations at sellers we are likely to shoot ourselves in the foot. Consumer and business interests are inherently intertwined via a voluntary trade that only occurs if sellers and consumers both agree to the terms of that trade. We consumers have a tendency to try to use government regulation to basically get something for nothing. But it's generally not possible to get something for nothing in a voluntary trade. Consumer protection regulation is most likely to be helpful if it is focused on encouraging businesses to supply products and making sure firms meet the terms promised to their consumers.

## LOOKING AHEAD TO THE REST OF THIS BOOK

The utter failure of consumer protection via price regulation was considered first largely because it is probably the easiest issue to debunk. However, the central thrust of this book is more about promoting product safety and quality. Of course, price and quality issues are inherently intertwined, just as consumer and producer preferences are inherently intertwined. In other cases, as we shall later see, regulation can lead to higher prices that render products unaffordable for many, especially the poor. Or, legally mandated quality improvement in one area can lead to declines in quality in another. Thus, despite common impressions, regulatory issues seldom boil down to a simple good versus evil, moral versus immoral conflict with an easy answer. Even if consumer safety and well-being are our only concern we have to consider the impact on producers, to make certain they remain motivated to bring their products to consumers while maintaining needed quality. Unrealistic regulatory pursuit of a hypothetically cheaper, safer, more perfect product can easily become the enemy, the destroyer of a very good actual product. Consumer protection is vital but regulation can so easily backfire, harming rather than helping consumers.

Government has a useful role to play; establishing appropriate tort law is particularly crucial. With that in place, in a system where both buyer and seller naturally guard their own interests, it is sometimes possible to give buyer and seller more room to creatively figure out and negotiate how to help themselves and thereby help each other. With government acting more like a partner and less like a dictator we can unleash a good deal of creativity to better protect and benefit consumers.

## NOTE

1. There are some scholars who argue that it is actually better to have a private system of law. See, for example, Benson (2011) and Boudreaux (2003).

*Chapter 2*

# New Medicines and ( Dangerous Quest for Certainty

## WHY CAN'T WE GET OUR BEST MEDICINES TO THE TERMINALLY ILL?

Abigail Burroughs was diagnosed with a deadly cancer at the age of nineteen. Her loving and highly supportive family arranged treatment with a top oncologist at world-renowned John Hopkins. However, conventional medicines proved to be basically fruitless and, just after Abigail turned twenty-one, in early March of 2001, all proven treatments had failed. It was clear, barring a miracle, Abigail had only a few months left to live. Her oncologist actually found two possible miracles in the form of two promising medicines—Erbitux and Iressa, both with a good chance of being effective against Abigail's particular cancer. But, there was a major problem; the government had not yet approved these cutting-edge treatments. Fortunately, the Food and Drug Association (FDA) recognizes the wisdom of allowing such desperate patients, with no other hope, access to potentially lifesaving, but unapproved, new medicines. However, the process turned out to be much more complex in practice than in theory. She and her family began a massive media blitz to call attention to not only her case but the general problem of denying access to developmental medical drugs even when patients are terminal and have no other hope of avoiding impending death (Tovanche, 2009).

Abigail herself, despite tremendous fatigue and other health problems, participated in numerous appearances and interviews. She and her family also met with a number of elected government officials as well as leaders of the pharmaceutical companies whose medicines held such promise for her. Virtually everyone was supportive. Who couldn't see the logic of trying to save Abigail's life with promising, even if not completely proven, medicines? An uncertain chance at life was obviously better than no chance at all. However, system, trapped in a sort of "paralysis of analysis," could not function fast enough; she never received either of the medicines. Consequently, Abigail Burroughs died on June 9, 2001. Years later, the FDA did approve both of those medicines Abigail's doctor had sought for her; these treatments lived up to their promise, preserving many lives (Tovanche, 2009).

In a heroic example of building something good out of heartbreaking personal tragedy, Abigail's father, Frank Burroughs, along with Steve Walker, cofounded the Abigail Alliance for Better Access to Developmental Drugs, devoted to spurring faster patient access to new, lifesaving medicines. The Abigail Alliance, among other related activities, carefully investigated developmental medicines and mobilized support for quicker distribution to patients like Abigail (Burroughs, 2018; Abigail Alliance, 2018).

Pharmaceutical companies exist to sell medicines to patients; the FDA did not forbid the sale. Why didn't Abigail gain the medicine everyone seemed to want her to have? The answer, we will eventually unravel, is complicated, with plenty of blame to go around. One thing is clear, the present system is failing miserably. Abigail's experience was fairly typical, not an aberration at all. "Expanded access" is the name of the government program which is supposed to allow terminal patients and those suffering great morbidity, with no other useful options, access to unapproved, developmental drugs. Analysts at the Abigail Alliance found, for example, that from 1997 to 2005 about 4.8 million Americans died from cancer. Since there were promising cancer drugs winding their way through the FDA pipeline throughout that period, there were millions of terminal cancer patients alone who could have benefited from expanded access.[1] Yet, the FDA reports actually granting effective access to less than 6,000 total patients during this entire period, a meager 650 per year, at most (Trowbridge and Walker, 2007).

One obvious problem, though not the root one, is the extreme level of paperwork required of doctors trying to get access for their patients. It takes doctors about 100 total hours of work to complete all the government forms (Huelskamp and Wilkerson, 2018). FDA officials recognize the absurdity of such a cumbersome system and have been working, within the sometimes odd constraints of government and politics, to streamline the process (Burroughs, 2018). Legislatively, in May 2018 President Trump signed into the law the "Right to Try Act" which attempts to streamline the whole process (Huelskamp and Wilkerson, 2018). It is too soon to tell how much difference this will make. Critics of the "Right to Try" movement point out that the FDA already approves 99% of the expanded access applications they receive, though, as we have seen this does not necessarily work to deliver the medicines (Caplan, 2016). In any event, our society's routine failure to deliver the best possible medicine to patients whose lives are in the balance has more fundamental problems than cumbersome paperwork.

## OUR PSYCHOLOGICAL FLAWS IN
## DEALING WITH UNCERTAINTY

Modern medicine is truly amazing but is also full of uncertainties and trade-offs. The treatment that cures one patient will kill another. Drugs with the highest benefits sometimes entail the highest risks. Is it better for a patient to just live with some pain and settle for a lower quality of life or is it worth taking a chance on an expensive treatment that may prove ineffective or even make things worse? These are all tough calls for the most rational human but it turns out we may not always be able to count on our rationality in wrestling with these dilemmas.

The following quotes from FDA leaders illustrate how our political process fails:

> In all of FDA's history, I am unable to find a single instance where a congressional committee investigated the failure of FDA to approve a new drug. But, the times when hearings have been held to criticize our approval of new drugs have been so frequent that we aren't able to count them. . . . The message to FDA staff could not be clearer.
>
> —FDA Commissioner Alexander M. Schmidt in 1974 (Kazman, 2010, 102)

> In the early 1980s, when I headed the team at the FDA that was reviewing the NDA for recombinant human insulin, . . . we were ready to recommend approval . . . my supervisor refused to sign off on the approval—even though he agreed that the data provided compelling evidence of the drug's safety and effectiveness. "If anything goes wrong," he argued, "think how bad it will look that we approved the drug so quickly."
>
> —Dr. Henry Miller, FDA regulator 1979–1994 (Miller, 2000; Klein and Tabarrok, 2018d)

Underlying these political failures are flaws in our own nature. At times, it seems our brains short-circuit a bit and just don't process and deal with situations of uncertainty logically. To illustrate, suppose I were to ask you how much would you pay for a $50 gift certificate to a given restaurant? Suppose your answer was $25. Later, after asking you other questions, I then asked you, how much would you pay for a gift certificate otherwise identical to the first except the value rather than being $50 will be somewhere between $50 and $75? Logically, your answer should not be less than $25 since this certificate has a value, at minimum, of $50. It can't be worse than the first $50 certificate, which was worth $25 to you, and it could be better.

Yet, it is verified that in these sort of economic experiments we routinely value the $50 certificate more than one for $50 to $75! We have a tendency to grasp for certainty even when there is absolutely nothing to be gained from certainty with a strong possibility of loss! We act as if a bird in the hand is worth more than a bird in the hand plus one in the bush—we have a predisposition toward an irrational pursuit of certainty. One might be tempted to dismiss such results as flukes of a survey where stakes are low. On the other hand, higher stakes, though causing us to give more thought to a decision, also increase stress which can magnify illogical reactions to uncertainty (Kahneman and Tversky, 1973; Barberis, 2013).

Obviously, we can work at overcoming this tendency, especially in situations that we repeatedly encounter. But consider how this problem will tend to interact with the problem of rational political ignorance discussed in chapter 1, the tendency for voters to respond to issues "off the top of their heads," rather than carefully studying every issue. That is exactly the situation where our rationality is most likely to break down under uncertainty.

Another illogical prejudice we tend to exhibit in uncertain situations is a preference for doing nothing when taking action is a better strategy, but has uncertain outcomes. It is a common human impulse to move slowly, think everything through before taking a step in a potentially dangerous situation. This is not always the optimal strategy, but it is often instinctive. Just as a squirrel crosses a street extremely hesitantly, and thereby multiplies the risk of getting flattened by a car, sometimes decisive action with uncertain outcomes is a superior strategy to waiting, gathering information until we are surer what we should do. Bad action seems worse than bad inaction. This whole scenario is referred to in psychological terms as "the status quo bias" (Samuelson and Zeckhauser, 1988).

Bad actions are what a statistician would call a type 1 error, such as allowing someone to take a bad drug, one with harmful side effects greater than any benefit. Bad inaction would be a type 2 error, such as failure to provide a good lifesaving drug, leaving a patient to die while we continued to study the new medicine's effects. Obviously, dying from *not* taking a good medicine leaves one just as dead as dying from taking a bad medicine that actually caused the death. Yet, it somehow seems worse, more scandalous if we kill someone with bad medicine rather than leaving them to die as we study the problem and withhold the cure that would have saved them.

Presumably, many health care professionals that routinely face these trade-offs would likely overcome this irrational bias. We should expect that most good doctors would have just as much concern for type 1 deaths and injuries as they would those of type 2. But, once again, it is much less likely that the average voter, or perhaps the average reporter, will reliably rise above this biased, exaggerated concern for type 1 errors with too little concern for type 2 errors.

Another important aspect of all this, as Aaron Wildavsky pointed out, is that our safety concerns, and therefore government safety policies, focus mainly on trying to minimize the occurrence of bad things. We do this even though the remarkable safety increases (measured, for instance, in the dramatic increases in life expectancy) we've experienced since the Industrial Revolution are due almost entirely to the new development of good things. We've benefited from new inventions and discoveries in medicine, food production/nutrition, safer housing, modern sewage treatment, and other innovations. Almost all of this stemmed from discovering new good things and had virtually nothing to do with simply avoiding bad things. In other words, improved safety is more often a process of discovery rather than something that can be cautiously established with more rules. But we love the clarity, the certainty of those firm rules (Wildavsky, 1988).

In the second quote above, from former FDA regulator Dr. Henry Miller, it appears the FDA manager is the villain, holding back a beneficial medicine based on the slight chance approval might backfire and harm his career. The first quote, from former FDA Commissioner Alexander M. Schmidt, suggests Congress is the real villain, since they are the creators and masters of the FDA. But, taking it one step further, Congress responds to political pressures from voters. However, we know voters have trouble overcoming irrational biases against uncertainty, and also tend to be too uninformed to deal with these matters efficiently. The root problem may be having decisions driven by voters collectively rather than by individual patients/doctors.

## BEGINNINGS OF THE MODERN FDA:
## THE ELIXIR SULFANILAMIDE DISASTER

The Food, Drug, and Cosmetic Act of 1938 gave the Food and Drug Administration, among other things,[2] power to hold back new medicines from patients until the agency deemed them reasonably safe. Prior to that, government regulation operated only through liability enforced by courts, a significant motivator for drug inventors to behave responsibly. The new law grew out of the 1938 Elixir Sulfanilamide tragedy. The drug itself had been carefully tested and was not the root problem. However, the manufacturer, Massengill, produced a liquid form that, in probably the most foolish and horrific blunder in U.S. pharmaceutical history, was not tested at all. This solvent, diethylene glycol, essentially the antifreeze we use in cars today, had a deadly impact on patients' kidneys. Before Massengill's hasty withdrawal, the drug killed 107 people, mostly children. The chemist behind the disaster committed suicide (Krauss, 1996; Klein and Tabarrok, 2018a).

There is some tendency to blame a disaster of this sort on an evil obsession with profits. But such behavior is always certain to generate huge losses rather than profits. Massengill suffered massive financial losses, not just in terms of depressed demand for the products and damage to their reputation, solid up until then, but also from courts finding them grossly negligent (Krauss, 1996). *If only Massengill had been so obsessed with protecting their profits that they had simply tested their modified product before selling it.* This case reflects the flaws in human nature rather than a flaw in the free enterprise system. Profits flow to companies that sell helpful medicines to people who continue to buy them via doctors who continue to prescribe them. The desire to gain profits from sales of medicine translates to a desire to help patients—killing your customers is not a profitable strategy.

Analogously, consider the poor soul who somehow thought he could impress the actress Jodie Foster by shooting President Ronald Reagan. The moral of that story is not that we should try to prevent men from doing things to impress women. Men generally do a lot of good things in attempting to impress women: taking showers more often, dressing more nicely, graduating from college, and working harder on the job, to name a few! If a man does something evil and, crazy, like shooting someone, that doesn't impress at all, the problem is simply that man's flawed nature. His goal to impress was not evil, he just choose a stupid, evil way to pursue the goal.

Likewise the pursuit of profit through voluntary trade is honorable, the system is generally fine. If only everyone at Massengill had indeed behaved in a profit-maximizing way. But humans sometimes do incredibly foolish, destructive things that ruin profits and everything else, and it seems no system can completely prevent that. Removing profit maximization from the Soviet Union's society didn't prevent the Chernobyl nuclear disaster, but so far, profit maximization has not caused, possibly even prevented, any similar calamity here.

Even so, it probably seems reasonable to most to have the FDA augment profit incentives, attempting to make absolutely sure no one ever again does anything as foolish as adding antifreeze to a medicine. Yet, this is not so clear cut as it seems. When we tack on government inspection to catch the "bad" medicines we also delay the delivery of "good" medicines, meaning some patients suffer and even die as they wait for the new treatment that can save them, the type 2 errors we often tend to minimize or overlook. Also, paying for tests increases costs for the manufacturer which increases prices for patients. Revenues are also reduced since there are no sales while the government inspection and testing continues; this also depresses supply, raising the prices of medications further. Worse, the prospect of both higher costs and lower revenues means investment in medicine is reduced, so fewer new medicines are discovered.

Thus, people die when government approval of medicines is not required but other people die when it is, and the approval process also depresses supplies and keep prices higher for all patients. Charting the best course for patients, with dangers on both sides, is not so simple. It is difficult to conclusively judge how well or poorly the FDA balanced these concerns in the early years, partly because there is no reliable way to estimate the medicines that are suppressed, never coming into existence or being invented only many years later. In other words, we can measure approval delay but we cannot easily measure discovery delays caused by regulation. However, it does not seem that the FDA safety approval process was at all crippling to innovation. In the twenty years after the Food, Drug, and Cosmetic Act of 1938, the industry prospered and the number of new drugs coming to market annually grew (Weimer, 1982).

Though the costs of regulation seemed small, so too did the benefits. In that same twenty-year period he FDA did not prevent another Elixir Sulfanilamide-type disaster or anything remotely close to it, nor has that happened to this day. That is the FDA has never detected anything anywhere near as foolish as adding antifreeze, or any other poison to medicine. After eighty years of history, we have confirmation of what many would say was obvious from the start—Elixir Sulfanilamide was indeed the anomaly of anomalies. It may well have been an overreaction to impose a regulatory innovation slowdown in reaction to that single tragedy.

On the other hand, the late 1950s brought another disaster of much greater magnitude that seemed to greatly strengthen the case for greater caution and a more sluggish embracing of new medications.

## THE THALIDOMIDE TRAGEDY RESHAPES THE FDA

Thanks to FDA procedures at the time, the United States avoided the heartbreaking tragedies inflicted on the rest of the world by the drug thalidomide. This is undoubtedly the greatest achievement in the history of FDA medical regulation. The key regulatory official responsible for this result, Dr. Frances Kelsey, eventually received the President's Award for Distinguished Federal Civilian Service from President John Kennedy in 1962. Dr. Kelsey became somewhat of a folk hero at the FDA, with an annual performance award named after her (McFadden, 2015).

In 1957, a West German pharmaceutical manufacturer introduced, thalidomide, a sedative which also relieved the symptoms of morning sickness in pregnant women. By today's standards and state of science it seems unimaginable but the drug was not significantly tested on pregnant women. At the time we were basically unaware of how sensitive the developing human fetus is to drugs. By 1962, thalidomide had been sold in forty-six countries, and it had become evident that the drug caused a disproportionate number of miscarriages, still births, and serious birth defects. These birth defects generally involved babies being born with deformed limbs that were basically flippers. Worldwide there were about 10,000 babies born with this condition; the media published many horrifying and alarming pictures of these tragically deformed babies. The United States was generally spared these horrors, except for a few tragic test cases. Had we been an early adopter of thalidomide total casualties, deaths and serious injuries would likely have been around 10,000 and maybe as high as 19,000 (Gieringer, 1985; Klein and Tabarrok, 2018a).

It can be argued that the United States avoidance of this catastrophe was largely a matter of good fortune and bureaucratic inertia. Dr. Kelsey and her colleagues were not specifically investigating the drug's impact on pregnant women and unborn babies; no one was. Other countries generally approved new medicines much faster than the United States at that time, not so much these days. The tendency of America to be a laggard in approving newly invented medicines was, of course, often harmful. However, since we were often among the last ones to benefit from innovative and helpful medicines we would also naturally be the last to receive any "bad" medicine. It isn't always a good thing to be years behind other countries but in this instance, being behind state of the art medicine, giving us time to learn from others' mistakes, was a massive blessing (Gieringer, 1985).

After dodging the thalidomide bullet, voters, horrified by the pictures of deformed babies, pressured politicians to "make sure" nothing like that would ever happen here. The result was the Kefauver-Harris Amendments (to the Pure Food and Drug Act) of 1962 which, for the first time, tasked the FDA with verifying the *effectiveness* of new medicines before approving them. This was a somewhat surprising, some would say, irrational twist of politics. That people might waste money on ineffective medicines did not appear to be a major concern. The whole zeitgeist of the time was to make sure drugs wouldn't harm us, especially our children (Gieringer, 1985; Peltzman, 1973; Klein and Tabarrok, 2018a). Perhaps, adding in tests for efficacy provided a good excuse to just slow down even more, let the rest of the world adopt new medicines first, functioning as guinea pigs for us before we tried those newfangled medicines.

Obviously, it is harder, more time consuming, and more expensive to legally prove effectiveness than it is to establish basic safety. Innovation would clearly be impaired by the requirement to take the necessary time to legally prove efficacy. However, slamming on the brakes of medical drug innovation appealed to those human biases of trying to wait for certainty and worrying first about preventing the bad rather than enabling the good. In this particular case, a stronger status quo bias might have been helpful and promoted a more incremental approach to legislation. After all, the system we already had in place had worked, whether from better insight or just general sluggishness; there was no disaster in the United States. But, given those pictures of "thalidomide babies" the rush to protect children from potentially very bad drugs was emotionally paramount. Extending our quest for certainty to verifying effectiveness would likely keep U.S. consumers last in line for new medicines, appealing to our understandable, if not entirely rational, obsession with avoiding a repeat of thalidomide at any cost.

## THE 1962 KEFAUVER-HARRIS AMENDMENTS, NEW TRAGEDIES WITH LESS VISIBLE VICTIMS

The stifling impact on medical drug innovation was immediately apparent. The average number of new drugs introduced in the period 1948 to 1962 was forty per year. After the FDA began holding back medicines to test for effectiveness, the average plunged to only sixteen new medicines per year in the 1963–72 period (Peltzman, 1973). Figure 2.1 shows the number of new medicines approved annually, before and after Kefauver-Harris. Over time, pressures began to build against this excessive impediment to innovation. However, politically overcoming the lingering memories of the thalidomide birth defects was a difficult, long haul that actually is still far from over. It wasn't until the late 1970s that government began to officially admit that public health was jeopardized by excessively testing medicines for safety and efficacy.

The U.S. General Accounting Office, under President Jimmy Carter, confirmed this conclusion in a report entitled, *Drug Approval—A Lengthy*

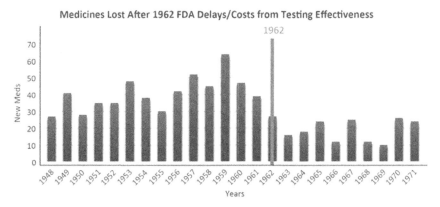

**Figure 2.1   Medicines Lost After 1962 FDA Delays/Costs from Testing Effectiveness.** *Source*: Author.

*Process that Delays the Availability of Important New Drugs, Report to the House Committee on Science and Technology* (U.S. General Accounting Office, 1980).

But, it was indeed a protracted journey to that, actually fairly obvious, conclusion. In the early post-Kefauver-Harris period the FDA commissioner claimed the dramatic 60% plunge in new medicines was basically a coincidence, and that drug companies were simply running out of ideas (Kennedy, 1978). But this was clearly incorrect as demonstrated by our experience in the late 1960s and early 1970s. Several studies confirmed the damaging delays imposed by U.S. regulation compared to both our own history and in terms of comparisons to other countries (Peltzman, 1973; Wardell, 1978; Wardell and Louis Lasagna, 1974; Kazman, 1990; Klein and Tabarrok, 2018c).

Dale H. Gieringer conducted, perhaps, the gold standard of this sort of analysis. Using data from 1950 to 1980 he compared results here to other countries that generally approved new medicines much faster than the United States. This was the basis for estimating the beneficial side of the FDA's extensive deliberating, fewer type 1 injuries. He also incorporated data on mortality rates before and after beneficial medicines were approved by FDA to estimate the type 2 deaths caused by the FDA's sluggishness. The estimates are inherently complex since many factors are changing over time. For example, reduced mortality rates over time are partly due to better medicines becoming available but may also be partially due to better patient education that leads to them seeking treatment sooner, before problems become fatal. Thus, the estimates provide a broad range, not a precise number. Another problem was that available data for the benefit side of the U.S. super slow approval approach was measured in casualties while the costs of delay only captured deaths, ignoring nonfatal suffering and casualties (Gieringer, 1985; Klein and Tabarrok, 2018c).

Geiringer found the FDA reduced type 1 casualties by about 500 per year, or for the worst case scenario up to 1,000 per year. This turned out to be a very trivial benefit compared to the massive, deadly costs of FDA delays— *Annual deaths from the FDA's delays were at least 2,100 per year and could have been as high as 12,000 per year* (Geiringer, 1985).

Again, keep in mind the benefits of regulatory delays are measured in reduced injuries while the costs are measured in fatalities. So, to be blunt, the above study indicates the FDA, compared to other countries' regulators at the time, *inadvertently killed four times more people per year than they substantially benefited* (500 reduced casualties vs. 2,100 increased deaths). In *worst case feasible scenarios, the regulatory delays killed 12 times as many people annually as benefited (1,000 fewer casualties versus 12,000 more deaths)*.

Also, if we focus on the impact of the 1962 change requiring proof of effectiveness, then we subtract the thalidomide casualties that occurred before 1962, which were the lion's share of those casualty estimates, that is the lion's share of the benefits of slow approval. So, working with Geiringer's data, subtracting out the thalidomide injuries knocks down reduced type 1 casualties to an average of around 160 per year post-Kefauver-Harris. So, *after requiring proof of effectiveness regulatory delays likely killed about 13 times as many people per year as received substantial benefit* (2,100 more deaths, 160 fewer casualties.) *In the worst case, FDA delays causing deaths annually were more than 18 times the number of reduced casualties* (12,000 increased deaths, 660 reduced casualties).

Of course, there is nothing to say that these other countries were approving medicines at an optimal speed. After all, the uncertainty biases discussed earlier are universal human tendencies, implying other countries also will tend to obsess too much on reducing bad drugs, approving the good ones too slowly. Moreover, these other countries generally had approved thalidomide, had experienced the horrifying results that the United States had mainly just read about, and seen pictures. They were less sluggish than the United States but not likely fast enough. Therefore, the damage done by FDA delays, compared to an optimal policy, is probably much larger than suggested by this study (Klein and Tabarrok, 2018c).

Moreover, the above figures estimate only a portion of the harm done by the FDA's procedures. Deaths from delays are estimated but nonfatal casualties are not. Even worse, probably, far worse, *we have ignored the deaths and nonfatal casualties caused by the FDA's inevitable suppression of new medicines.* That is, there is no accounting for the medicines that were not invented because inventors couldn't raise the capital to cover the massive development costs created by the greater burdens of regulatory procedures. Recall, the estimates discussed earlier suggest that the rate of new medicines being introduced fell 60% post-Kefauver-Harris through the 1970s. Unfortunately, there is no way of knowing exactly what those unborn medicines would have done.

## ADDING ESTIMATED DEATHS FROM THE SUPPRESSION OF NEW MEDICINES

Perhaps, those suppressed medicines would have been less productive, because inventors sensed their relative weakness, and emphasized getting the most effective drugs approved. But this tendency is weakened by the reality of pervasive uncertainty. When firms begin the process of FDA approval they have not begun any human trials, and human impacts do not reliably track results with lab animals at all. So, there is a great deal of guesswork in choosing which drugs to invest in with limited funds in the face of massive costs. One of the few certainties is that the suppressed medicines will tend to be those that treat diseases that relatively few people suffer from. The cost of getting a medicine approved to treat a "small" population disease is identical to costs entailed to obtaining FDA treatment approval for a "large" population disease but revenues will obviously be greater with the "large" case. Though a harsh reality, it probably makes sense, other things equal, to spend roughly ten times as much trying to cure a disease that affects ten times more people. But with identically high, up-front costs, spending on the small population drug may not be economically sensible at all; investment can become zero rather than being 10% of the large disease drug investment (Klein and Tabarrok, 2018c).

This has come to be known as the "orphan drug" problem; promising medicines are abandoned, or never pursued, if it is obvious that projected revenues have little chance of covering the costs of getting them approved because there are relatively few potential patients; "orphan" class is 100,000 patients or fewer. It's estimated that about 10% of Americans suffer from such a disease (Hemphill, 2010). The severe orphan drug problem finally reached a critical political mass in the early 1980s with passage of the Orphan Drug Act of 1983, which gave orphan drugs stronger patents with more monopoly power so as to attract more investment (Klein and Tabarrok, 2018a).[3]

So, the FDA's inadvertent suppression of new medicines is likely to be particularly lethal for anyone dying from a small population disease. Especially after 1962, a drug that treats heartburn may have been pursued and eventually approved while a drug to cure a less common, deadly cancer is abandoned and "orphaned." Thus, it is well within the realm of possibility that the suppressed medicines would have saved more lives on average than the ones which were sought and approved simply because the population targeted by approved drugs was so large, even if few or any were terminal.

In other words, we have no way of knowing whether these aborted medicines would have saved more lives or fewer compared to those which were approved. Splitting the difference, let us simply posit that the suppressed medicines were equally likely to save lives. Our next problem is assigning a number on the overall suppression rate. The 60% estimate in drug suppression after 1962 relative to pre-1962 understates total suppression since the market was still somewhat suppressed before the 1962 change in law. After all, the extremely slow rate of approved innovation in the United States relative to the rest of the world was the very factor that happened to save us from thalidomide; the two-edged regulation that caught the "bad" drug no doubt blocked some good medicines as well. And, the rest of the world also suppressed innovation somewhat, just not as much as us. Since there is a strong consensus that the magnitude of delay and suppression fundamentally surged after Kefauver-Harris, let us pick a much smaller number for pre-Kefauver-Harris, say, 20%. Thus, we are guesstimating that an open market would have produced something like 20% more medicines pre-1962 and 100% post-1962.

This then implies for the period of Geiringer's estimates, about 1950–80, the rate of drug suppression was in the ballpark of 50%. So, let us adjust

Geiringer's estimates by simply increasing everything by 50%, both the type 1 casualties avoided, the good part of sluggish approval and suppression, and the type 2 deaths incurred, the costs of delay and suppression. Again, his original estimates, including the thalidomide impact, were that the FDA reduced type 1 casualties by about 500 per year, or for the worst case scenario, up to 1,000 per year. Annual deaths from the FDA's delays were estimated to be at least 2,100 per year and could have been as high as 12,000 per year (Geiringer, 1985). Thus, increasing everything 50%, we estimate the approval delays imposed increased *annual type 2 deaths of at least 3,150, more than four times greater than the reduced type 1 casualties of 750.* For the *worst case scenario, estimated type 2 deaths would be 18,000 annually, about 12 times the reduced type 1 casualties of 1,500.* Again, keep in mind we are measuring *costs of delay and suppression in deaths* while the *benefits are in terms of all casualties.*

The above figures are for the entire 1950–80 period, the net damage of delay/suppression would be much worse for just the post-1962 period, the sort of world we have today. Granted these are hardly precise estimates but this is not a close call. Even in a best case scenario, it is a virtual certainty that the 1962 Kefauver-Harris Amendments cumulative death totals in the United States far surpassed the casualties from thalidomide worldwide. More heavy-handed regulation did prevent some bad things from happening, the focus our emotions and instincts tend to take us toward. But those benefits were tiny compared to the costs of depressed and slower introduction of new lifesaving medicines. The barriers to innovation that come with that careful, plodding, "safe" pace, caused thousands of unnecessary deaths and untold increases in suffering. Ironically, our obsession with playing it safe made us far less safe.

Also, we shouldn't, amidst all this aggregated data, lose sight of the fact that medical decisions that do not center on an individual patient's characteristics and circumstances are fundamentally flawed. To simply illustrate: It would seem to be sensible to move extremely slowly in approving and embracing a new treatment for say, ear wax buildup. But, how can it make sense to spend years officially verifying effectiveness for a promising medicine's treatment of a deadly cancer? Do we just tell patients who will be dead before the tests are completed, "Hey, we just want to check and check again to make sure buying this medication is worth the money, just doin' our job. You'll thank us one day . . . er, well, not you . . . but posterity will thank us."

## REGULATION FAILED TO IMPROVE EFFECTIVENESS

In theory, there could be a little silver lining to this dark cloud of delayed and suppressed medicines—if it had turned out that approved drugs after 1962 were more effective, preventing us from wasting some money on unproductive medicines. However, there is no evidence of improved efficacy at all.

The likely explanation, as Sam Peltzman pointed out, is that normal market incentives preclude useless treatments. Patients are not interested in taking and doctors are not interested in prescribing ineffective medicines; therefore, drug companies are not interested in trying to market them (Peltzman, 1973).[4]

## DE FACTO DEREGULATION: OFF-LABEL PRESCRIPTIONS

Physicians and other private health care professionals invented off-label prescribing to partially overcome the damage from the fatal approval delays imposed by FDA testing for effectiveness. In other words, they found a loophole in the disastrous Kefauver-Harris Amendments. Once a medicine is approved doctors are technically free to prescribe it for any treatment they see fit. So, when FDA-approved treatments failed patients, physicians and scientists began experimenting with other available drugs that had been approved and declared effective for other uses but had not been FDA approved, or generally even tested at all for the new, alternate use. For instance, Amoxicillin was approved for treating respiratory tract infections but doctors discovered it was also very effective in treating stomach ulcers, in fact it became the standard treatment, though government regulators never at all tested its efficacy. The FDA has historically forbidden drug companies from advertising any benefit not verified by their approved testing; so they forbade the manufacturer from mentioning how useful amoxicillin was in the treatment of ulcers. The amoxicillin label couldn't say, "Great for treating ulcers," hence the term "off-label prescription" (Klein and Tabarrok, 2018c).[5]

Today, off-label prescribing is quite common, comprising, at absolute minimum, 20% of all prescriptions, and possibly as much as 39% (Kao, 2017).[6] Evidence and common practice indicate that there are no important differences in safety or effectiveness between off-label uses and FDA-approved uses of medicines. In fact, in an interesting recent study, a group of clearly skeptical researchers set out to show that there was at least a slight advantage to using on-label (effectiveness FDA approved) medicines rather than the off-labels. In an extensive survey of pediatric patients they ended up verifying the validity of off-label use. They found off-label medicines were 37.6% of the total prescribed and that adverse drug reactions were no more common from off-label treatments (Palmaro et al., 2015). The most certain proof of the efficacy of off-label medicines is probably the fact that government agencies themselves—such as Medicare and Medicaid—have, for decades, been just as accepting of off-label medicines as everyone else (Tabarrok, 2000). *The government's complete embracing of off-label medications, without any*

*FDA verification of effectiveness, clearly indicates this FDA certification is not necessary or worth the cost of waiting for it.*[7]

It seems the decentralized, voluntary system of informal regulation works quite well to establish effectiveness. This really shouldn't surprise us. The research scientists and doctors tackling these problems and sharing information through newsletters, peer-reviewed journals, lecture presentations, conferences, and various internet outlets are really doing the same things FDA employees do. The FDA has no monopoly on medical talent, and there is no reason to suppose that private health care professionals are less proficient or less dedicated.

## INNOVATION MAKES A PARTIAL COMEBACK

The afore-mentioned U.S. General Accounting Office report, *Drug Approval— A Lengthy Process that Delays the Availability of Important New Drugs, Report to the House Committee on Science and Technology* (U.S. General Accounting Office, 1980), marked the beginning of a moderate turning point. The year 1980 brought an attitude commonly less trusting of government regulation, while the AIDS epidemic brought in activists insisting that dying patients should have more freedom to choose their medicines. The eventual rise of the internet and the information age would later make it easier for desperate patients to learn about medicines not yet approved by the FDA. At long last, for probably the first time in U.S. history, there began to be some sizeable political pressure on politicians and regulators to allow new medicines a path less slow. Though not huge and not enough, this paid some considerable dividends.

In the 1970s it had taken over ten years (median period) for a medicine to get approved by the FDA (Thomas, 1990). Then, in the 1980s, approvals began to speed up, and by the late 1990s average approval was down to 7.3 years, not significantly far behind most countries (Kaitin and Healy, 2000). Again, given the general bias against innovation, all governments are likely to be too slow to approve new medicines. Being no less dawdling than other countries is not much to brag about, like doing respectably in a race against snails. Still, cutting average approval delays by three years, about 30%, was certainly a step in the right direction.

Unfortunately, we have made virtually no progress since the 1990s. In the period 2012–16, the FDA had incorporated rules to slightly speed the approval of medicines that seemed particularly crucial. Drugs in the FDA's various expedited programs, which generally include medicines with stronger lifesaving properties, took an average in that period of about 7.1 years for the FDA to sanction, while non-expedited drugs took 8 years (Hwang et al., 2017). Obviously, a wait of seven years is deadly for the multitude of affected terminal patients, so much for our current expedited approach.

## THE VIOXX DISASTER

The lack of progress since the late 1990s in reducing approval delays likely relates to our experience with Vioxx. The now infamous drug was approved in 1999 based on its pain relieving and anti-inflammatory benefits; it was especially effective in relieving acute pain for those suffering rheumatoid arthritis. The FDA "fast-tracked" approval, which, again, typically reduces regulatory delay by about a year. The drug was widely prescribed and a huge financial success. Unfortunately, it turned out Vioxx caused an increased risk of heart attacks and strokes; the drug may have killed as many as 55,000 patients, according to an estimate from FDA officials (Harrismarch, 2005).

The manufacturer, Merck, voluntarily (sort of) took Vioxx off the market on September 30, 2004, five years after approval.[8] The media and government leaders were virtually unanimous in their condemnation of the way the matter was handled by the manufacturer. One commonly alleged problem was that Merck needlessly dawdled in withdrawing the medicine from the market, despite obvious indications of the risks. *The New York Times*'s headline was *Despite Warnings, Drug Giant Took Long Path to Vioxx Recall* (Berenson et al., 2004). This was the typical, virtually undisputed viewpoint of media coverage. Politicians were generally part of this consensus as epitomized by Congressman Henry Waxman's article in the *New England Journal of Medicine*, "The Lessons of Vioxx—Drug Safety and Sales" (Waxman, 2005).

Moreover, another common media theme emerged, arguing that the FDA was hasty, not only in approving Vioxx, but too hurried in general in approving new drugs! The FDA decision to fast-track Vioxx was especially criticized since the drug was another "me too" pain reliever and was not likely to save anyone's life. The main evidence cited for the "too fast to approve" argument, in addition to the Vioxx example itself, was the increase in the number of approved drugs subsequently recalled over time. In the period from 1993 to 1996, 1.6% of new drugs approved by the FDA were taken off the market because of safety problems. In the 1997–2000 period this figure rose to 5.3%. An excellent summary of this "the FDA is too fast" viewpoint is the Boston Globe's, *Once "too slow," FDA approvals called "too fast"* (Henderson and Rowland, 2005).

However, it seems *none of the voices insisting the FDA approval process had become too fast included any estimates, or even much consideration, of deaths and injuries from approval delays and medicine suppression.* This reflects our classic, innate biases against innovation, discussed earlier. It is, in the end, senseless to evaluate a policy based only on costs without any consideration of benefits. Yet, virtually all the media leaped to the conclusion that Vioxx must be bad since it caused many heart attacks, and most leaped to the corollary view that the FDA must be approving new medicines too fast, since they let Vioxx through and had been recalling more medicines than in the past. This view completely dominated, indeed virtually monopolized, the public discussion. In keeping with typical human biases, just showing that bad things happened from approved drugs was thought to be persuasive proof.

Of course, there is a group of professionals where the vast majority, through training and practical experience, has learned to overcome these common biases, at least within their field.

## VIOXX: THE SURPRISING FACTS AND THE VIEW OF DOCTORS

The most serious deficiency in almost all the Vioxx reporting was the lack of any statement about the predominant view of the experts in a position to actually know the real costs and benefits of Vioxx.

> I believe Vioxx should not have been taken off the market. At least a million people, if told the truth about its side effects, would accept it because their lives could be lived with a lot less pain. There are a lot of people now whose lives are miserable because they have to live with arthritic pain.
>
> —Catherine DeAngelis, editor in chief, *Journal of the American Medical Association* (Heisel, 2010)

It turns out that in the above quote, Dr. DeAngelis was speaking for the vast majority of doctors, 80%, who opposed the recall, as reported in an extensive survey conducted by the Competitive Enterprise Institute (Kazman, 2010). One reason for this is that the added risk of heart attack was not as catastrophic as one would assume from the many breathless accounts in the media. Patients who used Vioxx saw their risk of heart attack rise about 1%, certainly significant, but not necessarily a showstopper for patients in acute pain who found no other medicine that served. Whether you are willing to risk a 1% chance of a heart attack depends largely on how much pain and suffering you will have to endure if you don't utilize Vioxx, as Dr. DeAngelis[9] concisely explained.

As discussed in chapter 1, increased safety isn't automatically worth the cost, assuring that the bad thing we fear most doesn't happen is not always the best course. Moreover, it's not at all clear that the withdrawal of Vioxx actually made patients safer! Extreme pain in itself can shorten life spans and lead patients to take other chances. For example, many former Vioxx users turned to opioids. Among other problems this apparently caused a marked increase in serious falls and fractures, a leading cause of death in this age group. Patients using opioids were about four times more likely to experience a fall or fracture. Most ironically, there are also indications that the risks of heart attacks for these patients may be greater for those who use opioids than for those who used Vioxx—so much for getting that "obviously bad" Vioxx[10] off the market to make America safer and better (Rolita, 2013).

There may be another bias in play in these situations. Reporters and their audiences alike are most captivated by a story with a villain we all love to hate. "Greedy corporation hastily pushes deadly drug to market then drags feet in recalling it" is great pathos, the kind of headline that draws us in. In contrast, the problem of deadly delays, in addition to not appealing to our other anti-uncertainty biases, also lacks an appropriate, dastardly bad guy. Consider that headline, "Government officials too thorough in their testing, fewer pre-marketing tests would save lives." Where's the fun in that? How can we enjoy being outraged at some government official testing for safety? These public servants probably don't even make much more money than we do.

## THE REAL LESSON OF VIOXX

*The uninformed medical opinions of amateurs should not be driving medical decisions.* To the average voter, as soon as we learn that a drug causes people to die from heart attacks our mind tends to follow a biased path toward the hurried conclusion that this bad drug needs to be taken off the market. Reporters are subject to the same bias, and even those who rise above it work in a system where the biases of the target audience heavily influence, if not completely dominate, the selection of how the "news" gets reported. Again, we just seem hard wired when facing something "bad" under complex situations of uncertainty, to frantically seize on the option that promises to eliminate the "bad." As soon as we learned that Vioxx likely caused thousands of people to die from heart attacks, we "knew" the FDA was wrong to ever approve it. What decent person would approve heart attacks?

Imagine this scenario: A long-suffering arthritis patient in constant, excruciating pain, after all less risky treatments have failed, is in her doctor's office carefully considering her options. After a long discussion with her doctor she decides Vioxx is her best option, fully understanding and willing to accept the increased risk of heart attack. But meanwhile, a mob of "concerned citizens" has formed outside the office. The angry crowd, led by a reporter, contains people from every walk of life, except maybe doctors. The mob bursts into the doctor's office and angrily snatches the prescription pad out of his hands, "Are you out of your mind," the mob leader snarls, "or just easily manipulated by evil drug company propaganda? You can't prescribe Vioxx, you fool; it causes heart attacks! Don't you ever read the paper or watch TV? Wow, I never went to medical school a day of my life yet I know what's best for your patient better than you do!" The anguishing patient, in tears, tries to explain why she wants the medicine, risks notwithstanding, but the mob won't listen and drags her away to "safety." This, in essence, is pretty much what actually happened.

Furthermore, Vioxx is not at all an isolated case. The pattern is the same, as soon as a medicine is known to have substantial lethal side effects the mob drives it out of the market—whether through the FDA or through looming liability (judges and juries are affected by the mob mentality.) As soon as we know there are significant costs we lose all interest in finding out if the benefits might be greater than the costs for at least some patients (Weimer, 1982).

This mob, of course, has only the best of intentions. Members of this massive gang are united in a pure, simple desire to protect themselves and all of us from "bad" medicines. But each member of the gang is full of deadly biases and lacks the education and training to overcome or even recognize their biases. The mob demanded, in the early 1960s, that we "make sure there are no more thalidomide babies, ever again." Ideally, our elected officials would stand up to the mob. If they stood together, in complete unity, they could probably pull it off. But, it seems politics just doesn't work that way.

Perhaps, unity was impossible because there were some politicians, less amenable to reason, drawn in with the uninformed hordes themselves, or perhaps some pols gave in to the temptation to join the mob for career political gain even though they knew better. In any event, politicians caved in and gave the mob the Kefauver-Harris Amendments, average drug approval times blew up to more than ten years, causing the deaths of thousands and thousands. It was some two decades before politicians dared to even begin to pull the FDA approval times down a little. By then, the mob had inadvertently killed and seriously injured many, many more people than thalidomide ever did. Uninformed good intentions proved to be far more deadly than the worst medical drug side effects in history.

This mob doesn't mean to kill anyone or cause anyone's quality of life to decline so badly that life is hardly worth living. But, of course, that doesn't reduce the pain and suffering of anyone or make the mob's dead victims any less dead. The real problematic villains are not drug companies just trying to sell medicines to patients or FDA regulators following the dictates of Congress. The villains are closer to home. We the people are collectively demanding an obsessive compulsive reduction in the "bad" which inherently sabotages the greater good.

## DRUG APPROVAL DELAYS ARE STILL PROLONGED AND DEADLY

There is clear proof that the FDA, without any additional resources or radical innovations, could reduce approval delays by several years. In this chapter's introduction we discussed the work of the Abigail Alliance for Better Access to Developmental Drugs. They began to avidly recommend promising drugs to the FDA (and others) for quick approval not long after Abigail's death in 2001. The twenty-nine medicines recommended by the Abigail Alliance are shown in table 2.1. The FDA itself has proved that they were right in every

**Table 2.1    List of the Drugs and Vaccines that the Abigail Alliance had Pushed for Early Access, and that Were Finally Approved Years Later by the FDA**

| | |
|---|---|
| 1 | Eloxatin colon and others |
| 2 | Erbitux colon, head and neck, others |
| 3 | Advair—COPD—GSK |
| 4 | Revlimid MDS (blood disorder) and multiple myeloma |
| 5 | Velcade multiple meyeloma |
| 6 | Tysabri multiple sclerosis, Crohn's |
| 7 | Nexavar kidney cancer, liver cancer |
| 8 | Avastin many cancer uses |
| 9 | Tarceva lung and pancreatic |
| 10 | Bexxar non-Hodgkin's lymphoma |
| 11. | Sutent kidney cancer |
| 12 | Alimta two types of lung cancers: non-small cell lung cancer and a rare cancer—malignant pleural mesothelioma 02–08 |
| 13 | Lapatnib (Tykirb)—breast, brain, lung GSK |
| 14 | FragminR—cancer—symptomatic venous thromboembolism (VTE) |
| 15 | Torisel—kidney cancer |
| 16 | Abraxane—breast, head and neck, prostate, gastric Abraxis—AstraZeneca |
| 17 | Ixabepilone—breast cancer |
| 18 | Provenge—(patient specific vaccine) prostate cancer |
| 19 | Ipilumumab—Melanoma |
| 20 | PLX-4032—melanoma, Plexxikon with Roche |
| 21 | Zactima—thyroid, lung cancer, AstraZeneca |
| 22 | T-DM1—trastuzumab attached to a new drug delivery molecule |
| 23 | DM1—breast cancer, Genetech |
| 24 | Pertuzumab 12–11 breast Roche/Genentech |
| 25 | Axitinib—pancreatic cancer, Pfizer |
| 26 | Pazopanib—various cancers, GSK |
| 27 | PD-1 advanced or unresectable melanoma—Keytruda |
| 28 | Harvoni (ledipasvir and sofosbuvir), chronic hepatitis C virus |
| 29 | Eteplirsen—Duchenne Muscular Dystrophy, Sarepta Therapeutics |

*Source*: Abigail Alliance for Better Access to Developmental Drugs.

case, since every one of these twenty-nine medicines was ultimately approved by them. But FDA approval happened, in each case, two to four years after the Abigail Alliance recommended approval. When private experts can analyze the same data that regulators see and predict FDA approvals years before they finally become a reality, the regulatory system is clearly malfunctioning (Burroughs, 2018).[11]

The added years of deliberation are not generally adding important insights but are simply reflecting excessive caution driven by a society that systematically undervalues innovation and is hyper phobic regarding any possible bad outcome.

## A MIRACLE DELAYED IS A MIRACLE DENIED: THE SLUGGISH APPROVAL OF GLEEVEC

Perhaps, the single best example of excessive regulatory hesitancy is the history of the true miracle drug, Gleevec. Prior to the discovery of this silver bullet patients with chronic myeloid leukemia were basically told to get their affairs in order and prepare for their rapidly approaching death. But in the Phase I clinical trials of Gleevec something virtually unheard of happened. After some jiggering with the dosage, 100% of the patients responded; soon all the cancers were in remission by the end of the trial in 1999. Patients literally sprang out of their death beds and went dancing! Moreover, the high-tech treatment was molecularly targeted, it destroyed cancer cells but apparently left healthy cells unchanged; patients experienced essentially zero side effects (Dreifus, 2009).

Like everyone else, FDA officials were thrilled, promising to complete the approval of this miraculous medicine in record time, planning to truncate usual procedures which require lengthy Phase II and Phase III trials. In a literal sense, the FDA kept its promise, a modern-day record was set when Gleevec was approved—two and a half years later. Yes, despite every effort to expedite the process the government held back, for two and a half years, a virtually sure-fired cure for a disease guaranteed, without that medicine, to be quickly fatal in essentially every case (National Cancer Institute, 2018; Burroughs, 2018).

## WHY OUR SYSTEM FAILS TERMINAL PATIENTS

As one might suspect, there appears to be a virtually unanimous consensus that dying patients, who have exhausted all alternatives, should be able to try promising developmental medicines that have passed the FDA's Phase I tests on safety.[12] The FDA supports this position and reports that it grants (eventually) 99% of expanded access requests (Caplan, 2016). Yet, as mentioned earlier, only a few patients, about 650 per year, out of the millions who want them, actually get these cutting-edge medicines. The requirement of 100 hours of onerous paperwork for doctors and the slow response of the FDA are parts of the problem. But, a more key reason the FDA expanded access program generally fails is the massive costs imposed by regulatory delays. The average cost of developing a new medicine, as of 2015, and shepherding it through the FDA approval process is $2.6 billion, with a little less than 12% of drugs that start FDA trials actually becoming approved (Sullivan, 2018).[13]

Consequently, with billions per eventually approved medicine tied up in the long pipeline to FDA approval, companies cut costs as much as they possibly can. While in trials, they typically produce only enough medicine for those trials. Thus, there are no extra supplies readily available. Producing more, relatively small amounts is likely to be much more expensive per dose than full-scale mass production would be, but mass production without FDA approval is senseless. Of course, that problem is surmountable with a high enough selling price, though, of course, affordability for patients becomes an issue.

But the real issue is the company's problematic quest for FDA approval. If a company provides the medicine to desperate patients outside of the rigorously monitored trials, there is probably not much regulatory upside. If the patients do well the results will likely be deemed unscientific, unproven, will not help much in gaining approval (Weimer, 1982). In contrast, if patients have a bad reaction to the medicine that is well publicized this will likely reduce the probability of approval, or at best, significantly delay it. Even if evidence eventually supports the conclusion that the patient's problems were not related to the developmental medicine they took, that delaying effect will likely be substantial.

FDA officials maintain that they simply ignore results, good or bad, outside of the trial, and that these outside results have never affected approval processes (Burroughs, 2018). However, there has not been, to this point, a case of adverse patient reactions sensational enough to put the FDA to the test, inventors are understandably wary. Realistically, that same afore-mentioned mob that drives politicians, and through them the FDA, to be excessively risk averse would certainly react to any publicized negative results. Looking back at the Vioxx template, one can envision the headlines if some patient dies, even if already terminal, while taking a developmental medicine. "Anxious to make a buck, greedy company charges Sally Goodperson a fortune for risky, unapproved drug that kills her after causing days of torturous agony. Once again, the FDA fails to protect us from big pharma." It seems pretty certain that politicians will respond to such headlines and make sure the FDA does as well.[14]

Other reforms may be worth trying along the way, but it appears only more rapid approval will reliably get new, lifesaving medicines to terminal patients. We have seen that the FDA's expanded access program is very close to a meaningless gesture since so few patients actually ended up receiving not yet FDA-approved medicines. Eventually, "Right to Try" may marginally improve the situation but if we really want to stop sacrificing lives to regulatory delay we must dramatically increase the pace of bringing new lifesaving medicines to market. This would also slash the costs of all new medicines and unleash rapid innovation. This is most important for terminal patients but would be a huge boon to everyone. Far more medications would be invented each year, dramatically increasing competition and reducing prices.

## FOSTERING INNOVATION IS SAFER THAN OBSESSING ABOUT AVOIDING MISTAKES

Sometimes we are harmed by "good" medicines, even penicillin can harm patients allergic to it. There is a small chance of "bad" medicines, truly harmful on net, making their way to us. But significant occurrences of this are truly rare. The Elixir Sulfanilamide disaster was indeed the anomaly of anomalies; even if nothing like the FDA existed you're probably far more likely to get crushed by a meteor than to suffer from medication inadvertently laced with antifreeze or other poison by the manufacturer. Manufacturers have, for eighty years and counting, made certain there is no repeated tragedy of this sort; the FDA has never discovered a similar case and nipped it in the bud and probably never will. The greater danger by far is not the Elixir Sulfanilamide or even the thalidomide that makes it to us but rather the miraculous medicines like Gleevec that reach us too late.

The key to medical progress is not long, deliberate, protracted premarket testing to make sure we avoid the bad but rather a nurturing of innovation that gets new lifesaving medicines to us *fast* (and, hence, much more inexpensively, also). Politics, alas, tilts us in a tragically anti-innovation direction. Slow approval of lifesaving medicines regularly kills thousands of Americans each year, dwarfing the damage of unforeseen side effects from approved medicines. But voters notice and object to bad actions much more so than the deadly inaction of failing to approve. This bias, where we rage at bad actions (or at least seemingly bad, in our amateur opinions) but barely notice far worse inaction, seems hard wired into our instincts,

However well intentioned, the average voter is not medically well informed and prone to grossly overreact to problems with medicines that have substantial risks along with great rewards. Vioxx is a tragic example of how the political mob drives medicine in irrational directions. Doctors, and their affected patients, overwhelmingly favored keeping Vioxx available, despite the fact it increased heart attack risk about 1%, because it was the only effective pain reliever for about one million or so of those patients suffering the agony of severe rheumatoid arthritis. Unfortunately, most of the media and the public could not fully grasp the idea that people in misery could logically be willing to tolerate some risk of a heart attack in order to have a far better quality of life. They rushed to condemn Merck, the manufacturer of Vioxx, for "making a drug that killed people." In politics, doctors and other health care professionals are vastly outnumbered by uninformed amateurs, but a confused, uninformed vote counts just as much as a doctor's (or an affected patient's). In this world, many medicines with benefits far exceeding costs are driven from the market or, far more often, never reach it in the first place.

In terms of drugs that have overcome the initial FDA entry barrier of Phase I testing, but are in caught up in the lengthy regulatory pipeline, the FDA's current "expanded access" program appears to offer a limited, partial solution to the problem of patients dying while waiting those long years for permission to take known, potentially lifesaving medicines. In reality, though, expanded access is a chimera that almost always fails to deliver. It failed Abigail Burroughs and is unlikely to ever work well. We can hope for the best but it is unlikely the recently passed "Right Try" law will be markedly more successful than expanded access has been.

Any program designed to get patients access to drugs mired in the approval process is likely to come up short. More fundamentally, it's impossible to get access to medicines that simply don't exist because prohibitive regulatory costs preempted their creation. *The only real solution is to rapidly bring innovative medicines to market, get them through the pipeline quickly, allowing doctors to freely prescribe new medicines without any special procedures or paperwork.* How to best accomplish this is our subject for the next chapter.

## NOTES

1. Sometimes the FDA does directly bar terminal patients from trying potentially lifesaving medicines. Attorneys for the Abigail Alliance challenged this in court, basically arguing that a patient had a right to try to save their own life with developmental medicines. This seems a reasonable argument in a country supposedly devoted to life, liberty, and the pursuit of happiness—this issue hits all three of those. However, in 2007, the D.C. Circuit Court of Appeals disagreed in an 8-2 vote (Trowbridge and Walker, 2007).

2. The law also greatly increased FDA regulatory authority over advertising. Prior to this, commercial speech was generally uncensored. Drug manufacturers, shocking to today's sensibilities, had the same freedom of speech as we see expressed

today in newspapers and television news, with their wildly varying accounts of the truth. Fraudulent claims were illegal but it was about as difficult to prove fraud legally as it is today to prove a newspaper or television reporter guilty of libel. The regulations clearly reduced drug companies' exaggerated and borderline fraudulent claims (Weimer, 1982). On the other hand, these regulations have also been used to suppress the truth, especially as regards "off-label" (that is FDA unapproved) uses of medicines (Klein and Tabarrok, 2018c).

3. The law is very inefficient, increasing profits by boosting monopoly power and prices rather than by reducing costs. Also, it is sloppily structured such that companies can sometimes just submit new paperwork for already existing medicines to gain orphan status for the patent, or they can subdivide the paperwork for non-rare diseases, turning one disease into several rare diseases. And, of course, the gains for inventors do not nearly equal the costs of regulatory delays; the orphaned drug problem remains serious. But, at least the law has been estimated to increase the number of orphan drugs seeking FDA approval, by about a third (Yin, 2009).

4. In other words, using government regulation to stop doctors from prescribing ineffective medicines turned out to be a bit like using government rules and red tape to prevent the sale of square tires. Regulation to prevent the manufacture of products that no one wants doesn't have much of an upside potential. It's true, of course, that we can easily deduce square tires are ineffective on our own while we need some expert advice to gauge likely effectiveness of medicines. But, since that is the very reason we go to doctors and other professionals, that distinction has little significance.

5. Courts have recently ruled that the FDA prohibition against advertising off-label uses serves no useful public purpose and is therefore an unconstitutional infringement of free speech (Miller and Conko, 2018).

6. The fact that no one bothers to keep track of exactly how often off-label prescriptions are used is itself evidence of the apparent uselessness of the FDA's testing for effectiveness.

7. There are some studies suggesting on-label medicines perform somewhat better than off-label (Cuzzolin et al., 2006). However, such findings generally have two major weaknesses. One is that they don't differentiate between deliberate off-label prescribing and unintentional errors in dosage or in medicines selected. The second problem is that the basis of comparison is usually the number of adverse drug reactions. By this measure water would be judged a better treatment for pneumonia than penicillin, since there will be a few allergic reactions to penicillin. We need to get past that bias that focuses only on bad outcomes, and look at benefits, not just costs.

8. Most likely Merck was understandably worried about liability costs. Even after the voluntary recall they ended up paying out a $4.9 billion settlement (Heisel, 2010).

9. Dr. Angelis might be viewed by many as a heroic figure, not only because of her bold statements about Vioxx and medical trade-offs but also because of the fact that she is the first pediatrician, and also the first woman to serve as editor in chief of JAMA.

10. As of this writing, a small company, Tremeau Pharmaceuticals, has announced plans to bring Vioxx back to market for severe joint pain caused by hemophilia (Ross

et al., 2018). If that happens, then presumably the million or so patients harmed by its withdrawal would be able to obtain it off-label.

11. It should be noted that the Abigail Alliance was evaluating when medicines were *proven safe and effective*, in a practical attempt to influence particular medicines' approval. In other words, they were essentially employing the FDA's own standards, just more quickly and decisively. They generally favor allowing terminal patient's access much sooner, after Phase I trials show reasonable safety (Burroughs, 2018).

12. There is less consensus regarding nonterminal patients. A significant minority of health care experts think drug approval times are reasonable or possibly even too hasty at times for medicines that are not lifesaving and that offer treatments similar to established medicines. An excellent, concise presentation of this view's leading proponents and their basic arguments, as mentioned earlier, can be found in *Once "too slow," FDA approvals called "too fast"* (Henderson and Rowland, 2005).

Generally, these arguments center on the number of type 1 casualties and the number of drugs the FDA approves and subsequently recalls. However, to my knowledge, these works do not make any rigorous, convincing comparison of type 1 and type 2 errors; they generally just dwell on type 1 errors. Another common weakness is that people with this perspective seem to routinely dismiss any notion that some patients might be rationally willing to risk a significant chance of death in order to improve their quality of life.

13. This is a widely accepted figure but a few studies argue the cost is significantly less. Since there is tremendous variance across the industry it seems the size and composition of the sample is crucial. Biotech firms, for example, often have to invest less while traditional chemical manufacturers spend more. Lower cost estimates generally have small samples and a sample biased toward biotech. Also, lower estimates are often using older data, very relevant since these costs have risen much faster than general inflation. Lastly, it is important to look at average costs rather than incremental costs. That is, we have to average total R&D costs, including the vast spending on drugs that are abandoned, over the relatively few medicines that make it to market (Herper, 2017).

14. Liability exposure, of course, is another factor that discourages companies from selling medicines before FDA approval.

*Chapter 3*

# Saving Lives with a Better, Safer FDA

## A PROVEN REFORM: FDA APPROVAL
## BASED SOLELY ON SAFETY

To begin with the fairly obvious, we could repeal the 1962 Kefauver-Harris Amendments, returning to the policy of basing FDA approval only on safety, rather than on safety and effectiveness. Just as the earlier discussed evidence clearly shows the shift to Kefauver-Harris caused innovation to plunge and many thousands of people to die from that slower innovation, repealing Kefauver-Harris would speed discovery of new lifesaving medicines and save many thousands annually.

In fact, as explained in chapter 2, *we have extensive current experience with this reform because private health care professionals came up with a* de facto *partial repeal of Kefauver-Harris decades ago with the invention of "off-label" prescriptions.* The decentralized system of researchers and doctors that discovers off-label applications does an excellent job of verifying efficacy. In fact, theses researchers and doctors are as effective as the FDA and more efficient in that they take far less time. Of course, they have a major advantage since, unlike the FDA, they are not driven by the political mob. FDA officials have politicians constantly looking over their shoulders, anxious to assign blame to regulators if the mob believes an "evil drug like Vioxx" is labeled effective. Most likely, this is why private researchers can verify effectiveness so much faster and more cheaply than FDA regulators. (Earlier, we saw the private system, as exhibited by the Abigail Alliance, can, using the same data as the FDA, also verify *safety and effectiveness* much faster.)

Again, our government's full embrace of off-label medicines appears to be very solid proof that the private regulation of effectiveness works quite well. There is no government agency, apart from, perhaps, some in the FDA itself, railing against the use of these privately regulated treatments—not the health managers of Medicare, Medicaid, veterans hospitals, or anyone else. In modern times, even the FDA has been focused on stopping the advertising off-label applications, not really strongly opposing off-label medicines themselves.

*Does it make any sense at all to insist that we need lengthy FDA sanctioned testing to verify amoxicillin's effectiveness in treating respiratory infections but that we don't at all need the FDA to verify amoxicillin's effectiveness in treating ulcers?* Logically, it seems we either need the FDA to approve effectiveness or we don't. It is only happenstance that amoxicillin's effectiveness was FDA tested for respiratory infections rather than ulcers. If it had first to come to market as an ulcer medication it would have been the other way around; it would be off-label for respiratory treatments. Delaying medicines for years to test effectiveness in their first known (or at least first applied for) application but then potentially allowing all subsequent applications free market access is logically inconsistent. The off-label market demonstrates the waste of our long regulatory delays in this regard.

There is simply no evidence—not today, not in the past, not ever, that there is any sort of net benefit from the FDA regulating the effectiveness of medicines; private regulation is a proven success. The costly and sometimes deadly delays of waiting for FDA approval of effectiveness is something virtually all health care professionals, again, including those at government agencies such as Medicare, avoid whenever possible through off-label prescriptions. In reality, moving to an FDA approval system based only on safety is not a new idea but something we already did decades ago, and do today for 20% to 39% of our prescriptions, those that are off-label (Kao, 2017). We have every reason to do the same for the other 61 to 80%.

## UNIVERSAL EXPANDED ACCESS WILL SUCCEED WHERE ALL ELSE HAS FAILED

So, with no lengthy FDA assessment of effectiveness, once a medicine passed the Phase I trial for safety, the company could mass produce and sell the drug. This overcomes the problems that have caused the FDA's "expanded access" program to fail Abigail Burroughs and many millions like her. Medicines for terminal patients, and others with no other hope from older medicines, would become available at lower prices, thanks to both more mass production and more competition in a world with many more new medicines coming to market each year to compete with established drugs. Also, the onerous paperwork necessary in expanded access, and presumably reduced by Right to Try, would utterly disappear. Once the Phase I trial was passed the medicine's sales would not be restricted. In essence, the failed, ultra-expensive, extremely complex and pigeon-holed expanded access of today would become a simple, far less expensive, and universal standard procedure, that would therefore actually work.

Although terminal patients will be especially benefitted, universal expanded access will help everyone. It's very difficult to estimate exactly how much faster innovation would be; however, we can be certain that the effect will be quite large. As a first approximation, recall that in the first decade after the passage of Kefauver-Harris the average number of new medications introduced each year was sixteen, while in the previous decade the average had been forty (Peltz, 1973). *If those same proportions held today then this reform would increase the stream of new medicines to a rate two and a half times greater than the comparative snail's pace of today.* In the five-year period from January 2012 through December 2016 the FDA approved 174 new medicines, 34.8 per year (Hwang et al., 2017). Multiplying that by the 2.5 proportion means *new drugs introduced annually would surge from 34.8 to 87!* However, given the gigantic leaps in medical technology, and also in society's wealth, since 1962, it is likely that the increase would be much, much higher, almost certainly well over 100, quite possibly over 200. We're talking about a creative revolution in medicine, leaving the comparatively dark ages of today behind.

The rate of innovation would especially surge for "orphan" drugs as well as for medications that substantially duplicate existing medicines since both of these serve smaller markets, hence have smaller revenues that are often insufficient to cover the massive cost of proving effectiveness to the FDA. Thus, with those enormous proofs of efficacy costs gone, people suffering deadly but less common diseases would be especially benefitted. In all likelihood, we are talking about obtaining cures for these "orphaned" maladies many years, even maybe decades faster. Of course, everyone would benefit from the lower prices brought by the increased competition. Far fewer medicines would have monopoly power as the reduction in the FDA barrier to entry costs would allow many more competing treatments to enter the market.

It is interesting that, even though companies selling their medicines for off-label use are not required to seek FDA approval for effectiveness, they sometimes do. While obtaining the FDA seal of approval appears to have no medical value, it does seem to aid in marketing medicines (Kao, 2017). Thus, while it *apparently makes no sense to require FDA approval of efficacy, it does seem sensible to keep this as an option.* So, firms could begin sales right after Phase I but could choose to continue on to Phase II and III and ultimately FDA approval of efficacy when they considered this to be worth the cost. Thus, the FDA would remain *The* regulator for safety but would become an advisor for effectiveness.

Support for this universal expanded access approach is overwhelming. The vast majority of doctors, at minimum over 70%, support a reform that goes at least as far as ending the FDA delays imposed by verifying efficacy (Kazman, 2010). There are also a multitude of studies by economists and others strongly concurring with this conclusion. Summaries of their positions along with links to the studies are concisely presented in *Quotations: Economists' Judgments about the FDA* by Daniel Klein and Alexander Tabarrok (Klein and Tabarrok, 2018b). Of course, as already mentioned, every relevant government agency, even the FDA itself to some degree, has implicitly endorsed this reform through their embrace off-label medicines.

## UNIVERSAL EXPANDED ACCESS WOULD BE GREAT, BUT WE CAN DO EVEN BETTER

However, there is reason to believe this reform does not go far enough. There are two major limitations to leaving the FDA responsible for vetoing "bad" drugs to "keep us safe." First, this will still leave some terminal patients to die waiting (and others to suffer great morbidity), while a promising medicine works its way through the FDA safety approval process, though this amount will be small compared to the numbers currently dying and greatly suffering from regulatory delays. Second, the political mob remains empowered as long as politicians and regulators can overrule doctors and patients in the medical judgment of when a treatment is "safe." Wary of the mob's, and therefore Congress's, bias against innovation with its increase in type 1 errors, regulators are likely to simply take longer and longer to conclude that a new medicine is safe enough. Remember, the thalidomide mob discussed in chapter 2 that produced Kefauver-Harris was really demanding more "safety," or more precisely, fewer type 1 errors. Congress threw in "effectiveness" regulation on their own, perhaps because they felt uncomfortable passing legislation that simply required us to wait around longer, letting Europe and the rest of the world function as our guinea pigs a few more years before Americans took a chance on those scary, new, often high-tech medicines.

As we have conclusively seen, it is very dangerous to leave the political mob standing between patients and innovative or riskier treatments. Just ask the million or so people suffering acutely from rheumatoid arthritis that saw their quality of life plunge from the anti-Vioxx hysteria.

## OPTIMAL REFORM: MEDICAL
## DECISIONS WITHOUT POLITICS

Ben Harris passed away in August 2013; we'll have more to say about this good soul shortly. For now, let us just note the problem he succinctly states.

> We simply don't have time to wait for the results of [clinical trials]. Our life spans are much shorter than the [FDA] approval process.
>
> —Ben Harris, a medical physicist diagnosed with ALS
> (Lou Gehrig's disease) in January 2011 (Marcus, 2012)

When limited trials take too long we need a different system that deals better with uncertainty.

Medical decisions are often messy with no clear right or wrong answer; the safest or most effective course is often unknown. For example, an operation might or might not substantially reduce excruciating back pain for a given elderly patient. It might also kill her. The probabilities of success, ineffectiveness, or death vary with each individual patient and are not objectively known. Estimates of these probabilities will often vary significantly from doctor to doctor with equal expertise. Should she opt for surgery, take some risk for a chance at a much better life? Or play it safe, live with the pain, and the foggy mental state that her not fully effective pain medicines produce. No one can truly tell her what she "should" do; people can offer a subjective opinion but there is no objectively optimal course of action, or inaction. Patients, guided by health care professionals and the advice of loved ones, must make a decision in the face of massive uncertainties. This is inherently a subjective decision with severely limited information where reasonable and competent adults will make different choices depending on their unique personality, individual situation, religious beliefs, and other individual factors.

Thankfully, Congress has not tasked the FDA with deciding when surgery would be safe and effective. The mob, compassionate and well intentioned but dangerously confused, doesn't try to drag you out of surgery to keep something bad from happening to you. However, as we know, the mob will snatch risky medications out of your hand, without taking the time to learn that not taking that medication may be even more risky for you. The decision calculus involved for a dying or greatly suffering patient contemplating the use of a developmental medical drug, after conventional, approved options have failed, is essentially identical with that of the patient contemplating back surgery. In the case of a possible surgery we leave the decision to her, with the advice and consent of her chosen health care professionals. In the case of a cutting-edge medicine we implicitly bring in the opinions of voters, generally a nice bunch, but still nothing more than a well-meaning but woefully uninformed gang of amateurs. The mob does not vote to determine the fate of each individual patient, instead, they vote politicians into office to carry out their orders. In turn, politicians hire the professionals at the FDA to act as their agents. This is probably better than direct mob rule but that's not a certainty. After all, as we saw earlier, even the mob would likely have delivered the lifesaving Gleevec to dying cancer patients about two and a half years faster than the political process did!

What if we always left these complex decisions on cutting-edge medicines to the patients and the health care professionals the patient chooses to advise and guide them? This is exactly what we do and have always done with decisions regarding choices among already approved medicines, surgery, and most every other aspect of medicine. Suppose we simply make the FDA's opinion on both safety and effectiveness nonbinding advice rather than a universal, one size fits all diktat? How about we *always* let the patient, along with her doctors, decide which treatments are the safest and/or most effective for her, giving whatever weight she chooses to the FDA's recommendation? We can still benefit from the FDA's expertise, as we would from any health care professional, without having the stifling effects on innovation that come with political regulation. The FDA should still assess the safety of every new medicine, but during that testing period a doctor could prescribe the medicine for patients with no other hope.

Most doctors favor exactly this system, shifting the FDA into an advisory role. Through the 1990s and 2000s the Competitive Enterprise Institute conducted a series of surveys of doctors, with each one focused on a different medical specialty, such as oncologists, cardiologists, and, in the last survey, orthopedic surgeons. The vast majority of doctors surveyed in all specialties made it clear they would consider unapproved medicines for certain of their patients based on information from medical journals, colleagues, foreign countries' regulators, and other sources. In the most recently available survey, of orthopedic surgeons, 78% said the FDA prevented them from giving their patients the best possible care (Kazman, 2010).[1] This reform also has broad support from economists and other researchers (Klein and Tabarrok, 2018b).

In the latest data, about 12% of the medicines that begin human testing (FDA Phase I) were eventually approved by the FDA (Sullivan, 2018). This implies, if there is a medicine in Phase I trials intended to treat dying and/ or hopelessly suffering patients there is, on average, a roughly 12% chance those patients would indeed be helped by that medication. Isn't a 12% chance much better than none? Furthermore, something is still gained even in the cases where the developmental medication proves ineffective. Letting more patients try medications sooner will help us to more quickly reject ineffectual treatments so that we can more rapidly shift human and financial resources into more promising treatments.[2] Remember also, in a system where medicines are brought rapidly to market, where regulatory barriers to entry no longer exist, there will be far more new medicines, a much faster pace of innovation. So, if that 12% portion holds it will be 12% of a much, much larger number of treatments, conceivably several times as many treatments as we currently see.

The current approach under the FDA starts with just a few patients in Phase I, some time to analyze and process results, then, if approved at that stage, a wider test in Phase II, more analysis then, if favorable, much wider trials in Phase III, then a long study of all the results and finally a decision to approve or disapprove. There is an expedited process for more urgently needed medicines, but this still leaves average time to approval at 7.1 years (Hwang et al., 2017). This extraordinarily slow, cautious approach to innovation is reasonable for testing a new treatment for toenail fungus. But does this make sense for terminal patients certain to die unless, perhaps, they get the medicine being tested? Isn't it sensible, for patients with no other hope, to have immediate access, basically combining all three phases into a much larger, faster trial? When patients are literally running out of time it seems better do less studying and more learning through actively treating patients with no other viable options. Sure, sometimes these unproven medicines would make things worse. But if dying a little sooner is the worst case scenario, trying for a possible treatment might be the better option as many would see it. Some might prefer waiting for more tests, just staying sick, playing it safe, and clinging to a life that is soon to end. How about we let each patient choose?

## SHOULD WE LET TERMINAL PATIENTS TRY MEDICINES BEFORE USUAL PHASE I TRIALS?

Patients, as well as their doctors, would naturally prefer established medicines that have clearly helped others suffering the same malady. But, again, a one size fits all sort of approach does not seem logical. Desperate times sometimes really do call for desperate measures. Imagine, for example, you were living long ago, before the availability of antibiotics, and that the person you loved most was dying of pneumonia, in fact would likely perish that very night. A friend of yours, Alexander Fleming, stops by and says, "I know how strange this sounds but I stumbled upon this discovery that a certain sort of mold, penicillin, kills bacteria in petri dishes in the lab. I've brought you all the penicillin mold I have and I think there's a chance it could save your spouse's life. But I haven't had a chance to test it on anyone, or even on lab animals. What do you two think?" Doesn't it seem that would be the time to give mold a chance?

In essence, unrestricted consumer choice means we could sometimes begin some Phase I testing much sooner in desperate situations. Isn't that appropriate? Again, rigidly following the same general procedures for new cancer treatments as we do for wart removal solutions seems absurd. Someone always has to be the first human, or cohort of humans, to try a new medicine. Current Phase I FDA tests, the first human tests, are conducted on a small, carefully monitored group. Completely free patient choice basically means anyone could, with the advice and consent of their doctor, join this test group, if the inventor is willing. Compare this to our current policy where we tell the desperately ill, "Sorry, we realize you're dying but we have enough test subjects, you can't try this medicine. Plus, you have so many health problems you're not a good test subject. Try to hang in there a few more years while we finish the testing." Ben Harris, the ALS patient, quoted in the opening of this section began to desperately produce a "home brew" version of the medicine being tested because the present system denied him access to that most promising treatment (Marcus, 2012). As is often the case, the FDA granted him an expanded access that was useless because the cash-strapped inventor didn't have the medicine to supply and wanted to focus limited resources on gaining FDA permission to market, hence mass produce, the medication (Akst, 2017).

Frustrated patients frequently resent inventors for this situation but remember—*these companies always want to sell patients medicines; this is their entire purpose*. Government regulation stops them from meeting patients' demand for their product, their natural impulse. If we grant producers automatic access to markets, knocking a billion or two off the investment required to bring medications to market then we really will expand access! Essentially, for patients like Ben Harris we would compress the current three-phase, seven-year plus testing process to one large single process where marketing and testing are concurrent; every patient in the market is also in the test. Keeping dying patients from their best options with lengthy premarket testing would never happen. Since we would sometimes move up human testing this would actually shave more than seven years off the current lag from discovery to marketing.

Letting terminal or dreadfully suffering patients have access to any medicine they choose, even joining in on very early testing, will undoubtedly result in more deaths and suffering from type 1 errors of approving medicines with harmful effects, at least to some. However, a significant number will be helped, some greatly helped, and at least a few will even be cured. Imagine if all the leukemia patients seeking to try Gleevec had been allowed to do so, rising from their death beds to go dancing.

## Facing Reality: Subjectivity and Individuality

You might say that before enacting this reform we should carefully estimate both the costs and benefits of such unbridled freedom to assure there is a net gain, but that's actually impossible in cases of this sort. Even if we could overcome the pervasive uncertainty there is no objective way to aggregate results. Most likely this system would be an unambiguous gain for terminal patients overall but, to make it more interesting, suppose the results are more mixed. Imagine, for instance, it turned out that patient life expectancies appear to fall slightly with this policy while average quality of life improves substantially. Does it automatically follow that we should deprive patients of a choice, just to make sure they live slightly longer, but more wretchedly painful, lives? If we say "yes," since life is sacred we must always increase life spans then we should also ban swimming, skiing, driving faster than 15 miles per hour, childbirth, and so on. Obviously, many of us agree life is sacred but to live joyously with some meaning we need to accept some risks, like sharing life with friends and family even though humans are all dangerous germ-carriers who occasionally turn violent!

Taking a medicine that reduces our pain and increases our joy might be more valuable than living a little longer. Is 94% chance of a pain free, great life worth a 6% risk of death? Different people will give different answers, and no one has to be wrong. We cannot objectively say when a complex medication is safe enough any more than we can say when a complex surgery is safe enough. There is no objective basis for preempting patient choices with regulatory commands and controls.

When the FDA, or anyone, declares a drug is "safe" all that really means is, "it seems safe enough to us." Asking the FDA to judge when a medicine is deemed appropriately safe is like asking them, "What's the prettiest color, the catchiest song, or the coolest hairstyle?" They can provide us with their opinion, and the relevant data considered, but the government, like all of us, is not capable of reporting the objectively "correct" decision in these complex cases because it doesn't exist. The FDA is entitled to its opinion on a medication's safety and virtually all patients would want to hear that opinion. But *there seems no basis, ethically or in practicality, for the government to dictate that we are not free to seek a second opinion, and make our own decision.*

## A Fly in the Ointment: Liability Law

Recall, Merck withdrew Vioxx *before* the FDA had a chance to order it to do so. In all likelihood, Merck did this to limit their liability exposure. This seems to have been a very wise move in light of the fact that Merck still ended up paying out a $4.85 billion settlement (Krauskopf, 2007). The political mob that sabotages innovation and patient access to state of the art medicines also sweeps up or greatly influences juries and judges, not just politicians and regulators. The U.S. liability system is a significant obstacle to getting developmental or riskier medicines to terminal patients, and others who are similarly desperate. So, to fully unleash innovation and especially to best aid terminal patients or those experiencing great morbidity we would also need tort reform. Manufacturers will be reluctant to sell riskier, less proven drugs, just as they often are now, if they face standard liability rules. Doctors, who face their own liability concerns, may also be hesitant to prescribe unproven, riskier medicines.

David Weimer suggests an elegant but conceptually simple solution: Suppose laws were updated so that pharmaceutical firms selling developmental medicines were only liable if they concealed relevant information or were somehow misleading, likewise for doctors (Weimer, 1982). Thus, for example, you could not have sued Alexander Fleming if that crazy mold triggered immediate death. More realistically, imagine the seller of a medicine truthfully said, "This worked great on lab animals so far, 99 were cured while the other 13 weren't but did not appear to be any worse off. But you would actually be the first human to try it; it's hard to even guess at the risks or the probability of success." In this case, the manufacturer and prescribing doctor could not be sued regardless of any adverse reaction to the unproven treatment. So, they are motivated to supply these medicines to patients with no other hope.[3]

The running theme in all of this is that we end up killing people because our laws governing innovation in medicines are so rigid, so hostile toward rapid innovation even when a rapid response is the only possible way to save lives. If inventors know they run the risk of being financially crucified anytime they move fast, before all the facts about cutting-edge medicines are in and carefully checked and rechecked, then they simply aren't going to move fast. Moving slowly and hesitantly is frequently a good life strategy, and often a good policy in medicine. But, there are certain times when hesitation and extreme caution are deadly, we need better liability rules for those cases.

## How Would the FDA Evolve In Its New, Advisory Role?

We know the FDA's advice has value, as evidenced by off-label sellers that choose to work with the FDA to become on-label. The FDA's expertise, experience, and historical gravitas guarantees that companies will, whenever it's financially feasible, generally prefer to have the FDA seal of approval— for safety and also for effectiveness, to aid in marketing their medicines. Patients and health care professionals will also look first at FDA-approved treatments. The vast majority of prescriptions will likely be written for drugs safety approved by the FDA exactly as they are today. What patient wants, and what doctor would prescribe, a risky, unproven medicine when tried and true remedies are available? Removing the rigid gatekeeping function of the FDA will be a tremendous benefit for some but with a much less radical overall impact than one might initially imagine.

The demand for those drugs not safety certified by the FDA will be limited mainly to terminal and a few other desperate patients who have not responded to established medicines, and probably not even 100% of those patients. For this group, right from the start, freedom for innovation will sometimes be a godsend. Over time, the massive increases in supply will slash prices, and increase the pace of innovation, greatly benefiting patients more broadly.

While some inventors would pursue FDA approval for effectiveness, if the system in place today doesn't adapt it is likely that off-label prescriptions would become even more common, would probably become the norm. However, it is very likely that the FDA would adapt. For one thing, isn't a yes or no answer on effectiveness inherently inefficient, bordering on silly? We don't really go from effectiveness being completely unknown one day to being approved and known the next day, though FDA procedures sometimes essentially operate that way. In reality, we judge efficacy in a continuous process where our estimate of the probability of effectiveness is steadily updated as we gain new information. The FDA could, for example, estimate the probability of effectiveness as testing proceeded. So, rather than remaining officially silent for years then suddenly proclaiming they are virtually 100% sure a medicine is effective, regulators-cum-advisors could provide continuous estimates, with details about the test results the probability estimate is based on.

It seems likely that going from, say, 80 or 90% certainty to 100% certainty would often require great expense, sometimes even greater than the expense of going from 0% to 80–90%. There might therefore be a very high demand for getting that 80–90% official FDA score. In some cases, inventors might settle for 50–60%. Orphan drug inventors might not be able to afford any formal FDA effectiveness tests but the FDA could still rate them based on available evidence. Thus, rather than an off-label/on-label dichotomy (a less than 100% vs. 100% dichotomy) the FDA could grade every medicine. Some firms would go through the time and expense to get that 100%, as off labelers sometimes proceed to do today, while others would stop at 80% or 90% or likely much lower for some orphan drug inventors and others with very limited resources. The point is, it seems more reasonable to have the FDA provide effectiveness judgments on all medicines rather than issuing a somewhat grumpy "no comment" on every single off-label use. Likewise, rather than running around trying to stop amoxicillin producers from mentioning how well their medicine works on ulcers, the FDA could tolerate more free speech but also state its own opinion. *In this information age, a good advisor freely dispensing valuable information might be more beneficial than a rather secretive naysayer guarding the entrance.*

Of course, information would be especially precious to dying or otherwise desperate patients considering brand new medicines not yet safety approved.

They could get information on unapproved drugs directly from the FDA as well as indirectly from their doctors and others who incorporate that FDA information for them. Again, the advisory system would allow the FDA to express more nuanced, complex opinions, rather than the basically crude pass/fail approach in place now. For example, when forced to say either yes or no to the apparently safe and virtually 100% effective Gleevec, the FDA ended up taking two and a half extra years to get to "yes." This, of course, caused significant suffering and death, needlessly. But, perhaps such problems are inevitable when we require one small group of people to take on the extraordinarily heavy responsibility of making a complex, subjective, potentially dangerous decision for our entire society.

In this reformed, advisory system the FDA recommendation might have begun with something like, "Early reports on Gleevec are astounding. We have never seen a more promising new medicine coming out of a Phase I trial. But, as with all developmental medicines, there is a chance of some hidden risks. Consult your doctor, and proceed carefully. But, if your health is failing, your situation desperate, Gleevec certainly appears to be worth considering." That sort of recommendation, unlike long regulatory delays, is not likely to kill any patients. However, there is a cautionary tone that alerts patients to consider possible type 1 problems as they consult with their doctors. This more diversified system reduces overall risk, an FDA mistake in either direction (type 2 or more likely type 1 errors) is not so catastrophic, can be corrected by each patient's doctor. The FDA becomes a depository and clearinghouse of information but the new system recognizes the individual patient is the decision maker, guided by health care professionals that know the relevant specifics of each of their patients. We stop our current pretense that borders on pretending that drugs are good or bad (approved or unapproved) and consistently deal with the reality that a given medicine is potentially good for some patients but bad for others.

Even if we don't formally convert the FDA from dictator to advisor, advancing technology is likely to do something like that anyway. Ben Harris was suffering a deadly disease in that "orphaned" category; ALS victims in the U.S. number only about 30,000. There were no useful approved medicines for him—remember, our current regulatory approach is especially devastating toward the development of orphan drugs. An unapproved, developmental medicine was promising but, like many victims, he couldn't get in the clinical trial, and expanded access failed, as it normally does.

So, Ben joined an online group that was using its own home brewed version of the medicine the system denied them. The group knew their crude version, of the medication known as NP001, wasn't the best but hoped it would buy them enough time until they could get access to NP001. Another ALS patient, Eric Valor, researched and produced the homemade drug, knowing his health was too poor for him to be eligible for trials. Ben kept and shared meticulous records, and analyzed overall results of the group. Establishment researchers, though sympathetic, were displeased by this do-it-yourself approach, concerned the group could hurt themselves, and fearful that the establishment could lose control of its rigorous testing process (Marcus, 2012).

In the age of the internet and widespread international travel it doesn't seem realistic to expect patients too sick or otherwise unable to join FDA clinical trials to just suffer or die quietly. There is no telling what informal production and black markets in medical drugs may develop in the future if we cling to the FDA dictator model.

However, all that can be prevented by moving the FDA to advisory status. Perhaps, in that arrangement, the FDA could, in certain urgent cases, even publish multiple analyses from different perspectives that make varying recommendations. Those internal differences of opinion are largely suppressed today, as massive amounts of time are spent behind closed doors to get a consensus in the simplistic world of approved/not approved. How about more transparency in FDA deliberations and more free speech?! Isn't it better to face uncertainty and controversy, and deal with it, than to more or less pretend it somehow doesn't exist?

## CONCLUSION

We have placed the FDA in an impossible position, making a single, one size fits all decision as to whether a new medication is "safe and effective" for our society. Safety and effectiveness, in this context, are inherently individualistic, subjective concepts, yet we pretend there is an objective answer, and we pretend the FDA can find it, given enough years of delay. Complex, sometimes life or death, medical decisions are best made by patients, with input from their loved ones, guided by the advice and consent of their doctors and other health care professionals. Although we generally recognize this in most health care decisions, we have unwisely blundered into a system where we allow politicians to dictate to doctors which medicines professionals may consider for their patients. In this case, we are implicitly trusting our politicians more than our doctors![4] Of course, FDA regulators handle the nuts and bolts of restricting the medical choices of doctors and their patients, but they are creatures of and report to the U.S. Congress.

Since patients and doctors alike naturally prefer old, proven medicines, patients' freedom to choose will not lead to a reckless embrace of risky, unproven medicines. But when tried and true treatments are useless, when taking a new medicine is less risky than doing nothing, then we can give new treatments a chance.

One specific reform possibility is to return to the standard where the FDA simply judged and approved safety, rather than safety and effectiveness. This means, in current parlance, approving drugs after they pass Phase I trials, with Phases II and III optional. This would cut regulatory delays of innovation from seven or eight years to about one or two, assuming Phase I procedures remain unchanged. In reality, we have already done this for many medications through the process of off-label prescriptions, which by definition have not been approved by the FDA for effectiveness in the treatment for which they are prescribed. Our ongoing off-label experience, as well as overall historical experience, indicates that the benefits of having the FDA judge effectiveness are insignificant. Thank goodness doctors were allowed, for example, to use amoxicillin as a standard treatment for stomach ulcers, without waiting for the FDA to conduct a single test of effectiveness. The fact that government programs such as Medicare and Medicaid have covered off-label medicines for decades is obvious confirmation that it is *not* worth waiting several years for regulators to verify effectiveness.

However, repealing the FDA authority to judge and approve effectiveness does not go far enough. Retaining the FDA as a safety czar holding new drugs back for a year or two still abandons many terminal patients to a certain death as we study whether the latest medicine is safe enough for them to choose. Furthermore, keeping politics involved in medicine is inherently dangerous. However well intentioned, the average voter is not medically well informed and prone to grossly overreact to problems with medicines that have substantial risks along with great rewards. Vioxx is a tragic example of how the political mob drives medicine in irrational directions.

The only way to keep the political mob out of the equation is to leave all medical decisions to patients, guided by health care professionals.[5] Thus, the ideal reform is to convert the FDA into an information clearing house that makes recommendations but has no power to veto patient's choices by unilaterally banning the sale of medicines. The FDA would still be very influential and could provide more complex advice, rather than the narrow and simplistic approved/unapproved message they send now. But, the expert advice of the FDA would no longer preclude patients from seeking a second opinion and making their own choice.[6] Thus, the decision of what medicine to take would become like the decision of whether or not to have surgery, purely a medical choice not a matter of politics.

Just moving to a system where the FDA judged/approved only safety is likely to multiply the annual introduction of new medicines by two and a half times the current rate, at bare minimum, which means the introduction of new medicines would go from a current rate of about thirty-five to at least eighty-seven annually. But this projection is based on 1960s data, given the explosive growth in medical technology as well as far great levels of wealth today, it seems more likely new medicines would surge to over 100 or even 200 per year. Moving to a wide open, depoliticized system with FDA advice but not diktats would likely multiply innovation even more than that. We would probably preserve some of the slow, protracted testing procedures before embracing new medicines to treat, say, toe nail fungus. However, new cancer treatments for otherwise doomed patients, would follow an entirely different path. These would generally be available to all patients at the time human testing begins, and the point of human trials might also be moved up sooner when time is literally running out for dying patients. This would be an expanded access program that actually works. Our FDA advisors could deliver a constant flow of information, providing a report on estimated safety and effectiveness that is continuously updated.

The resulting surge in newly invented medicines will save lives and slash prices. Treatments that largely duplicate existing medicines will especially become much more common, exponentially increasing competition. Unlike today, where such medicines often are incapable of generating enough revenues to cover the massive expense of gaining FDA approval, therefore are never brought forward. Similarly, the problem of orphan drugs will largely disappear. Like duplicate medicines, those treatments that target smaller groups, such as ALS patients like the late Ben Harris, often simply can't generate the $2.6 billion or so it takes to bring a medicine out of the lab and through the current FDA approval process. Moving the FDA to an advisory role vastly shrinks that huge, up-front cost. A straight-forward economic principle is that any major entry barrier retards competition and elevates prices. Our government's current seven- to eight-year average approval process is the mother of all entry barriers; moving the FDA to the role of valued advisor eradicates that barrier.

Imagine the devastation we would wreak on high-tech industries like computers or smart phones if we required their latest products to sit around for seven or eight years of testing before anyone could buy them! Innovation is nowhere more important than in lifesaving medicine yet this is where we make sure innovation is slower than virtually anywhere else.

If we remove the politics, leave the practice of medicine to the professionals, we can unleash innovation, as we already do with most products, that will save thousands and thousands of lives annually, greatly reduce suffering, and make prices far more affordable.

Keep in mind, that ultra-conservative doctors and patients are not at all required to participate in this complete freedom for patient choices of medicines. Any doctor would be free to continue to rigidly prescribe only proven medicines, completely approved by the FDA. In fact, any doctor is free to wait for years after FDA approval just to make sure nothing bad shows up with further experience. Any patient could avoid those they considered to be "wild hippy doctors" who sometimes prescribed newfangled, unproven medicines. Each individual is free to be as personally resistant, even hostile, to change and innovation as they choose. Note, these ultra-conservative patients would still benefit from the system of patient freedom because the prices of their old medicines would fall. That is, patients who more freely embraced innovation would drive companies with established drugs to cut their prices, or else lose many of those customers to newer medicines.

Innovative medicines would not be forced on anyone, but those more welcoming to invention would end up benefitting those who remain unreceptive. Of course, this is the complete opposite of our current system where those who oppose innovation, perhaps without even being fully conscious of their bias, harm everyone who would benefit from it. The opponents of rapid invention force desperate patients to stick with old medicines that are useless to them. If, gentle reader, you and I don't want to take newer, perhaps, riskier medicines, that is certainly our right. But how in the world do we justify forcibly withholding riskier but potentially lifesaving medicines from those patients who want to try them? Why does Abigail Burroughs or the thousands like her each year have to die, sometimes, because of our very cautious preferences, which are given dictatorial status via politics?

Patient freedom is surely optimal, would save many lives and slash costs/ prices, but it would not be heaven on earth; it will always be a dangerous world. At times, patients will err in one direction or another—sometimes suffering needlessly when they could have been saved by a seemingly risky new medicine, sometimes suffering more from a new medication than they would have without it, or dying sooner.

We would also lose our rigidly controlled testing processes in clinical trials, especially for lifesaving treatments. With universal expanded access no terminal or seriously suffering patient would be willing to participate in a trial featuring placebos, where there is a 50% chance they will be given a worthless palliative. Of course, we have survived and advanced without placebos in other areas of medicine. Surgeons have never conducted trials where, say, half the patients scheduled for appendectomies were actually stitched back up with their appendix still intact! Nor did we ever have trials where half of the heart defibrillators just tickled patients without actually affecting their hearts. However, most of life is an experiment, we learn as we go along. In testing new medicines we will have to learn by doing, as we have always done in most areas of medicine.[7] Of course, we will often learn faster anyway with earlier human testing involving many more test subjects.[8]

If we do replace our government medicine dictators with government advisors we can be certain families would no longer have to watch loved ones die for lack of a saving new medicine that is unavailable to them only because of government regulation, as happens thousands of time each year currently. No family would have to endure what Abigail Burroughs' did. No family would have to watch their daughter die, knowing that medicines exist to help but are denied her by a well-meaning but fundamentally flawed system of political regulation.

## NOTES

1. Of course, any doctor who wished to wait for the FDA verdict could still do so.

2. One can imagine some disadvantages to an open system versus the command and control approach of the FDA. For instance, suppose two drugs are ready to start human testing for the same malady but one worked a bit better on lab animals so everyone wants to try that one, the second has trouble attracting a test pool. The problem doesn't exist with the FDA functioning as a gatekeeper, limiting access. In a free system this problem might be combatted by the second inventor offering free trials with financial assistance while doctors point out that animal results often differ wildly from human, so the probability of success might not differ significantly. Even in a worst case though, when the second drug only attracts test subjects after the first one has been tried and failed, the open system will still be years faster overall than our current approach.

3. It's possible that even this sort of limited liability would sometimes not be enough to assuage the liability fears of inventors. Even if they are truthful they may not trust our legal system to verify that, and to do so without excessive legal costs. The only way to completely remove liability as a barrier to patient access is to honor a contract where the patient agrees the company is not liable under any circumstances, thus eliminating all possibility of an expensive court battle.

4. If you actually do trust your senator or congressional representative more than you trust your doctor then, gentle reader, you really should consider finding a different doctor.

5. In the interest of saving time and space we have not discussed issues with FDA approval of medical devices. Although some of the particulars will vary the same general logic applies to both devices and medicines. Massive barriers to entry always have the same general effects. If we let patients make decisions, guided by health care professionals, including the *advice* of the FDA we will enjoy the same rapid innovation and lower prices in medical devices as we've been envisioning for medicines. See (Klein and Tabarrok, 2018e).

6. It seems the political mob would not so easily corrupt FDA advice but if they did the damage would be minimal since that advice could be ignored.

7. Drug companies and, of course, patients themselves have long complained that the standard double-blind placebo tests are unethical, especially for terminal patients, and that any knowledge gained is not large and certainly not worth the cost. Happily, it seems the FDA has recently begun to move away from the use of placebos (Burroughs, 2018).

8. A major complication in all this, beyond our scope, is that neither government agencies nor private insurers will be anxious to provide coverage of medicines deemed too experimental. Currently, patients in FDA clinical Phase I trials generally get treatments for free, while private insurance or government programs cover more general medical expenses (Seattle Cancer Care Alliance, 2018). But current Phase I

patients are small in number, usually in the thirties. In this reform, virtually the entire terminal patient population may want the medicine but it's hard to imagine Medicare or private insurers rushing to cover a treatment that has only something like a 16% chance of working. However, as mentioned, removing the FDA as, perhaps, the world's most stifling barrier to entry will dramatically increase medicine supplies and result in plummeting prices. This helps patients forced to spend their own money and also frees up the resources of these third party payers, making the overall issue of coverage easier to deal with effectively.

*Chapter 4*

# How Uber Innovated to Save Lives and Why Taxis Never Did

## DRIVING A TAXI IS MURDER

The murder rate for taxi drivers is at least four times as high as that of police officers. Actually, the authors point out that driving a taxi is far more dangerous than even these numbers suggests because the Bureau of Labor Statistics (BLS) data lumps cab drivers and chauffeurs together, but it is only cabbies who are in great danger, picking up strangers off the street (Sygnatur and Toscano, 2000).

> Taxicab drivers and chauffeurs have the highest homicide rate of any occupation, 17.9 fatalities per 100,000 workers, or 36 times the risk of all employed individuals. This group comprises 0.2 percent of employed workers in the United States, but accounts for about 7 percent of work-related homicides. (Sygnatur and Toscano, 2000)

These figures are from 1998 but subsequent numbers as well as the latest available data show that taxi driving has consistently been and still remains the occupation with, by far, the highest risk of murder in the United States (BLS, 2017). It turns out that it truly is dangerous to pick up strangers, especially when these "hitchhikers" are aware you are probably carrying substantial amounts of cash, as cabbies normally do.

Of course, the danger is somewhat of a two-edged sword. Passengers are also hopping into a car with a stranger. There is no comprehensive data available on crimes committed by cabbies but at least three serial killers worked as taxi drivers, including David Berkowitz, "Son of Sam," who was a nighttime taxi driver for a time (Pulham, 2012) and Derrick Bird, "The Cumbria Killer," a self-employed cabbie in Whitehaven, England (Brown, 2011). Paul Durousseau was also a cab driver who murdered several of his passengers in Jacksonville, Florida (Ivice, 2003). Thankfully, though, serial killers are not commonplace in taxi driving or in any occupation. More commonly, unfortunately, sexual assaults against female passengers have been an ongoing taxi problem (Gonen, 2016).

There are some things that taxi companies could have done, even before the technological revolution ushered in by Uber and others, to better protect both their drivers and their customers. For example, since robbery was the main motive of those who murdered cabbies, companies could have established a policy where cabbies carried no cash at night, perhaps with some sort of ticket system for customers without credit cards. Taxi companies could, like truck companies, have had a prominent "How's my driving?" with a toll-free number to call. The toll-free number could also have been on the inside of every cab, for customers to readily report bad driving, improper advances, or any other problem. However, as we will discuss further, most of the world's taxi companies have been operating as protected cartels for many decades; they haven't felt competitive pressures to ensure that drivers and passengers are safe, cabs are kept clean, older vehicles are retired, and drivers are courteous or anything else.

## REGULATION AND THE TAXI CARTEL FIEFDOMS

In 2017, based on an analysis of about 50 million credit card receipts for U.S. business travelers, Uber had 56% of all ground transportation expenses, Lyft had 12%, car rental companies had 25%, and taxis (including limos and shuttles) only 7% (Goldstein, 2018). By comparison, in the first quarter of 2014, taxi-type services were dominant with an 85% market share (Bender, 2015). How did the taxi industry collapse so suddenly, from a market share around 85% to a measly 7% in less than three years? Anytime an established industry disintegrates so rapidly, a good bet is that said industry had somehow previously suppressed competition and new entry, then fell apart once new entry and competition finally occurred. This is exactly the case for the taxi business. The typical condition of the pre-Uber taxi world, except for the omission of safety problems, is nicely summarized above by the Washington, D.C. City Council.

> By restricting supply and creating high barriers to entry, there is an unmet demand for taxi service, longer wait times for taxis, more non-responses to phone requests, less clean vehicles, poorer quality of service, and higher fares. Taxicab drivers would refuse service to certain types of customers (for example, based on race) or to certain parts of the city.
>
> —Washington, D.C. City Council (Snead, 2015)

The full explanation begins with the fact that businesses are routinely tempted to conspire to eliminate competition. Every firm competing in an open market is constantly in the hot seat; at any time some innovative competitor may snatch away their customers, and destroy their livelihood. Even companies with a long history of dominating their market can lose it all tomorrow—ask the people at Sears or Kmart. It's a tough system but it produces the benefits of constant innovation, technological improvement, and a growing standard of living. Every business knows if they give in to the impulse to be lazy, to serve themselves too much, and serve their customers too little, they may soon find themselves out of business. We benefit by, in effect, fostering competition that holds companies' feet to the fire so that they serve us better. But who likes having their feet held to the fire? Businesses are virtually always interested in cooperating with rivals to make life easier and more profitable for every firm in their industry.

Fortunately, for the sake of consumers and the overall economy, it is generally difficult, often even impossible, for businesses to suppress competition. When firms attempt to cooperate to reduce competition, to act as a unified cartel rather than separate rivals, they face two gigantic obstacles. One is that there is always an incentive to cheat on the cartel agreement. If all cartel members agree to keep prices high, any individual business can generally make even more profit by selling at a price just below their fellow cartel members'. Usually, someone does exactly that, then others respond with lower prices themselves and so on. It's a "no honor among thieves" sort of thing. Even if they come up with a way to keep all the co-conspirators in line, the second, even larger problem, is that their artificially high prices and profits are like waving a red flag at all of the investor and entrepreneur bulls in the world, new entry into the industry is virtually certain. Any new entrant will likely receive a warm welcome from consumers tired of being ripped off by the incumbent cartel.

Realistically, there is usually only one way to make a cartel operation feasible—bring in corrupt, or sometimes merely naive and economically ignorant politicians, to the conspiracy. *If an industry can get government to make both price cuts and new entry illegal then they may have a workable cartel.* This is, of course, exactly what the taxi industry was able to do decades ago. In most cities in the U.S. local government regulation of taxis to prevent price cuts was established in the 1930s. Of course, it was difficult to get regulations abolishing price competition past vigilant, savvy voters. . . . Just kidding, voters generally accepted government price controls unquestioningly, probably assuming they were aimed solely at preventing price *increases*. Government also required taxi drivers to be licensed and used the licensing procedures as a way of limiting new entry (Snead, 2015).

The suppression of new entry via licensing has been particularly obvious in New York City where taxi operating licenses are transferrable, making it possible to easily judge about how powerful the entry barrier is by observing the price paid for a license, termed a "medallion." In 2013, a New York taxi medallion cost $1.3 million! Only severe limits on competition can make the right to operate a taxi so ridiculously high. So, anyone who wanted to become a taxi driver in New York City had a colossal entry barrier to overcome, facing an up-front entry fee well over one million dollars just to get started, or more commonly, working only for a company who happened to own an open medallion. What's more, in the heavily regulated market, even with new entrants there was often no pro-consumer impact, no increase in competition because the total number of medallions was generally held constant or nearly so. Often, each new driver merely replaced another one leaving the market, with very little new entry on net (Byrne, 2018; Snead, 2015).

In chapter 2 we discussed how voters, obsessed with avoiding safety mistakes and not fully cognizant about suppressing innovation, drove politicians to create a massive, deadly barrier to entry for new medicines. The continued years and years of delayed approvals, jacking up production cost into the billions, are costing us thousands and thousands of lives. This regulatory barrier for new medications slows what would otherwise be a powerful flow of new medicines into the comparatively slow trickle we currently see. But, for medicines, at least there is still substantial new entry. The regulatory barrier for taxi service was often worse, with little or no significant new entry. Though, of course, taxi service is less crucial than lifesaving medicines, there is considerable harm done to consumers, including reduced safety.

This cab licensing barrier is of a different ilk than that of the FDA, driven not by voters but by incumbent taxi companies. In this case, the role of voters is mainly passive ignorance. Politicians supporting taxi licensing generally claim this is aimed at keeping consumers safe. We tend to take politicians at their word whenever they play the safety card. Most economists have long been skeptical of the claim that occupational licensing is about protecting consumers from dangerous or poor quality service. It seems the true purpose is virtually always more to suppress competition, and keep incomes of suppliers artificially high at consumer expense. This is nicely summarized by Ryan Nunn of the Brookings Institute (Nunn, 2017). Furthermore, it turns out society's safety was actually impaired by the expensive, sluggish service of the taxi cartel. However, it would take the Uber revolution to expose that truth as we will see.

It is likely that many voters who actually rode in taxis would be dubious that the licensing processes accomplished much to make cab rides safer! But each voter knows how hard it is for one person to change much in government. Sensible taxi consumers-cum-voters did not research taxi regulation, organize protests, and try to do away with entry barriers. Consumers just don't do that sort of thing. While consumer voters are generally unengaged and ill-informed about regulations-cum-entry-barriers, affected businesses, and their employees, tend to be engaged and informed on the issue, since their profits and pay rates are at stake. As Nobel Prize laureate George Stigler put it, this asymmetric information and engagement problem producers a tendency for government regulatory agencies to be "captured" by the businesses they regulate (Stigler, 1971).[1] So, voters were basically neutral, not a cause of the suppressed competition but not fighting it either.

## IS THERE A CASE TO BE MADE IN FAVOR OF THE TAXI CARTEL SYSTEM?

Even before Uber revealed just how anxious consumers were to escape the taxi cartels, economists were overwhelmingly critical of taxi regulation (Moore and Balaker, 2006).[2] While local governments generally favored regulation a significant minority rejected the cartel arrangement. A U.S. Department of Transportation study in the early 1980s found 12% of U.S. cities had open entry and 23% didn't regulate fares (Shaw et al., 1983). This is significant since it seems virtually certain that political pressures had created a pro-regulation bias. The taxi industry was a well-organized special interest group paying close attention and politically focused on preventing competition. Consumers were inattentive and unfocused, not much of a countervailing influence. It seems the only reason local politicians would favor deregulation was because, like most economists, they thought it was truly beneficial for society. A Federal Trade Commission analysis of the results in those cities that successfully deregulated appeared to confirm this (Frankena and Pautler, 1984).

Even the minority of economists who argued there were important favorable aspects of taxi regulation generally did not favor the severe limits on new entry that cartel cities practiced. For example, it might sometimes be true that there is too much traffic congestion in a given area. However, economists agree that the optimal regulation is not to arbitrarily limit the number of taxis for the whole city at all times, but instead to employ some sort of congestion pricing system, where all vehicles on the road at certain times and places are charged. In other words, a problem of too many vehicles on certain roads at certain times needs to focus on exactly that problem. Raising the price at that time, perhaps by limiting traffic to those who purchase appropriate permits, or through the use of electronic toll systems. This can reduce road demand to meet the limited supply. The higher peak period price will ration the limited road space to those who value it most. The higher price will result in fewer vehicles at that peak period/place, but not necessarily fewer taxis. In fact, it is likely that taxi drivers would routinely outbid other drivers in these cases, especially a single driver without passengers (Snead, 2015; Moore and Balaker, 2006).

## THE TAXI CARTEL PERPETUATED
## AN UNSAFE SYSTEM

There is no better illustration of how important innovation is to safety than the taxi industry. Unfortunately, the taxi cartel system illustrated this by pretty much having a complete absence of innovation, regarding safety and everything else. In the early 2000s taxi operations were not much different than they had been in the 1930s. As smart phones became ubiquitous the potential for greater safety innovation, like cashless transactions, for instance, was generally ignored by taxi businesses the world over. Even as Uber and others led the way, the taxi industry mainly tried to simply suppress the competition rather learn from it and improve their product (Sundararajan, 2017).

Uber, which began as a licensed, upscale limousine service, had the technology to revolutionize the taxi industry but quickly ran up against the regulatory cartel. Like every would-be new entrant, Uber was trapped in a catch 22. Voters would likely love Uber's service and be great political allies but, of course, only *after* they experienced Uber's service. But most local politicians and their hired regulators, determined to stop that from ever happening, stood ready-to-use government power to arrest and fine any Uber driver who defied the regulatory cartel. The suppressed competition via licensing scenario in the big apple, though usually not as extreme, had been repeated in cities all over the United States and the world. Since "you can't fight city hall" the threat of arrest/fines is enough to generally prevent firms from even trying to break a government sanctioned cartel. Then came Uber. Lyft and others are part of the story as well. But it was primarily Uber, whatever its flaws, that overcame the corrupt licensing system, that broke the cartel. For one of the rare times in history, a private company fought city hall; in fact, fought city halls all over the planet. Eventually, they usually won (Sundararajan, 2017).

## CIVIL DISOBEDIENCE IN THE UBER REVOLUTION

Knowing that it would often be impossible or prohibitively expensive to buy medallions or other government taxi licenses to legally compete with the cartel Uber began to adapt. Their new strategy was simply to enter markets without the government permission they knew would be either denied or extortionately expensive. This was how they implemented Phase I of Kalanick's strategy as summarized in this quote, which came to be known within Uber as *Travis's Law.*

> Our product is so superior to the status quo that if we give people the opportunity to see it or try it, in any place in the world where government has to be at least somewhat responsive to the people, they will demand it and defend its right to exist.

> —Travis Kalanick, Uber's Founding CEO (Stone, 2017, 194)

Arguably, they generally had a legal loophole to slip through. Licensing laws do not forbid private parties from using their own cars to give acquaintances a ride. Uber maintained they simply facilitated exactly that sort of arrangement, providing the software that helped drivers and passenger to become acquainted. No taxi companies here! Just one private citizen using their own car to give someone a ride. A big part of the strategy was to boldly storm into a market and establish as much customer (and driver) goodwill as they possibly could before the local taxi cartel empire could work through the legal system's bureaucracy to strike back (Stone, 2017).

When the taxi regulatory empire did eventually strike back, usually beginning with a "cease and desist" legal order, Uber's standard procedure was to completely ignore the order, continuing business as usual. No one does that! Government regulators are accustomed to winning by intimidation and winning quickly. It would take time to process Uber's quiet rebellion and begin the next legal step because no previous business in most cartel's experience had refused to cave when confronted by the big gun power of government. Uber just continued to peacefully go about their business as the government stalked them. No one would confuse Uber's controversial founding CEO, Travis Kalanick, with Dr. Martin Luther King, Jr. Nor was Uber's cause breaking the taxi cartel for the sake of previously exploited customers, and Uber's own profit (not necessarily in that order!) as noble a cause as the fight against racial discrimination. But, there were some parallels as the stunned taxi cartel/regulatory alliance confronted this vexatious entrepreneur who refused to obey laws that he, as well as most economists and many other informed observers, considered unjust.

Of course, in this sort of confrontation, the government is going to eventually start arresting someone. Uber executives were in fact sometimes arrested, as happened in France. Kalanick himself avoided capture, largely because he stayed physically removed from any government, such as South Korea, that would, at the time, have loved to capture the brash CEO! Naturally, it was the drivers, driver-partners in Uber parlance, who faced the brunt of the taxi empire's wrath. But since Uber drivers' cars were unmarked it wasn't easy to catch them with conventional techniques, especially since they often would have passengers ride in the front seat (Stone, 2017).

Regulators eventually figured out they needed to pose as honest customers, then summon a driver through Uber's app and then finally arrest them. However, Uber frequently anticipated this scheme and thwarted it. Uber used sophisticated software to identify the cartel's law enforcers and evade them. Uber altered the apps on the phones of the cartel's would-be enforcers' so that drivers appeared to be unavailable, with their true locations hidden. Actual cars were replaced with nonexistent ghost cars in these apps! Thus, the Uber "underground" rebels could conduct operations right under the regulators' noses yet still slip away. In the cases where something glitched and a taxi cartel "narc" managed to make it into a driver's vehicle, Uber would often figure it out and quickly refund the fee and instruct the driver to end the trip, ruining the cartel enforcer's case that they had been charged for an illegal ride. Sometimes the undercover taxi police would create false identities on a new cell phone number. Even then, Uber quickly adapted. They would deduce (or perhaps be informed, since satisfied Uber customers were turning up everywhere in the growing Uber underground) where the batch of phones had been purchased and eventually identify them. When cartel enforcers did manage to catch a driver, Uber would pay all fines and legal costs (Isaac, 2017).[3] It seems that Kalanick just built these legal costs into the financial plan, and they were certainly cheaper than it would have been to legally buy the needed taxi medallions—which, recall, were sometimes over $1 million apiece.

However, the collapse of the cartel, though probably just desserts, set in motion more tragic problems than licensing fines. The decline in income was unpleasant, but not catastrophic, for most cab drivers. For one thing, they had the option of driving with Uber, a job they could get virtually instantaneously in Uber's system, and that generally paid better than taxi driving.[4] But, consider the cabbies in cartels where they personally had to purchase their license (medallion) at a wildly inflated price just before the cartel began to disintegrate. Recall, New York cabbies who bought their way into the cartel in 2013 had to pay $1.3 million. But by 2018, thanks mainly to Uber, medallion prices had plummeted as low as $160,000. This reflects huge gains for consumers as the number of for-hire vehicles available to consumers in New York surged from about 50,000 in 2011 to 130,000 in 2018 (Byrne, 2018).

This is great for almost everyone but certainly not for those hapless drivers who personally bought their way into the cartel at the worst possible time, most likely borrowing heavily to finance that $1.3 million asset now worth as little as $0.16 million. One could argue that buying a medallion was an inherently immoral purchase, representing value stolen from consumers; it was, perhaps, simply trading in stolen goods. However, it's hard to blame cartel drivers for not seeing it that way. The real villains, of course, were the politicians and cab companies that established the cartel ages ago. But, current cartel members only knew that they had paid a fortune for a legal medallion, then saw its value disappear because government couldn't stop new entry by unlicensed, medallion-less upstarts. It was wrong that these drivers were charged a fortune to bypass an unjust entry barrier, but now they wanted, perhaps, another wrong, the perpetual continuation of the medallion barrier system. They sought to make a right (to them) from the two wrongs.

The end of the cartel, though a great thing overall, meant, in worst cases, financial disaster and bankruptcy for some. Of course, many people go through personal bankruptcy and bounce back, going on to live happy, meaningful lives. There are no debtors' prisons here. Unfortunately, some of these cartel drivers did not bounce back. They basically fell into a rage, including some who were not in medallion type systems but became furious about any increase in competition (Stone, 2017).

This scenario played out in cities all over the world. Some of these furious cartel drivers let their rage control them and launched violent attacks against Uber drivers. The singer, Courtney Love, was riding an Uber in Paris when a mob of cab drivers-cum-terrorists surrounded the vehicle and began smashing the car with metal bats; she and the driver eventually escaped that mob with no injuries other than car damage (Isaac, 2017). However, a few of the attacks have been fatal. A former taxi driver was recently arrested for the murder of an Uber driver in Florida (Kogan, 2018). Another Uber driver was burned to death in Johannesburg, South Africa, when a gang of taxi drivers set his car on fire. In fact, in that area of South Africa Uber decided it was worth hiring private security to help protect their drivers (Burke, 2017). A single death is too many but thankfully these were very rare events. It should also be mentioned that Uber, as we will see, has saved many lives, primarily through reducing the risk to drivers as well as reducing drunk driving.[5]

Although physical attacks by the taxi cartel were not numerous enough, especially in the United States, to seriously dissuade Uber or its drivers, operating illegally forever was too expensive to be viable. In fact, that had never been Kalanick's plan. The idea was to first educate the public through positive experiences with Uber, then next harness the legions of satisfied customers and drivers to pressure politicians to reform unjust laws to eliminate, or at least moderate, the excessive barriers to entry.

## UBER AND FRIENDS FIGHT CITY
## HALL AND (USUALLY) WIN

One of Uber's earliest successful skirmishes with regulators occurred in Washington, D.C., in 2012. The D.C. City council was much less hostile toward cartel breakers than most, looking to weaken the cartel, to compromise, and to work Uber into the market. However, they wanted Uber, at least temporarily, to agree to a price minimum, to keep them from cutting prices too aggressively. Kalanick rebelled; he contacted Uber's customers and asked them to contact the council in support of Uber. Within a day the council members received 50,000 e-mails. Not long after that the council voted unanimously to let Uber cut prices as much as they liked. Similar confrontations with and triumphs over regulators occurred in Philadelphia, Chicago, and Cambridge, Massachusetts (Stone, 2017).

New York City, the largest taxi market with perhaps the strongest cartel in the United States loomed as Uber's next major challenge in 2015. The regulatory agency there, the Taxi and Limousine Commission (TLC), consisted of very strident cartel supporters who were generally hostile toward Uber. Earlier strategies employed by other cities' cartels had often tried to sell the idea that licensing promoted safety, therefore Uber should be licensed like everyone else (in the cartel.) The safety alarm scheme usually works quite well when voters are contemplating a hypothetical product. However, voters who had ridden with both Uber and in taxis simply did not buy the argument that taxis were comparative paragons of safety.

So, the New York TLC chose a craftier strategy, insisting that entry into the taxi/rideshare market needed to be strictly limited in order to avoid even worse congestion problems on the city's streets. The TLC also tried to frighten Uber away by insisting on several very onerous restrictions, including that Uber would have to agree that the TLC would have authority to review and approve any changes to the Uber app. They also planned to limit Uber's growth in drivers to 1% per month. David Yassky, a former TLC chairman himself from 2010 and 2014, agreeing with most observers, said the TLC's position in 2015 was clearly focused on suppressing competition (Stone, 2017).

Uber began with its usual tactics of mobilizing consumers and drivers to pressure the TLC and relevant politicians such as the city's mayor, Del Blasio, and New York governor, Andrew Cuomo. But, sensing how great this challenge was, and the value of setting a precedent in the big apple, Uber escalated the political pressure. They organized protests and demonstrations and paid for television ads. These ads emphasized the benefits of Uber for consumers but also for generating flexible jobs. In addition, Uber inserted a clever ad within its app called "De Blasio's Uber" which depicted a bleak future where New York Uber users would have to wait around for twenty-five minutes before their Uber ride finally showed up. In the end, Governor Cuomo responded to the pressure first, praising Uber's job creation and suggesting the state might intervene if the city passed the proposed stifling legislation. The next day the mayor caved, dropping the limit on the growth of new drivers. Eventually, a study by the city would show that road congestion was not caused by rideshare drivers but by increased construction, tourism and deliveries (Stone, 2017).

The stunning victory over the New York cartel set the stage for numerous Uber triumphs around the United States and internationally. But every victory is hard fought, and not every battle ends in victory. Sometimes the cartels are able to keep Uber out, or force them to more or less behave like just another cartel member (Stone, 2017). Even so, Uber's historical triumph over so many entrenched government-run cartels around the world is astounding and unprecedented.

## POLITICIANS ALIGNED WITH THE CARTEL STRIKE BACK, SNEAKILY THIS TIME

Market shares prove that people find Uber's product vastly superior to that of taxis. Thus, in most places politicians have found it impossible to convince Uber's satisfied customers that, for the sake of passenger safety, Uber needs to be regulated and licensed just like taxis. Thus, politicians embarrassed and defeated by the rideshare juggernaut have begun war on an entirely different front. The new wave of regulatory attacks on Uber is more cunning, designed to have broader surface appeal to voters and even some of Uber's drivers. The product is too good for government to discredit so better to play on anti-big business biases in general and common notions of employee exploitation in particular. Politicians can't stop people from appreciating golden eggs but they may be able to kill, or at least wound, the goose that lays those golden eggs.

For example, as of this writing, *New York City is trying to impose an extreme minimum wage that would apply only to rideshare drivers, not taxi drivers or anyone else.* The proposed minimum wage would be well over $20 per hour, specifically, $17.22 per hour plus all driver expenses—gas, mileage, and insurance (Siddiqui, 2018). Since the coerced wage hike would not fall on taxi drivers the intent seems obviously to be to protect the cartel by inflating the costs of the cartel's competitors only, and thereby reduce the number of rideshare drivers in the market.[6]

Another ongoing regulatory attack against Uber and other rideshare companies is the attempt to force them to reclassify their driver-partners as employees. Although some might benefit from this, the increase in labor and administrative costs would harm many workers and fundamentally weaken key attributes of Uber's service. A vital part of Uber's success stems from the flexibility of their driver-partners' schedules. In fact, a slight majority of their drivers make most of their income from some source other than Uber. Likewise, many drivers work temporarily to earn extra money or when they are between jobs—at any point in time about 68% of Uber drivers will not be driving six months later. When people are driving full time they generally drive for at least one other rideshare company; over 78% of Uber drivers double as drivers for Lyft or others (Campbell, 2018).

Consider how Uber has solved the problem of peak period demand that the flawed taxi cartel system handled so incompetently. In the old taxi monopoly days it was often virtually impossible to get a cab during peak periods, the most glaring example being after New Year's Eve partying. Uber solved this by contracting with an army of driver-partners with no minimum requirement of hours worked. So, many drivers normally work only a few hours now and then, often supplying rides mainly in peak periods when the pay for drivers is higher. To clarify, Uber's price rises when demand surges, which is standard efficient pricing as we saw in chapter 1, and the only way to avoid shortages and long wait times in peak periods. When price rises 80% of the price increase goes to drivers to induce them to work in those peak periods (Hall and Krueger, 2016; Stone, 2017).

The added administrative costs from forcing a formal employee relationship would likely make it uneconomical to keep many people who seldom work on the payroll, which is what regulators are, of course, probably hoping for. The Uber army would become smaller, making wait times longer, much like taxis' in the busiest times, and making it more difficult to respond to peak period demand, therefore forcing prices higher. Thus far, though, the point is moot, since Uber has won the key legal battles to allow them to continue under the contractual arrangements they signed with their driver-partners at the outset. There is currently no sign that Uber's enemies will succeed in forcing them to abide by an employment contract they never agreed to in the first place (Lee, 2018).[7]

## LICENSING AND SAFETY ISSUES

Again, the exponential growth and huge market shares of Uber and other ridesharers are probably the best empirical evidence that passengers do indeed feel safe. However, we want to examine this issue more carefully, in part, to understand exactly how consumers were persuaded to abandon safety-regulated taxis in favor of unregulated Uber.

### The Dearth of Safety Data

Government licensing officials and the taxi industry itself have loudly claimed that their licensing makes taxis safer, but consumers are not buying it. Part of the skepticism of regulators' safety claims probably stems from the fact that these regulators never present any comparative data on safety, indeed such data seems completely nonexistent. This in itself is revealing. Who is in a better position to gather comparative data on accidents, driver harassment of passengers, or anything else that might be relevant? The taxi cartel has been fighting a losing battle against Uber for several years, yet they still have produced no evidence to back up their perpetual assertions of the great safety of taxis. If they had truthful data on their side it seems they would be presenting it.

The taxi industry does maintain a website, http://www.whosdrivingyou.org/rideshare-incidents, which lists every report in the world of alleged incidents over all time involving their ride-sharing competitors. These allegations range from the more sensational vehicular accidents to alleged violent crimes such as murder and assault. Many of the reports are unproven allegations and the site reads rather like *The National Enquirer*. Still, the list of allegations is somewhat daunting, and some of them are certainly true; there are some listed convictions. Of course, there are millions of share-drivers worldwide; Uber alone had two million by 2017 (O'Brien, 2017). There are bound to be a few villains in any group that large. The fundamental question is, are taxi drivers worse than Uber drivers? One-sided anecdotal evidence is essentially meaningless and easily countered. For example, as mentioned earlier, at least three known serial killers were taxi drivers. In isolation, disturbing facts such as this have no clear implication. Interestingly, Uber, though about as feisty as they come, has not taken the taxi hoopla seriously and has never bothered to organize a website reporting evil deeds by cabbies.

Of course, if safety was just a red herring all along, merely an excuse to suppress competition, then it would follow that regulators who were never in the business of monitoring taxi safety would be pretty clueless about safety data. This appears to be exactly the case. As mentioned earlier, taxi drivers are more likely to be murdered than workers in any other occupation in the United States. All these multitudes of regulators never exhibited great concern for cabbies safety over the decades. It seems passenger safety was not much of a priority either. Consider the experience of Washington, D.C., in 2012. There was a rash of assaults by taxi drivers against female passengers, seven incidents in a few weeks. The taxi commission issued a public warning to female passengers, though the commission stated the scope of the problem was unclear. The commission's spokesman, Neville Waters, said, "It's not as if there's a standard procedure where we get all incident reports. A lot of it depends on the commander of the particular ward. That also doesn't necessarily mean that all assaults that are occurring in a cab are being captured or that we're even getting that information" (Lafrance and Eveleth, 2015). In other words, the taxi commission, safety watchdogs for the community for decades, had never established procedures for monitoring safety, and basically had no clear idea how safe or unsafe riding in their taxis might be! Ride at your own risk, ladies!

But, there may be something beyond government inefficiency behind the lack of data. In fact, a reasonable person might suspect that perhaps the taxi industry and its government allies very intentionally haven't kept and produced comprehensive taxi safety records because they know enough to realize that comprehensive data would not support their cause.

## Comparing Safety Procedures for Protecting Driver-partners and Cabbies

This is the easiest call, so we'll start with the safety of cabbies relative to driver-partners. With no comparative data, all we can examine and compare are the safety-related procedures involving these two groups. It seems certain that Uber drivers are safer from crime by passengers than are taxi drivers. Ubers do not pick up random, unknown passengers off the street, and they are less likely than cabbies to carry substantial cash since payments are generally automated through registered credit cards. (Drivers will accept cash but are not allowed to make change, the passenger would simply be given a credit.) Every Uber passenger leaves a clear paper trail, actually electronic, of who they are and where they hopped in the car, and where the car goes (Stone, 2017).

There could be criminals with elaborate false identities employing a credit card and phone in that false identity, perhaps like spies on television, with multiple passports in different names and all that. But, how often is someone like that going to expose themselves or be forced to abandon that identity in order to carry out a crime against an Uber driver carrying little or no cash? Robbery is the underlying reason cabbies are so frequently murdered, where killers are after the cash that cabbies normally carry (Sygnatur and Toscano, 2000). Although there is no data on murder rates of share-drivers the murder risk does not seem to be a significant concern.

An interesting example of how confident Uber drivers are of their safety was illustrated in a report by *Forbes* in the article, "The Uberpreneur: How an Uber Driver Makes $252,000 A Year." The driver depicted, Gavin Escolar, also owns his own jewelry store and displays some of his wares on his person as well as in the vehicle. If passengers comment on the jewelry and are interested then he brings out more samples, as well as a catalog. Uber fully supports Escolar and all of its driver-partners who mix in their own businesses with driving. After all, there is no concern that hard selling would irritate riders; the customer rating system automatically polices that and any other driver misbehavior, as we will further discuss. Indeed, Escolar is highly rated by his Uber customers, 4.87/5.00 on UberX. About a third of Uber drivers surveyed owned their own businesses, though there are no figures on how many of these *Uberpreneurs* also display valuable merchandise in their vehicle (Youshaei, 2015).

In addition, online reputation plays a key role in this. Drivers and passengers can easily rate each other, quickly building up online profiles. Before the driver accepts the pickup she can evaluate the passenger and the location at that time of day and then decide if that passenger represents too much risk for her. Uber will ban passengers if their behavior has been seriously problematic (Knowles, 2015). Once the passenger is in the car the procedures are pretty much the same for cabbies and drivers, though again, only the cabbie normally carries lots of cash and picks up basically unknown hitchhikers.

Consider, also, that Uber provides a virtually automatic outlet for anyone properly qualified who wishes to earn some money as a driver. Before Uber, if you couldn't afford to buy a medallion, or find a job with a company that had an extra one, your only choice was to drive illegally, become a "gypsy cab" driver. This was an especially dangerous job, no doubt far worse than conventional taxi driving. In, for example, New York City, the gypsy cabbies operated in poorer, more dangerous neighborhoods where licensed cabbies seldom bothered to venture, and where the gypsies knew regulators and police enforcing licensing laws were unlikely to find and hassle them. Of course, these "gypsies" had no dispatcher; they were on their own as they picked up strangers on dangerous back roads. *The New York Times* detailed the dangerous lives of the city's gypsy cabbies in the article, "Gypsy Cabs: A Hard, Chancy Life on the Side Streets of New York" (Hernandez, 1992). Today, people whose life circumstances would have forced them to become gypsy drivers back in the day are now, thankfully, Uber drivers, and far safer.

## Passenger Safety Procedures of Uber versus Taxis

The incentives for safe driving are likely much stronger for Uber drivers. Uber's GPS system and electronic recordkeeping make it easy to monitor driver speeds. Uber also makes use of smart phone gyrometers which can more exactly measure car movements such as sudden stops or sudden swerving (Warren, 2016). Taxis have none of this. Uber customers can very conveniently report bad driving and give their driver a bad online rating right through their phone app. It's much more of a hassle for cab riders to do likewise. More fundamentally, in Uber's system no driver is guaranteed a customer, rather the customer can evaluate the driver's online reputation and either decline or accept the ride offered.[8] Taxi customers take either the luck of the draw on the street or whoever the taxi company sends; there are pretty much no reputation effects for drivers to worry about (Sundararajan, 2017).

A possible safety plus for taxis is the fact that their drivers have to be commercially licensed and may receive additional training while Uber's need only a standard driver's license. But, of course, there is no empirical evidence that this licensing improves driving safety. Even if one accepts that it takes greater driving skill to get a commercial license, the greater issue is driver habits and attitudes. Think of this analogy: Truck drivers with the "how's my driving? Call this number" sign are constantly monitored by every driver on the road. If you've spent much time on highways you've probably noticed that the unsafe truck drivers one occasionally encounters virtually never have such a sign on their truck. Similarly, Uber drivers are constantly monitored electronically by the Uber "home office" as well as by passengers that can so easily report unsafe driving. Very much like having a "how's my driving" sign on the back of the driver's seat. It is likely that this makes Uber's drivers safer, which probably explains why the taxi industry has never seemed to specifically argue that their driving is safer. That, and the fact that, in making such an argument, taxi supporters might have trouble keeping a straight face!

## Data on Driving Habits: Uber versus Taxi

An analysis of drivers in San Francisco found share-drivers to be much safer motorists than cabbies, as one would expect given taxi drivers' inferior incentives for safety. The study was conducted by Zendrive, a California-based company that uses smart phone technology to help increase driver safety for businesses and also for some insurance companies.

> During non-peak hours, rideshare is both cheaper and safer than taxi. During peak hours, price-conscious passengers should probably take a taxi [if they can find one]. However, passengers that care most about safety should still prefer a rideshare service, as the safety gap is even bigger then.

> —Zendrive (Zendrive.com, 2014)

For several months in 2014 Zendrive employees rode with both taxis as well as rideshare companies, secretly recording data via their phones. Cabbies were far more lead-footed, speeding 50% more than share-drivers on average, 250% more during peak hours. Share-drivers actually sped slightly less than average drivers, perhaps reflecting their great concern for their online reputations (Zendrive, 2014).

## Vehicle Safety

Another possible advantage of taxi procedures is that taxi vehicles are regularly inspected for mechanical safety while Uber drivers generally own their vehicles and make their own maintenance decisions. Again, we have no data on mechanical failures of taxis versus Ubers so we have no way of judging whether mechanical checkups are useful. However, a number of studies have examined whether mandatory state inspections of private vehicles reduce accidents. It turns out these studies find that government inspections apparently have zero impact, do not reduce driving accidents or casualties at all (GAO, 2015; Feeney, 2015; Poitras and Sutter, 2002). Most governments have therefore abandoned these inspections. Matthew Feeney points out that in 1975, thirty-one states and the District of Columbia required regular vehicle inspections but as of 2015 only seventeen states continue to do so (Feeney, 2015).[9] Since they are so ineffective generally there is no reason to suppose that inspections of taxis do any good.

On the other hand, the fact that Uber drivers own their vehicles may in itself lead them to better maintain their vehicles than cab drivers who typically are driving company cars. Also, Uber requires that drivers use relatively new cars while taxi companies do not (Hyde, 2015). In addition, just as passengers continuously monitor how safe their Uber driver is, they also monitor the safety performance of the vehicle. A car that skids on bald tires or has piercingly squeaky brakes will likely be noticed and reported. Thus, in addition to driving around with an implicit "how's my driving sign," each Uber operator also has an implicit "how safe, dependable and clean is my vehicle" sign. Again, Uber drivers' strong concern for their personal reputation seems to be a key feature in promoting safety and efficiency in general. The term "driver-partner" is actually quite apt; drivers really do act more like entrepreneurs than mere hired hands. Even the fact that Uber drivers, though obviously in favor of tips, do not view tips as an entitlement the way cabbies often do, creates a feeling that the passenger is dealing with an entrepreneur/ owner rather than just a hired hand.

## What about Drivers Assaulting Passengers?

What about the risk of other possible dangers posed by drivers, such as sexual harassment, assault, or even murder? Sarah Buhr concisely states the safety advantage of Uber, and in more detail in her article, "Regulators should favor Lyft and Uber not Taxis for Safety Reasons" (Buhr, 2016), after a hair-raising taxi ride:

> I was scared and frustrated I had to think about things a man alone on the town wouldn't have to think about. I had so trustingly lined up and gotten in a random cab. There was no way of easily warning another lone woman who might also take a ride with that guy that night, or that week, or ever. No way to complain about inappropriate advances. There was no app for that and no way to trace him if he didn't deliver me back to my hotel, either. He was just a random cab driver in a taxi line and no one thought anything of it.

> —Sarah Buhr, a writer for TechCrunch, on her terrifying
> taxi experience (Buhr, 2016)

Once again, that electronic "paper trail" makes a difference. It will be clear who the Uber driver picked up, when and where they were picked up, and where the car was then driven. Conversely, the taxi driver can pick up someone anywhere, from an anonymous airport line or on a secluded street where there are neither witnesses nor electronic trails, with no one knowing the passenger was picked up or where she was taken. It is also worth noting that Uber suspends drivers as soon as they receive a complaint from a customer alleging assault, as they continue to investigate. Instead, many taxi commissions, such as Washington's, suspend taxi drivers only after criminal charges are filed (Lafrance and Eveleth, 2015).

Furthermore, although taxi regulation varies from city to city, Uber and other rideshare platforms generally enforce stricter rules in their background checks than those of the government. Uber and government regulators are concerned about the same general issues in an applicant's driving and criminal history, but governments are generally only worried about issues over the previous *five* years while Uber and Lyft analyze the last *seven* years. Thus, for example, someone with a DUI conviction six years ago would have no problem working as a taxi driver but would not be qualified to be a driver-partner with Uber (Feeney, 2015).

## The Issue of FBI Fingerprint Background Checks

Many cities, though not nearly all, use FBI background checks with fingerprints while Uber and Lyft background checks work with the applicant's named identity. This is principally where regulators rest their claims of a taxi safety advantage. However, despite the FBI connection this is not such a clear point in favor of taxis is it might at first seem.

> The big key is it is a voluntary process, so law enforcement agencies are not required to provide us their arrest data and criminal history information. We rely on the agencies to provide us the most accurate and up-to-date information, as we are just the repository.
>
> —FBI spokesman, Stephen Fisher, explaining defects in FBI background checks (Lafrance and Eveleth, 2015)

In 2013 the National Employment Law Project released an extensive study of the FBI's employment background checks which found that "FBI records are routinely flawed" (Feeney, 2015). Getting local authorities to provide the correct data to the FBI seems to be a large part of the problem, as explained in the above quote from the FBI's Stephen Fischer.

Even if the FBI system was perfect, would there be any real safety gain if Uber used fingerprints rather than named identities? It is surely true that a master criminal could sometimes create a convincing false identity that would hold up under normal background check scrutiny, and only a properly conducted fingerprint check would catch this sort of criminal. (Assuming he hadn't surgically altered his fingerprints or hacked into the FBI system and deleted his records, as I think I recall villains doing in an exciting Dean Koontz novel.) But it is hard to imagine why the proverbial evil genius would be so interested in driving for Uber! Would it make any sense for this cleverly incognito criminal to plan to commit crimes against his Uber passengers, knowing that there is a clear electronic record of every single passenger he picks up and where he drives them?

It is instructive to consider the behavior of city regulators that do not appear to have been "captured" by the taxi industry. These regulators are, naturally, not infallible but the usual bias of regulators is probably toward too much regulation rather than too little. When a regulator admits that a certain regulation is unlikely to help consumers they are probably telling the truth. Cities with non-cartel regulators have generally not tried to incorporate FBI checks through regulation once rideshare companies are established. For example, Dallas essentially verifies that private background checks have indeed been conducted and occasionally audits these private companies. Indianapolis concluded that costs outweighed any conceivable benefits to additional checks beyond what Uber normally does (National League of Cities, 2015).

Even more revealing, some governments that previously required FBI fingerprint checks, after observing Uber's operations, have changed laws in order to emulate Uber's background check procedures. Likewise, taxi companies are at last beginning to do what they should have done long ago—copy not only Uber's background checks but their entire approach. That is taxi companies have begun to use apps similar to Uber's, creating those electronic paper trails that are so key to ensuring safety as well as the best customer service (Canon, 2017; Daysog, 2018). The decision by Uber and Lyft, as well as many of their government overseers, to rely on private background checks and skip the fingerprinting appears quite sensible and is increasingly emulated in what's left of the taxi cartel.

## Cartel Safety versus Safety as a Competitive Advantage

Actually, it should come as no surprise that Uber has outdone taxi companies and their regulators, that Uber has focused so successfully on ensuring that passengers and drivers feel and are truly safe. Again, since most taxis have been operating as protected cartels for decades, they haven't felt competitive pressures to ensure that optimal safety is maintained for drivers and passengers, cabs are kept clean, drivers are courteous or anything else. Also, since safety is vouchsafed by the same government body for each taxi firm in a given city there is a sort of safety cartel within the overall cartel. To rephrase, just being a cartel suppresses taxi companies' safety concerns but the fact that all taxis in a given city are safety regulated by the same regulatory board more or less eliminates safety as a competitive variable. When the government is in charge of every taxi company's safety then consumers will logically tend to believe that safety will not vary significantly from one company to another.

This is an ironic aspect of government safety regulation—it actually reduces market pressures for safety. Thus, firms will sometimes seek safety regulation in order to take some of the pressure off. Robert Poole's *Instead of Regulation* discusses this in several industry settings (Poole, 1982). Uber, obviously not a regulated member of the taxi cartel, does face the full force of consumer scrutiny. Moreover, Uber is trying to persuade people to hop in a stranger's car, with each stranger an unregulated (by government) entrepreneur. They better have sound safety procedures! Think, also, of the tremendous value of Uber's worldwide brand name in terms of its reputation for both safety and reliability. Recently, as Uber moves toward an Initial Public Offering, the company's value has been estimated at $120 billion (Hoffman et al., 2018). A substantial chunk of that value is generated by their reputation, their brand recognition. Brand Finance, a company specializing in estimating the worth of a company's brand name/reputation, valued Uber's brand at $14.6 billion, 89th in the world back in 2017 (Liddell, 2017). It is likely that figure has risen as has the company's total estimated value. Certainly any weaknesses in Uber's safety measures risk the evaporation of those many billions in brand value.

If their safety performance ever broke down, imagine the media barrage, relaying the jubilant crowing of all those taxi companies and all those regulators who have fought Uber and generally lost. Uber is also despised by many on the political left who are upset that the company won't hire drivers and provide health care, union rights, and so on (Eidelson, 2018). On top of that, there have been well-publicized allegations of a hostile corporate culture to women, resulting in the firing of at least twenty people (Ohnsman, 2017). With the nature of their business—strangers picking up strangers, and with a multitude of enemies anxious to destroy them, Uber has unusually strong incentives to be safe, perhaps, greater than most any company in history!

## Uber's Broader Impact on Safety

One clear safety advantage of Ubering rather than taxi riding is the far more rapid and organized response of Uber. For example, a short wait time for a ride is of the essence for a woman alone with a broken down car in an unsafe neighborhood. Also, there is never a need to roam the street hoping to hail an Uber. In fact, since the app tracks the driver there is no need to wait outside at all. And Uber arrives far more speedily than taxis. For instance, a 2014 study in San Francisco found that Uber arrived in less than ten minutes 93% of the time, while only 35% of dispatched taxis made it that quickly. Uber riders never waited over twenty minutes while 22% of passengers who called taxis did, 33% waited over twenty minutes while hailing a cab on the street (Jaffe, 2014).

## Uber's Impact on Drunk Driving

The convenience of summoning a driver quickly with an easily operated phone app, knowing up front exactly what it will cost, not needing to fumble with cash or credit cards, and often saving money versus a taxi (with no automatic expectation of a tip for routine service) seems likely to encourage tipsy or exhausted customers to Uber home rather than drive themselves. Drunk passengers are a substantial portion of Uber's nighttime customers; tips on the best way to handle them are common topics among driver forums. Uber also offers a standard $200 compensation for cleaning when a drunk passenger vomits in the driver's car (Campbell, 2014).

Uber's market pricing, which allows prices to surge when demand jumps and/or supply is restricted, is a key aspect of reducing drunk driving in peak periods. The ultimate peak period for drunkenness is, of course, New Year's Eve. So, demand is off the charts then while simultaneously supply is severely limited because many would-be drivers prefer to celebrate the season themselves. In the old days of the taxi cartel, with a fixed price normally too high but way too low on New Year's, it would be almost impossible to get a cab. But, with Uber's system the price surges to induce drivers to be available and put up with inebriated passengers. Supply jumps to meet demand but that only happens because price goes so high. For instance, in Miami Beach in the early hours of January 1, 2016 Uber's price was nearly ten times the normal level (Muzenrieder, 2016).

Many formal studies confirm a substantial drop in DUI arrests once Uber is well established in a city. In one analysis of ten major cities just before Uber compared to two years later, after Uber entry, DUI arrest rates declined in all ten cities. However, the decline rates varied widely, from 37% in Las Vegas to 14% in Los Angeles (Chicago Car Accident Lawyers, 2018). Obviously, local conditions strongly influence the DUI arrest rate. For instance, in the ebb and flow of politics cities sometimes crack down harder on DUI drivers than in other times. Traffic fatalities may offer a more clear impact measure. One study focused on traffic fatalities in the 100 most populous metropolitan areas but found no significant effect from Uber (Brazil and Kirk, 2016). However, most studies do find an impact. One found that the entry of Uber into California was associated with a significant drop in the rate of motor vehicle homicides between 2009 and 2014 (Greenwood and Wattal, 2017). Another study found both fewer traffic fatalities as well as the usual declines in arrests for DUI post-Uber (Martin-Buck, 2016).

In perhaps the most comprehensive study to date Dills and Mulholland analyze the impact of Uber's entry into 150 cities and counties over a three-year period. They found no significant impact for about the first six months of Uber operations. After this start-up period, and the rise in consumer use and acceptance, there was a monthly reduction in fatal traffic accidents of 0.5%, a 1.6% decrease per quarter at the mean. After Uber had operated in a county for at least four years, fatal accidents declined by an average of 3.4 to 8% annually, for a total decline of 17 to 40% (Dills and Mulholland, 2017). These methodologies and results suggest these safety benefits may increase over time as more and more consumers become comfortable with utilizing Uber.

Unsurprisingly, with one notable exception, Uber's entry into a market is not associated with any increase in crime. There is, of course, a reduction in DUI arrests. Taxi companies have alleged that those dangerous Uber drivers are more likely to assault passengers, but there is no such increase. The taxi cartel, in sort of a left-handed compliment to Uber for getting drunk drivers off the road, has charged that the presence of Uber encourages more drinking binges, since drinkers know Uber can get them home. If this were true then we would expect the study to find an increase in disorderly conduct arrests—but it does not. In fact, there is a slight decrease in disorderly conduct arrests—perhaps because of fewer arguments about who should or shouldn't drive? Neither is there an increase in assaults or robberies—it seems those Uber drivers are not so dangerous. The one clear increase in crime after Uber's entry is car theft. This makes perfect sense—incapacitated people who would have driven home often take Uber instead, reducing traffic deaths, but leaving their vehicles in unsecure areas (Dills and Mulholland, 2017). Thus, the one negative result from Uber's entry, more car thefts, actually seems to reflect broader success in reducing drunk driving and vehicular deaths. An increase in stolen vehicles is probably a price worth paying for that life-saving result.

*Uber Ambulances?*

It turns out, in the cities they serve, Uber drivers generally arrive much faster than ambulances! In Manhattan in a 2015 study it took an average of six minutes for an ambulance to arrive after being called. Uber showed up in two to three minutes. However, the Uber time advantage is actually a couple of minutes greater than this since the ambulance phone call, not measured in this case, takes much longer than hailing Uber with the app. Similar speed advantages of Uber over ambulances were also documented in London. The advantage of having a widely dispersed army of drivers available almost instantaneously at the press of a button has led to some discussion among health care professionals of perhaps providing some basic medical training to willing Uber drivers, and maybe some equipment such as defibrillators, and possibly even issuing them emergency lights and sirens. Conceivably, Uber might one day revolutionize ambulance service as it has taxi-type services (EMS1.com, 2015).

Even now, Uber has emerged as an occasional substitute for ambulances. In a national study Leon S. Moskatel and David J. G. Slusky find that ambulance usage drops at least 7% when Uber enters a city. Uber arrives faster, is far cheaper, and will go to a preferred hospital, whereas ambulances normally go only to the closest hospital. Of course, in many medical emergencies a full service ambulance will be needed. Moskatel and Slusky envision a possible future system with a video link to a 911 doctor who would evaluate the level of service and expertise a patient needed and send the appropriate vehicle and personnel (Moskatel and Slusky, 2017). Uber has made strong statements that their services are no substitutes for ambulances; however, as Thulin points out, that is very standard procedure for any business in our litigious society (Thulin, 2018). In fact, the driver-partner status of Uber seems ideally suited to facilitating some drivers doubling as sometimes semi-ambulance drivers. Instead of a few ambulance drivers sitting at home base why not have a number of them dispersed in the city, perhaps picking up normal passengers until they are needed for emergencies?

## CONCLUSION AND IMPLICATIONS OF UBER'S RISE

In chapter 2 we discussed the historical reality that improved safety is primarily discovered through innovation rather than mandated by laws and rules (Wildavsky, 1988). There are few things, if any, that impede innovation more than a powerful barrier to entry. And there is no more powerful entry barrier than a corrupt or misguided government that stands ready to arrest any and all new entrants! It is therefore no surprise that there was zero safety innovation in the decades when the taxi cartel ruled. A cartel-monopoly that restricts supply so stringently that a taxi license is worth over $1 million, as it was in New York, is a cartel-monopoly where zero innovation is quite feasible. Note, again, that some safety innovations could have been embraced by taxis everywhere—like a toll-free number for complaints and cashless systems for late night, long before the advent of smartphones. Uber, of course, brought in the cashless system, with an app even better than toll-free calls for complaints, as well as a prescreening/identifying system so neither drivers nor passengers were strangers, an electronic "paper trail," and so on. Furthermore, drivers have no automatic right to pick up a passenger nor does the passenger have a right to a particular driver, instead, both of them choose whether or not to accept the other.

However, to accomplish that Uber had to succeed in its peaceful but relentless revolution against the corrupt government licensing laws that had utterly suppressed competition and innovation in most cities for so long. Travis Kalanick's bold experiment in business civil disobedience was a remarkable success. Uber made history by politely but firmly refusing to obey crooked government regulation, frequently outwitting cartel enforcers, and eating the legal costs of fines and such when the enforcers did manage to catch them. They brought a superior product to consumers, then eventually organized those consumers-cum-voters into a political force that often forced the repeal of those corrupt regulations. This was *Travis's Law*; their customers would fight unethical politicians for them once they experienced Uber's wonderful product.

## The Importance of Online Reputation

Driver safety, in all aspects, and the safety of the vehicle itself are continuously monitored by riders with the Uber app in hand, as well as the Uber "home office" itself. Of course, the same is true of the passenger, who may be banned by Uber in extreme cases, and just avoided by more cautious drivers in cases of more moderate misbehavior. This is truly a marvelous innovation for safety and for product quality in general. This technology brings a sort of "small town" individual responsibility to the large, modern world marketplace.

After all, what we commonly call "corporate misbehavior" is really individual misbehavior. Often, the nefarious deeds are very much against corporate policy and are completely contrary to the company's interests. This is an example of the well-known *principal-agent problem*, also referred to as *shirking* in this context. Workers (agents) have a tendency to act in their own selfish interests rather than in the interests of the owners (principals). Uber instead has used technology and their own policies to make every driver-partner a principal in their own right. Each driver basically has to compete for each customer in every instance since the passenger makes their own selection rather than having a driver assigned to them. In essence, this gives consumers double protection as Uber uses technology to monitor driver behavior to protect their own reputation and brand value, while every driver is simultaneously cognizant of protecting their own reputation and personal brand value.

## Broader Safety Improvements from Uber

Uber benefits society by getting drunk drivers off the road, resulting in fewer DUIs and fewer traffic fatalities. Uber is also sometimes a substitute for ambulances, largely because drivers arrive faster than ambulances but also because Uber is so much cheaper, and people can choose their own hospital. Although not specifically yet measured, there are likely some safety benefits from fewer sick and injured people driving themselves to the hospital. Obviously, to be a closer substitute for ambulances Uber drivers would need medical training and equipment, perhaps a possibility in the future.

## Lessons for other Licensing Reform

Corrupt occupational licensing laws in other fields are not rare; these laws tend to virtually always suppress competition, even if they sometimes actually do improve quality. For that matter, the taxi cartel still remains in power to varying degrees in some cities. Consumers aren't informed and engaged enough to prevent these occupations from "capturing" their regulators. We need a better reform system than just waiting and hoping that someone like Travis Kalanick and Uber will show up to somehow find a way to break all these other cartels. Taking a page from our FDA reform discussion, why not convert government licensing to an advisory system where government provides information, but consumers make their own decisions?

That is, rather than arresting Uber drivers suppose the government merely required the app to say something like, "This person is not licensed by the City of New York or any government body and we urge you to instead ride with a licensed taxi driver for your own safety. We rate Uber F for safety and our taxis A. Click here for more information." We should also allow a free speech counterargument from Uber along the lines of, "Our driver-partners are constantly monitored by us, as well as being rated by riders just like you, and our background checks and other procedure are more demanding. You are far safer with us than with some anonymous taxi driver taking you who knows where with no electronic trail. Don't trust these corrupt government ratings. Click here for more information."

This would initially be very cumbersome for new entrants, but not as cumbersome as being arrested! Moreover, consumers would, over time, come to ignore government ratings that are senseless and corrupt. On the other hand, without the power to arrest competitors, maybe the government ratings would sometimes evolve and become more truthful and actually be of some use to consumers. Thus, in the end consumers win no matter what. Either the fraud of occupational licensing as safety/quality control is exposed or the system reforms itself so that the ratings/information do reveal something useful about safety and quality. We could replace licensing laws with government advisories for carpenters, plumbers, and every other licensed profession, and usher in a new age of competition and innovation with lower prices and better, more innovative safety (Summers, 2007).

Trusting politicians to make our consumer choices for us is probably never a wise idea but the provision of information may be useful, and if not, we would be free to ignore bogus government advice.

## NOTES

1. If only medicine inventors could overcome confused voters and capture the FDA, to quickly bring new medicines to patients! As discussed in chapter two, it is virtually impossible to approve medicines too fast since approval only gives doctors the option to prescribe them, but doesn't compel them to do so. Doctors and patients alike will prefer time-tested medications, turning to new untried remedies only when all else fails.

2. In the pre-Uber world opinions were more evenly divided among engineers and other analysts who were not trained economists (Moore and Balaker, 2006). Post-Uber, defenses of the taxi cartel, apart from the cartel itself and its agents, are not so common.

3. Operating in a generally hostile, and in their view, corrupt legal environment, aware that anything they say can and will be used against them if at all possible, Uber is usually as vague as possible about operational details. They actually have never formally stated that they do cover drivers' legal expenses. It is widely assumed that they do, and in fact, this must surely be the case or their drivers would have abandoned ship.

4. Comparing pay rates is a little complex. Uber drivers do have higher cash income but have more expenses. On net, earning are likely substantially higher (Hall and Krueger, 2016).

5. Sadly, there have also been several suicides involving taxi drivers in financial distress in New York (Stewart and Ferré-Sadurní, 2018).

6. Although voters tend to accept politicians' claims that minimum wage regulation is a humanitarian effort economists are often more skeptical. Probably the most sordid aspect of some minimum wage regulation is that it has been used as a racist tool. Employers who don't wish to hire black workers have favored a minimum wage to drive up labor costs of competitors who were hiring blacks (Williams, 1982).

7. Of course, some drivers see such regulation as a way to coerce Uber into giving them something for nothing. They hope, for example, to keep the same pay and, perhaps, get health insurance as well. This is highly unlikely. Employers who deliberately cater to a workforce interested in flexibility and part time work will generally, in the face of mandated benefits for full-time employees, simply make sure they don't have any full-time employees (Cannon, 2016).

Thus, rideshare companies are likely, if strong-armed in this direction, to go with a workforce where everyone works something like 20 to 29.9 hours per week. The mandate to give health care to full-time employees translates to a ban on full-time employees. Thus, those drivers supporting the regulators against Uber, rather than coercing their way to a windfall gain, are likely to simply see their choices limited.

But these results, fewer drivers and higher rideshare prices are probably the real aim of this cartel friendly regulation.

8. Although this is commonly done, it is a bit inconvenient to keep turning down drivers and then requesting another until finding the preferred match. Uber is working on updating their app to allow customers to simply request a driver with a high rating or other characteristics, such as experience level. Passengers can request certain vehicles but that's usually focused on seating capacity. Uber is working on allowing other requests related to safety, such as anti-collision technology, and also to quality in general, like providing Wi-Fi (Pritchett, 2018).

9. Studies cannot conclusively explain why mechanical inspections of vehicles are so useless. Probably the main theory is that people simply drive safer to offset any mechanical weakness—such as driving more slowly and stopping earlier if the brakes aren't quite tip top.

# Chapter 5

# Business Reality versus Cultural Perception

## THE GOOD, THE BAD, AND THE CONFUSED

We've explained in chapter 1 how a lack of economic understanding can lead to complete misperception of the morality of some business practices. However, we've really only scratched the surface regarding the theme of unwarranted cynicism toward business. Business practices are certainly imperfect but are generally much more ethical than they often first appear. Much of our cultural confusion stems from our common assumption that companies' pursuit of profit is inherently corrupting. Corruption and dishonesty are universal human temptations and tend to infect, to varying extents, all of our institutions. But the profit motive, constrained by voluntary trade and appropriate government regulation to assure that trade is indeed voluntary, generally guides businesses to act in the public interest. In chapter 1 we explained, for example, how "price gouging" after hurricanes and other disasters, though springing from the self-interest of sellers (and consumers) actually benefited society as well.

When really bad behavior by businesses does occur it consistently stems from a lack of truly voluntary trade. For example, a firm that secretly dumps harmful chemicals into a river rather than paying for their proper disposal is simply forcing the cost of that pollution on society. This is essentially theft; the company is stealing clean water from us. Similarly, a company that attempts to weasel out of their agreement to provide "complete refunds to any dissatisfied customer" is also attempting theft. Such conduct is not the norm but neither is it extremely rare. People care more about themselves and their families than they care about the strangers and casual acquaintances with whom they trade. Businesses are tempted to cheat customers, and their customers are tempted to cheat them, and we are all prone to give in to this temptation often enough to create significant problems. Of course, any business that establishes a general reputation for cheating customers is soon out of business; this reputation effect tends to keeps most businesses in line most of the time. But, for the rest of the time, economists generally agree government liability laws as well as laws against fraud, pollution, and other forms of business theft are useful to minimize damage.

The key point here is that normal business activity, voluntary trade, is generally not at all corrupting. A free trade is inherently somewhat self-policing since both trading partners must sign off on the deal. Profit seeking boils down to seeking to please customers, hardly a scandalous activity. And correct government policies can help minimize the tendency for trade to sometimes slyly mutate into theft.

Consider, for instance, the common view that commercial activity is inherently ignoble. Perhaps you've seen a movie with a theme that goes something like this: An artist struggles for years to earn a living by painting abstract depictions of "what he feels" until finally he "sells out" and accepts a job where he draws kitsch illustrations for children's books. Such stories often spin this as a greedy betrayal of true art. Since art is subjective such a spin may not be inherently incorrect.

However, another viable interpretation could be that the struggling artist stopped selfishly painting whatever he "felt like painting" because he realized his work was not pleasing enough to others for them to be willing to adequately pay him. So, he took a job where his work did please others, he offered something that people valued, thrilled children, unleashed their imaginations, and drew them deeper into children's literature. Profit seeking drives us to find ways to please others, not just ourselves. Isn't this more often uplifting rather than corrupting?

Nobel-winning economist Paul Samuelson reportedly once said something like, "An intelligent person can learn the key economic ideas in one course, but you have to get a Ph.D. in economics to actually believe it." While we can't turn reading this book into the equivalent of obtaining a PhD, it probably is useful to address more of the cultural myths and biases that make it difficult to trust the logic of economics that underpins the efficacy and morality of free enterprise.

It is important to remember ours is a *mixed* economy, with large elements of government command and control as well as substantial elements of free enterprise. When something goes wrong in our economy it is sometimes because of government intervention; there is no basis to reflexively blame "greedy" free enterprise for every failing in our economy. It is interesting to note that overall government control of the U.S. economy is about equal to the level of government control in the economy of Sweden. The Heritage Foundation's 2017 ranking of economic freedom has the United States with a score of 75.1, in a tie with Denmark for 17th place in the world. Sweden is next, with a score of 74.9. Sweden has higher taxes and government transfer payments, but has less regulation and is otherwise generally more free enterprise oriented than the United States (Heritage, 2017).

No U.S. business is free to conduct operations as it sees fit to best serve its customers and others. Politicians exert a great deal of influence over business behavior, and as we have seen, it is not always a beneficial influence. For better or worse every business is in effect in a partnership with government. In chapter 2 we saw how harmful government policies slowed innovation and caused massive increases in the price of medical drugs. In chapter 4 we saw the impact of corrupt occupational licensing laws in the taxi industry-cum-cartel. We now turn to some other sectors of the economy where government regulation has had similar devastating effects.

## WHY CONSUMERS LOVE THE RISKIEST BANKS AND HOW TO FIX THAT

> We don't care what risks you might take with our money—we have perfect peace of mind through Federal Deposit Insurance. We don't care what you do with our funds, where you invest or who you lend it to, don't bother us with details, just bring us good returns—no questions asked. Roll the dice all you want.

The implicit command of depositors throughout the United States. A major difficulty banks have is that all their depositors are relentlessly pressuring them to take on too much risk. We stand ready to boycott any bank that is less risky than the others. Consumers do not consciously have this intention but nonetheless we all systematically drive banks to take imprudent risks. We will choose the bank that pays the best interest on deposits or offers the best free services. But do you have any idea what the balance sheet of your bank looks like? When you've chosen a bank, have you ever investigated which bank seems to have the less risky loan portfolio, or asked a friend which bank seems the financially safest? Me neither. We depositors care only about the rate of return on our deposits; we don't care much about risk at all. The above "quote" is a realistic summary of the message we send to our banks and other financial institutions. When it comes to selecting a bank or credit union we all tend to be riverboat gamblers. We are only conscious of demanding the highest possible returns, but an unbridled demand for the highest returns for our deposits inevitably translates into demand for our bank to make the highest risk loans/investments.

Our insatiable, if unconscious, appetite for risk stems, of course, from federal deposit insurance—we know taxpayers will bail us out if we trust the wrong bank with our life savings.[1] Basically, when we drive our banks to gamble and they win, our share of the rewards go right into our private account. If they gamble and lose then our share of the losses gets billed to the taxpayers. Private enterprise rewards with socialist losses, a financial system that is half socialist is kind of like being shot in the heart with half a cannon-ball. The definition of financial free enterprise is a system where the people who enjoy the fruits of financial gains are also responsible for bearing the losses; since we don't have that, we don't have a truly private system. When government takes over and shifts risks from depositors to taxpayers they have established a fundamentally government system. Having sabotaged market incentives to fully control risk, only government is positioned to protect us from financial crises in the banking system.

We have this strange, hybrid socialist set up where government guarantees us riskless returns through banks that can only generate the high returns we demand by taking risks! Fortunately, there is still some degree of market pressure against excessive risk-taking coming from the bank's stockholders. However, the inexorable inclination of any business is to give their customers what they want, government bank regulators must try to force banks to swim against that tide. Direct government bank regulation must attempt to replace the void left from consumers' being induced to abandon their normal risk reticence. Actually, it would be more accurate to say government attempts to push back against the unrelenting push for maximum return risk from deposi-tors who have been warped into wild, risk-taking junkies by the incentive of socialism for any losses.

In other words, government deposit insurance destroyed the free enterprise risk management system, which, to avoid even more chaos, was replaced by a risk management system of regulation run by the federal government. Therefore, *every banking crisis since 1933, the commencement of deposit insurance, is unambiguously a failure of this government regulation.* It cannot possibly be a failure of free enterprise since free enterprise banking only exists if any severe bank losses fall on depositors. Since such losses are socialized, falling on taxpayers not depositors who chose their bank, banking crises are ultimately a failure of socialism. Command and control regulation attempts to stop banks from taking the excessive risks that naturally come with a system of socialized losses. But from time to time regulators utterly and disastrously fail, and we get results like the financial crisis in 2008. Ironically, one reason the mortgage crisis and resultant recession of the 2000s was so severe is that regulators rigidly drove banks toward making lots of mortgage loans because regulators "knew" people hardly ever default on home loans (Ely, 2009).[2]

By the way, if your bank or credit union didn't sustain large losses from the 2008 crisis then you probably picked the wrong bank. Your stodgy, old-fashioned bank is too worried about balancing risk and returns when they should be jacking up returns for you and letting the risk fall on taxpayers. Your tax dollars went to bailing out other depositors, who probably enjoyed better deals and returns than you in those high risk banks. Maybe you can try to find a bank more readily pressured into taking great risks so that you too can properly enjoy looting taxpayers!

A natural solution to this mess would be to require that federally insured deposits be used exclusively to buy U.S. treasury bonds. Lending to the federal government is essentially risk free since they can raise taxes, borrow even more, or ultimately print money to pay back the loans. Of course, this allows the government to borrow at much lower rates than businesses or homeowners, which means lower returns to the banks and affected depositors. That's the main downside; of course, returns on risk-free deposits would be much lower since the loans generated from those deposits would be risk free to the banks as well. Separately, banks could still offer depositors the higher returns we like but we would have to accept the commensurate risk that generates those returns. So, if the bank uses our deposits on risk-free loans only, those are guaranteed. To get higher returns we would deposit in different accounts and accept the risk that comes with lending to private parties.[3] This concept is known as *narrow banking* and the general problem of socialized losses leading to excessive risk-taking is known as *moral hazard*. Details of all this are discussed by George Pennacchi in his book, *Narrow Banking* (Pennacchi, 2011).

Depositors would no longer get something (higher returns) for nothing (no risk). On the other hand, as taxpayers and participants in the economy we would gain much, much more than we lost as depositors. We wouldn't have to fund so many bailouts, and we would all benefit from a more stable financial system with fewer and less severe recessions. With banks' incentives returning to a natural concern for risk, regulation would be far simpler; we would no longer need an army of regulators impeding financial innovation as they cast about in a perpetually futile attempt to consistently control risk in a system where government subsidies constantly encourage excessive risk-taking.

The theme of politicians' regulations sabotaging free enterprise is a very common one in our economy. Ironically, the failure of regulation is often unfairly attributed to the very companies who are the victims of government blunders. This stems mainly from voters' being so misinformed, and also from the often subtle inter-relationships of an economy. An economic system, like an eco-system, can often be wrecked by seemingly minor interventions. For example, did you know the key problems in private health insurance today were caused by errant government wage controls during World War II?

## HOW POLITICIANS WARPED PRIVATE HEALTH INSURANCE

In some sense there is almost no such thing as private health insurance in the United States. The health care that is provided through employers is referred to as "private" but is actually mutant, quasi-socialist health care. Strangely, private health insurance was inadvertently strangled to death in its infancy by the federal government's system of wage and price controls foolishly instituted during World War II. Price controls make no more sense in war time than they do after hurricanes or any other time, but the harm done is this case has long outlived the misguided price controls. The specific culprit in this case was federal regulation that would not allow wages to be raised; firms could not compete for labor by paying a higher salary than their competitors. Again, this is senseless in its own right; allowing labor to go to the highest bidder results in labor generally going to where it is most productive for firms and their consumers, exactly as it should.

As routinely happens when regulations impede profit maximization, firms found loopholes to evade the rules. They were forbidden from paying higher wages but the law did not prohibit them from giving things to their employees. A few firms began giving away health insurance, and it quickly caught on (Buchmueller and Monheit, 2009). The good thing about this loophole is that it allowed some firms to attract labor to where it could be most productive, a harmful regulation was at least partially evaded. However, the side effects of all this would ultimately sabotage the entire structure of health care and insurance.

Wage and price regulators were upset that their rules were being evaded, and the IRS agents were also upset that this form of employee compensation was not being taxed at all. However, by the time legislators were preparing to close this loophole it had become so popular that the politicians were afraid to change it. Wage and price controls ended shortly after the war, but the tax-free status of employer provided health care became permanent, more or less the same to this day (Buchmueller and Monheit, 2009).[2]

But it is only tax free when your employer pays for it. If you want to buy your own health care/insurance you must generally use after tax dollars, the income you have left after payroll taxes, federal income taxes, state income taxes, and in many cases local income taxes. Consider, for example, an individual with taxable income of $38,701 to $82,500, who is fortunate enough to live where there are no state or local income taxes. That worker is currently in the 22% federal tax bracket and faces a payroll tax of about 15%. So, basically, that's a 37% subsidy you get if you buy health care/insurance through your employer rather than on your own, too large a subsidy to resist in most cases. Of course, the subsidy is much larger for many workers, especially if they live in high-tax states and cities. Thus, government clumsily herded us into a system where we lose our health insurance if we lose our jobs.

It's worth noting that, strictly speaking, there is no such thing as employer paid health care. Though employers often write the checks, the cost of health care is ultimately paid for by workers in the form of lower wages. In fact, employers don't "give" their workers retirement benefits, paid vacations or anything else—all such things are part of the compensation package, earned by workers, and essentially deducted from what their cash pay would otherwise have been without such benefits (Leibowitz, 1983). So, employees indirectly pay for their own health insurance, but in a company system where they lose the freedom to choose the terms of that insurance and tailor it to their own particular needs, and risk losing it if they switch jobs.

Probably even worse, this tax bias causes these employer health care plans to be idiotically structured. Insurance can only function smoothly when claims are relatively rare, only covering major, unforeseen expenses. This is how auto insurance, homeowner's insurance, or any other kind of truly private insurance function. To grasp the absurdities of our distorted employer-based health insurance imagine auto insurance was set up in a similar fashion. That is, imagine auto insurance covered every expense occurred in operating a car, including buying gasoline, with only, say, a $100 annual deductible. So, virtually every time you filled up, got an oil change, or replaced a light bulb in your car, you, or the seller of these products, had to fill out detailed insurance forms. The insurance company would have to hire an army of administrators to process these mountains of claims pouring in every day. Since most of these claims would be way too small to justify the cost of a claims adjuster investigating them, insurance fraud would be a major concern. With no good way to discourage fraud desperate insurers would use more complex insurance forms and would try to reduce fraud by often adopting a fairly hostile attitude toward claimants. After all, those with legitimate claims will typically persist, even when a claim is initially denied, while those attempting fraud are more likely to back off when insurers argue with them.

In reality, this crazy form of auto insurance would never exist. Conventional auto insurance, covering only major expense of accidents or theft, would cost only a fraction of what this ridiculously broad coverage would cost. Of course, with conventional insurance we have to pay directly for our own gasoline and all the other routine expenses of operating a car, but cutting out the middleman would be far more efficient, saving us a lot of money overall. Normal insurance plus operating expenses would be far less costly than mutant car insurance that covers fill-ups and everything else. So, there is no way this insane form of auto insurance would ever show up in the real world, unless, of course, politicians blundered into providing a big fat tax exemption just for this mutant car insurance.

Fortunately, government does not provide a tax subsidy for employer provided auto insurance; we dodged that bullet, but we took it right between the eyes in the case of health insurance. The next time you're annoyed at all the paperwork in health care, and how your insurer seems to argue about almost every bill, remember you have the federal government to thank for that. While employer-centered health care is referred to as private, it's really much closer to socialism since each consumer pays only a tiny portion of the cost of their own care directly. In fact, in the United States in 2016 the average patient paid only about 6.7% of their health bill. Businesses' employees paid 19.9% of total health care[4] costs through the mutant, quasi-socialist employer system, with government at various levels paying the lion's share of health care costs, 73.4% (The Centers for Medicare & Medicaid Services, 2018). Given these figures it's rather silly to think of U.S. health care as fundamentally private, or to automatically assume that government errors are unrelated to any shortcoming we observe in health care.

A full explanation of how to fix health insurance is beyond our scope. However, the key reform needed is simply to equalize the tax treatment for private expenditures. We could provide a full tax credit for the purchase of private health insurance as well as private health care expenditures, as we do now when employers write the checks. Health insurance would begin to look more like true insurance, with most health care consumers paying directly for routine, smaller expenses so that claims would become far less common. Once consumers begin to pay more directly, we will also get more price competition and efficiency in health care generally. John C. Goodman discusses this and many other aspects of health care reform more fully (Goodman, 2015).

## SOME NOTES ON MORALITY AND EFFICIENCY IN EMPLOYMENT PRACTICES

Since our focus is on consumers we haven't said much about the profit motive in relation to employer behavior. However, employer/employee behavior is inherently relevant for consumers. Furthermore, if one believes the commonly accepted myths concerning business misbehavior in employment it is probably difficult to fully accept that those same businesses can be driven by profit to properly serve consumers. So, let us briefly analyze a few key misconceptions in businesses' dealings with workers.

Consider how rarely one hears words like this, "I have to admit; I deserved to be fired." Instead, fired employees will often say something like, "It was just politics, my boss is so unfair and just doesn't like me. Nice guys finish last." While, no doubt, people are sometimes unjustly fired, there is reason to believe that most firings are actually justified. Each employee is an investment by the firm. If someone is fired for no reason this will cost the firm some money, including the case where there is no government involvement at all. After firing someone a firm must go through the expense of recruiting, hiring, and training a replacement. Part of that training cost includes the fact that new employees are less productive than experienced hands, and they may also reduce the productivity of other workers who must take the time to guide the newbies. Moreover, if the firing really was arbitrary, this will usually trigger a wave of eventual resignations as other employees decide to move on to a more reasonable employer.

No one likes working for an employer that might suddenly fire them for no reason. Many employees who believe a coworker was unjustly fired will immediately start looking for a new employer, and the better employees will typically find new jobs the quickest and be the first to resign. So, arbitrarily firing one worker sets off a domino effect which will cause a huge increase in recruiting, hiring, and training costs. For this reason, and others, *a truly profit-maximizing employer will never fire a worker unjustly*. Undeserved firings most likely do occur sometimes, but always in spite of, not because of, desire for profits.

## The Bright Side of Layoffs

Sometimes, business behavior that clearly is profit motivated can seem worse morally than it is. Many seem to see layoffs in pursuit of profits as inherently immoral, unless the layoffs are absolutely necessary to prevent complete collapse of the firm and an end to all jobs there. Keep in mind, though, the purpose of the economy is to generate abundance for consumers; jobs, though very important, are secondary, a means to an end. For example, a true cure for cancer—take a pill and the cancer is gone—would be a miraculous, wonderful blessing to humanity, saving countless lives and ending massive suffering. But it would destroy all the jobs people now have offering imperfect cancer treatments such as chemotherapy or radiation treatments, as well as all the jobs involved in researching a cure for cancer. Of course a cure, not jobs for researchers, is the entire purpose of cancer research. Jobs are never central; they are always the means to an end. As a society we may sometimes need to assist those, usually relatively few, people who suffer great hardship in the transition to new jobs. But it wouldn't make sense to end all progress so we can end layoffs and freeze people in the same jobs forever.

More generally, we can't consume more per person unless we produce more per person. Increasing abundance for consumers mainly happens when we improve technology, broadly defined, such that we generate more output per worker. More output per worker means, of course, we sometimes need fewer workers in some areas. An advancing economy will inherently generate some layoffs and render some jobs obsolete as new ones are created. Consider U.S. employment history in agriculture. In the year 1800, 68% of all U.S. workers were employed in agriculture (Lebergott and Brady, 1966, 118). Producing enough food just to survive was difficult in such primitive times; it took the lion's share of our workforce to do it. But by the year 2012 modern technology made food production a comparative breeze, with only 1.6% of U.S. workers employed in agriculture by then (Employment Projections

Program, 2017, table 2.1) The enormous job loss in agriculture was, overall, a great triumph, not at all a tragedy. As we needed fewer people making food we could begin employing those people to create trains, indoor plumbing, automobiles, washing machines, modern medicines, airplanes, and eventually computers and smartphones.

Of course, within this flourishing there were some hardships. Most of the people who lost jobs on the farm got new jobs that ultimately paid better; we know this because we know average wages surged compared to their starting point in the year 1800. However, there were no doubt some tough times, at least initially, for some of those laid off farm workers. Even the cancer researcher who rejoices that someone else has indeed found a cure may still face some personal hardship as her job ends. Again, as a society, we want to help people who have a very tough time finding a new job, which we do. But we do want them to move on to those new jobs rather than somehow jury rigging the economy to preserve jobs which make nothing properly useful for society. Labor is a resource, like energy, but even more crucial; it is intrinsically beneficial to use less of a resource whenever possible, to make the resource more available for other unfulfilled needs.

Let's take this a step further. Since we know replacing some workers with machines is the key to raising our living standards; is it any different if some workers here are replaced by people in other countries? No, in fact the economic impact on us is exactly the same. Imagine this alternate history: Suppose somehow there were never any breakthroughs in U.S. agricultural technology but such breakthroughs did occur in other countries. Suppose then we imported this increasingly cheap food from abroad which generated the exact same employment trends, agricultural employment tumbling from 68% of our workforce in the year 1800 to 1.6% in 2012. Once again labor is freed up to start making trains, cars, modern medicine, and so on. The key thing is to produce food at the lowest possible cost using the least amount of our labor, regardless of exactly how that is achieved, whether by machines, foreign labor, or whatever.[5] The key to every advance we desire, from curing cancer to ending world hunger, is related to using fewer resources, especially labor, to produce the things we already enjoy.

It's true, of course, that *any employer who replaces some workers with machines or foreign labor in order to reduce costs and make their products cheaper is chasing profits. But it is also true that such employers are advancing society, freeing up labor to make something else, and raising our standard of living.* Just as all those farmers did beginning centuries ago. So, the image some have, of heartless firms sabotaging our country with merciless outsourcing or cruel layoffs is not at all warranted. Again, as a society we need to continue to offer and possibly improve things like unemployment compensation and/or private charity to help those who are laid off and having trouble finding a new job. But we do want them to bounce back to a new job, not always stay in place with the old. Let's hope we need to help out a few former cancer researchers in the not too distant future.

## Employer Discrimination

The economics of employer discrimination encompasses some shocking surprises. Perhaps most surprisingly, *racist employers have been known to favor equal pay for equal work laws*! This stems from the fact that discrimination is a sort of brain disease that contains the seeds of its own cure. If employer bias against certain workers is strong, it will depress the market demand for those workers and, in turn, depress their wages. This was exactly the situation faced by black workers in South Africa in the apartheid system of the 1970s, as explained by Walter Williams. Discrimination, including strong bias on the part of the government itself, depressed black workers' wages. But even racists like bargains. Firms found they could hire some very productive workers at cheap wages and thereby make a lot of money. Hiring black workers triggered some consumer boycotts and even strikes by racist labor unions, but many firms persisted in hiring black workers. The money they lost from labor headaches and some consumers moving on was less than what they could gain from tapping into a pool of labor available for bargain-basement wages. People will do almost anything for enough money, including sometimes even setting aside their own racism, at least in business, and rebelling against a rampantly bigoted society (Williams, 1982).

Moreover, the firms who hire black workers will have lower labor costs and be able to cut prices for consumers and gain market share. In turn, growing market share means they will demand more labor and continue to drive up the wages further for black workers. The process continues with better profits for those hiring more black workers unless ultimately the wages are bid up to equality for equal work. This is a dramatic example of the redemptive power of the *invisible hand. In a free enterprise system deeply flawed people can be motivated purely by self-interest to do the right thing.*

However, there were also some employers whose racist impulses dominated even their desire for profit; these refused to hire black workers no matter how inexpensive they were. But these worst of the worst racists faced a dire threat from their competitors who were willing to hire black workers. With much lower labor costs those competitors could sell their products at lower prices than the ultra-racist businesses could afford to match. They were wasting too much money paying premium wages to white employees whose productivity wasn't proportional to their wages. This is actually a key point: bias not only makes wages artificially low for victims, it simultaneously elevates the wages of those favored by it. The only way the racist employers could have competed in the marketplace would be to reduce their own labor costs, but the only way to do that would be to also hire black workers, anathema to them (Williams, 1982).

Firms engaged in pure profit maximization will defeat firms sacrificing profits for the sake of bias every time in open competition. The optimal profit maximization strategy entails treating workers based solely on their productivity and how much it costs to hire them. Inserting employer bias always conflicts with profits. So, the ultra racists banded together to get politicians to protect them from market pressures against racism; they passed an equal pay for equal work law that required black workers to be paid the same wage as their white counterparts! This did not end all opportunities for black workers, but it did slow advances as firms employing blacks now had to also fight legal battles and search for loopholes in the law to make it affordable to hire blacks, and withstand the costs of some consumer boycotts and all that. Fortunately, this equal pay law did not protect racists enough. It did not stop market pressure from helping to cause the collapse of the apartheid system, though equal pay laws helped hold it up longer (Williams, 1982).

## Pay Gaps in Reality

So, the more firms focus on maximizing profits the quicker they bid wages to equality for equal work. But, what about wage gaps we hear about in the U.S. economy? For instance, the latest figures indicate the average woman earns about 83% of what the average man earns (Bureau of Labor Statistics, 2018). But such comparisons commonly reported by the media are completely misleading because they ignore all differences in labor markets. For example, suppose we compare the earnings of men and women at hospitals across the United States. There are two main categories of employees, doctors and nurses, with about 2/3 of doctors male while over 90% of nurses are female (Erikson et al., 2012, 7; Bureau of Labor Statistics, 2018). So, the hospital male/female wage gap only proves doctors earn more than nurses, hardly surprising and not a clear indication of discrimination or anything else.

More sophisticated studies that adjust for education and experience show a lingering but much smaller gap, around 5 or 7%[9] (Christianne and Hill, 2012). But such small pay gaps may be explained by a number of factors. For example, men are disproportionately employed in more dangerous jobs, about 92% of workplace fatalities happen to men though women are almost half the general workforce (Bureau of Labor Statistics, table 1). So, the slight pay gap may reflect, at least in part, compensation men receive for taking more physical risks and tolerating less pleasant working conditions. We really can't get data good enough or adjust for every factor so we cannot conclusively prove how much pay differences stem from discrimination.

However, the key takeaway here is that *employer discrimination always conflicts with profit maximization*. Again, profit maximization entails treating workers based solely on their productivity and how much it costs to hire them, inserting employer bias always conflicts with profits. Relentless pursuit of profit means a firm will always refuse to pay a man an unwarranted premium and would prefer to hire an equally productive woman if she's available at even only a slightly lower wage. This means, if the pay of equally productive females is even slightly lower, then demand will always drop for men and always rise for women until the wages equalize for equal productivity. In fact, a truly profit-maximizing employer would also refrain from sexual harassment and other bad behaviors that would hurt profits in various ways. Fines and lawsuits are possible consequences of sexual harassment but even without those, profits would be harmed as good workers would sometimes quit, requiring expenditures to recruit, hire and train replacements. We, of course, are not saying that employers never discriminate or never harass employees, but such bad behaviors have their roots in other human failings, and completely conflict with the desire for profit. The desire for profit actually helps constrain baser desires, when these ugly behaviors occur it is in spite of, rather than because of the yearning for profit.

So, just as the desire for profit generally drives firms to satisfy consumers as best they can, it also prods firms to use labor efficiently, generally fairly, and in ways that benefit society.


## WHY OPTIMAL BUSINESS BEHAVIOR IS NOT PERFECT

In 2016 employee theft and shoplifting by consumers cost U.S. firms over $48 billion (Reilly, 2017). Given modern technology, and the fact that firms generally struggle to earn enough to just stay in business, these figures might seem astoundingly high. Indeed, it is likely that firms could set up modern security systems to virtually end consumer and employee theft. There's only one thing stopping them: to virtually eliminate this $48 billion worth of theft they would likely have to spend far more than $48 billion. Sometimes eliminating human imperfections is too costly, more expensive than tolerating those imperfections. In such cases it makes more sense to just sit there rather than doing something. Spending another, say, $1,000 to stop some thieving consumers makes no sense if they only would have stolen $900; cost/benefit analysis is hardly utopian but when the numbers are correct the logic is inescapable.

This is a central fact in human cooperation: anything worth doing is worth doing imperfectly. We do what we can to reduce bad behavior but we cannot hope to eliminate it. This includes employee actions that harm consumers or other employees, such as sexual harassment or discrimination or anything else. Such bad behaviors, as already explained, always conflict with profit maximization. Still, businesses can no more eliminate these evil flaws in human nature than governments can end all crime. But the profit motive does work some wonders in constraining some of the worst human impulses. The $48 billion in theft that retailers didn't stop is smaller than it might seem. In 2016 GDP was 18.57 trillion, meaning thieves only made off with far less than 1%, about 0.26% of the GDP total. We can restate: firms are about 99.74% effective in eliminating employee and consumer theft. Getting to 100% even if possible, would cost more than it's worth.

## ON HUMAN NATURE AND THE
## ECONOMICS OF THE MEDIA

Bad news sells. Television ratings soar when the cameras are covering horrible acts of terrorism, deadly accidents, cataclysmic natural disasters, or extraordinarily scandalous behavior of prominent people. There is seldom, if ever, a headline story in the papers about the remarkable safety record of commercial airlines; however, in the rare event of a tragic airline crash front page coverage is a certainty. Perhaps part of our fascination for the macabre stems from our self-preservation instinct, we don't have time to learn about everything so maybe we often focus on learning about potential dangers in hopes that knowledge gained might help us avoid the fate of the victims we see on video. Possibly, we sometimes enjoy seeing the failures of others more wealthy and famous than ourselves.

Whatever its roots, our demand for negative news has consequences. One is that news reporting has a relentless bias; reporters will bring us the worst possible news as much as possible and are not above gross exaggeration, relaying unverified gossip or even outright fabrication in order to draw our attention. An infamous example of media fabrication was NBC's News' secretly rigging GM trucks with explosives, and presenting a video of a staged "test crash" as evidence the trucks would naturally explode in a collision. Only after GM proved the conspiracy and launched a lawsuit did NBC confess at length and profusely apologize on air, whereupon GM dropped the lawsuit (Kolbert, 1993).

It turns out there are several known instances of television news shows rigging vehicles to artificially generate sensational films. ABC did this to try to exaggerate safety risks in Ford vehicles in 1978, while the *60 minutes* show on CBS acted similarly in a 1980 film of a Jeep and in a 1986 attack on Audi. Experts like Walter Olson point out that even when there is some safety issue with a vehicle it is seldom if ever something you can readily generate and film on cue—if the car was that bad no one would be driving it! Staging illustrations is a practical necessity to manufacture the desired video, which wouldn't be so bad if they honestly admitted the filmed incident was staged for illustration purposes (Olson, 1993). Even so, media lies that can be proven wrong are probably not common.

It is generally easy for the media to create a completely false impression through selective reporting without resorting to lies. A good example of this in general economics is perception versus reality in the case of foreign investment. Most people in the United States, and certainly my own students initially, have great concern about the imagined strong trend in U.S. job loss stemming from businesses, on net, moving operations to foreign countries. The media creates this impression by harping on particular cases where this happens.

However, in reality, for decades, there have been more firms moving into the United States than moving out, more jobs gained from international capital flows than lost. The United States generally leads the world in Net Foreign Direct Investment, which is foreign investment in factories and other operations in the United States minus factories and other assets owned by the them operating in other countries. In 1994 foreign-based companies invested about $46 billion more dollars into the United States than we invested abroad. By 2016 that net figure had ballooned to about $425 billion (World Bank, 2017). So, it is selective reporting, not outright falsehoods, that has played on the public's fears to create the mythical belief that international capital flows are hugely flowing out from the United States when they are in fact flowing in at a massive rate. Furthermore, in reality, it is not harmful when there actually are capital outflows. We had massive net capital outflows from 1945 through the early 1980s to no ill effect. Capital naturally flows to where it's most productive; the higher productivity shows up in cheaper, more efficient products that help drive the economy up. Thus, thanks to the fear-mongering media we are greatly afraid of something that isn't happening and wouldn't be harmful even if it was happening!

## OUR BIASED PERCEPTIONS

Returning to common perceptions of business ethics, based on decades of experience with those students who have little or no formal education in business, it seems misperceptions of industry practices commonly stem from a failure to fully filter the media bias toward a steady drumbeat of negativity. Psychologists have well documented a frequent cause of misperceptions known as the *availability heuristic*—meaning under uncertainty, particularly in areas well outside our expertise, people tend to estimate probabilities based largely on the examples that happen to come to their mind. Of course, spectacularly negative examples more readily stick with us and often come to mind. Thus, for example, people tend to wildly overestimate the probability of shark attacks (Tversky and Kahneman, 1973).

Similarly, what most people recall about businesses they don't know well is whatever was in the news headlines. Probably most everyone realizes the media has a negative bias but most don't fully account for this bias, especially as it flows through their own biased memories. If, for example, 90% of business stories allege truly malicious business behavior most students are not so foolish as to assume 90% of business executives are truly malicious, but they still vastly overestimate the frequency of such behavior. We know that the rare airline crash makes news and the frequently safe landings don't, but we still greatly overestimate the risk of flying. Similarly, people know that few who wade into the surf will be seized by a shark, but still erroneously assume a shark attack is far more likely than it is. This sort of bias seems wired into us (Tversky and Kahneman, 1973).

If you watch local television news constantly and don't get out much it may seem like most people in the town must be either rapists and murderers or the victims of rapists and murderers. Likewise, anyone whose opinion of business ethics is drawn substantially from media reports will have a much more negative view than is warranted. The media naturally focuses on bad news; we know this and discount the news somewhat but not nearly enough.

This warped, overly negative view of business leads to an unwarranted, though common, assumption that profit seeking is automatically corrupt, that greater profit must signify greater corruption. This distorted view permeates our culture, including our interpretation of history. Let's take a brief look at some businesses from the past that we so often like to blast.

## ROBBER BARON MYTHOLOGY

Widespread economic illiteracy is rather universal, not unique to our time and place. Most historians have been shaped by the dominant culture, not well versed in economics, and it shows in common versions of U.S. history. Many historical stories told of the "Robber Barons" are filled with economic misunderstanding and, at best, exaggerations, and, often even outright myths and untruths.

Consider, for example, the case of John D. Rockefeller's Standard Oil. According to common myth and many historical accounts, Rockefeller epitomized the ruthless, unethical capitalist, illegally dominating oil refining by using predatory pricing to monopolize the market before engaging in heartless price gouging to rip off consumers. Only toward the end of his life, so they say, driven by guilt, did Rockefeller show a kinder side as a generous philanthropist (Josephson, 1962).

In fact, Rockefeller, though a very tough, politically incorrect competitor, was a generous philanthropist his entire life and was a godsend for consumers of kerosene (The key events took place in the late 1800s and early 1900s, before the importance of gasoline). Here are the facts: Before Standard Oil, oil refineries were essentially little mom and pop operations. We know now, as Rockefeller first showed us, this is not an efficient way to produce oil products. Standard Oil employed economies of scale and superior technology to reduce costs and make kerosene available at markedly lower prices. Many of those tiny refineries were indeed driven out of business but not because of some nefarious "predatory" manipulation, but simply because they were too inefficient to match Rockefeller's low prices. At its height, Standard Oil had a 90% share of the kerosene market. But even if they'd had 100% of the market they would have had no monopoly power since, at that time, whale oil was a very close substitute for kerosene, and Standard Oil had zero share of the whale oil market. In retrospect, perhaps Standard Oil was persecuted simply because they were an inviting political target, the first huge corporation, with a lot of disgruntled, inferior competitors to fan the flames (Chamberlin, 1974; Folsom, 2018).

Perhaps, the most amusing aspect of Robber Baron mythology is the importance played by Upton Sinclair's 1906 novel, *The Jungle*, depicting incredible horrors in the meatpacking industry. Though enthusiasts of Sinclair's ultra-negative view acknowledge the work is fiction, there often seems a faithful belief that conditions described were accurate and meticulously researched. However, consider this excerpt from Sinclair's novel, "There would be meat stored in great piles in rooms; and the water from leaky roofs would drip over it, and thousands of rats would race about on it. It was too dark in these storage places to see well, but a man could run his hand over these piles of meat and sweep off handfuls of the dried dung of rats" (Sinclair, 2017, 164). Does it really seem likely that greedy meatpackers would disinterestedly let thousands of rats run about eating up their inventories? Sinclair also fantasizes that firms use a sort of magical alchemy to render spoiled meat palatable, with absolutely no limit on just how badly spoiled the meat might be. Forming a view of business, and a theory of regulation, based somewhat on a Sinclair novel seems little different then believing we should have a government employee in every lab to make sure scientists aren't assembling parts of cadavers and bringing them to life with a lightning bolt à la Frankenstein.

The whole Jungle paradigm rests on assumptions that consumers are easily manipulated and fooled while the competitive process always reduces quality, never driving firms to attract consumers by increasing quality. In this fevered vision of business rather than car companies inventing antilock brakes and anti-collision technology, they would have invented cars that fall apart while you drive them and explode if you hit the brakes too hard!

In the real world, as opposed to Sinclair's wacky dystopia, a firm that routinely sold spoiled meat would make many customers sick and would soon be out of business. Even before that, every employee involved in the disgusting production process with mountains of rat dung and all that would boycott the meat and tell all their family and friends to do likewise. Such a situation is unlikely to remain secret. Some firms seeking profits would recognize consumer willingness to pay more for meat supplies that are healthier and safer, and would maintain such quality in order to be able to charge higher prices. In this case, quality control would likely be meticulous since one episode of selling bad meat would typically destroy their reputation and end their ability to charge higher prices.

Firms would also accept inspections by credible private parties that verify quality control. Rabbis who inspect firms to assure that kosher standards that are met are perhaps the oldest example of this. Eating kosher would have been a simple, immediate solution for those consumers suffering nightmares after reading Sinclair's rat army horror. Government liability laws would also prevent the kind of systematic, extremely hazardous abuses featured in Sinclair's wild tales.

Of course, no human system is perfect. No doubt contaminated food sometimes slipped through and was sold in Sinclair's day. Just as the FDA and other regulators have failed to prevent all contamination of our food supplies today, despite all the enormous wealth and technological advantages they have compared to that of 1906. The CDC reports, for example, that Salmonella causes about 1.2 million illnesses, 23,000 hospitalizations, and 450 deaths in the United States each year (Centers for Disease Control and Prevention, 2018). Incidentally, kosher foods have been shown to be less prone to Salmonella, probably because of the use of salt in the cleaning process. Kosher procedures are also, in at least one sense, superior in that firms must agree to surprise inspections at any time (Berkeley Wellness, 2017). This is not an indictment of government food regulations. An examination of the limits and possible improvement of government regulation in this area is beyond our purview. The point is simply that private businesses serve society far better in reality than in Sinclair's novels or other Robber Baron myths, and government regulation is hardly a failsafe panacea.

## WHY INNOCENT FIRMS COMMONLY LOOK GUILTY

This quote, though not sympathetic to the particular bank discussed in the article, summarizes the tendency of U.S. regulators to employ their considerable power to extort companies into paying fines without any sort of due process:

America's legal system looks like an extortion racket. . . . There are no meaningful checks on this process, let alone a plausible procedure for . . . appeal . . . bosses cannot even publicly criticize deals they agree to under extreme duress. No precedent is set and no guidance provided as to the limits of the law and the proportionality of the punishment.

—*The Economist* (*The Economist*, 2014a)

Government can deny or delay approvals of licenses or other mandatory forms, require endless paperwork or even bring less than solid lawsuits that are often prohibitively expensive to fend off (The Economist, 2014a). The upshot of all this is that innocent firms often have great incentive to pay fines and settle charges even if those charges are baseless.

This might be an analogous situation—imagine you are falsely charged with a felony. If you go to trial it will be expensive and very stressful. Your lawyer is confident you would likely be vindicated in the end, but reminds you juries can be unpredictable and fickle, and there is still a chance you could be convicted and imprisoned for years. The government agrees to drop all charges if you pay a fine without admitting guilt, and agree to a gag order where you can never proclaim your innocence. The fine is not trivial but is far cheaper than your legal costs would be if you go to trial. Your trusted attorney advises you to accept the settlement, save money and avoid the chance of being thrown in prison. What would you do? Me too. Vindication is sometimes not worth the expense and risk. *If you are an innocent business in the United States proving your innocence is often a luxury you can't afford.*

Most people probably assume that firms agreeing to pay regulatory fines or compensation for alleged damages, though admitting no guilt, must in fact be guilty. It seems the media headline is often something like "Acme fined $200 million for killing grandmother." As opposed to, "Acme admitted no guilt but agreed to pay $200 million in settlement, avoiding massive legal costs." In fact there are several overwhelming reasons why innocent firms routinely pay off government regulators and/or consumers armed with lawyers rather than go to court, even if victory is highly likely. Legal costs are high on the list. This is not just attorneys' fees, though those can quickly become enormous. The costs in terms of employees' time are often astronomical, especially high level employees, as they laboriously gather mountains of subpoenaed documents and data, and, worse, prepare for high stress testimony.

Then the trial begins. Government gets to go first so in the early days and weeks of the trial, they get front page news coverage with headlines such as "Prosecutors maintain Acme's can openers turned deadly as lovable grandma died screaming in blood bathed kitchen." Finally, the prosecution rests and Acme can at last make their case, but the media headline of, "Acme insists can openers are safe," just doesn't garner the same attention, especially in the case of a long trial where people are tired of hearing about the case. Given that reality, the Acme defense coverage is placed on the bottom of page 13. Suppose, at long last, the trial ends, and the firm is declared innocent. The title of the page 16, section c article is likely something like, "Jury acquits New Jersey can opener manufacturer despite tragic death of grandmother."

## Regulators Inherently Suppress Free Speech

Think, for example, of the tremendous power the FDA has over pharmaceutical companies. Would a company really want to rock the boat too much with harsh, if honest, criticism of them? Why tick off the monopoly regulator that can easily add another year or two of testing, and hundreds of millions in costs "just to be really sure it's safe" to every new product you invent? Consider also that the nature of government regulation in general resembles common traffic regulations in that normal activity commonly violates some regulation. Virtually every driver exceeds speed limits now and then or doesn't always come to a "complete stop" at stop signs. There are similar picky regulations for most businesses that are routinely violated.

For instance, it is likely that pilots technically violate some Federal Aviation Regulations (FARs) on most every flight. In fact, when union airline pilots want to engage in a work slowdown to pressure airlines in contract negotiations a common technique is to follow FARs exactly (Herlehy and Ingalls-Ashbaugh, 1993). Just as traffic cops are generally not so unreasonable as to hand out speeding tickets to drivers going 6 MPH over the speed limit, the FAA and other powerful regulators are usually not so unreasonable to fanatically look for technical, inconsequential violations. But, it seems there is nothing to prevent traffic cops and regulators from acting against technical violations if they feel like it. Any company that offends its regulatory master is risking quite a bit more than a speeding ticket.

## Regulators' Ultimate Threat

The clincher in all this is the modern trend of government prosecutors threatening executives with criminal charges if they refuse to settle out of court. Even if the probability of conviction is low, a criminal trial is inherently terrifying. Many have said the threat of criminal charges is a sort of extortion; even in a case where a CEO believes shareholders might be best served by going to trial, the highly stressful threat of criminal charges is likely to motivate a settlement (Jensen and Meckling, 1978; DiLorenzo, 2000; The Economist, 2014b). The capricious power wielded by U.S. regulators has been likened to the manner in which China's government shakes down business (*The Economist*, 2014b).

## The Ford Pinto Case

The infamous Ford Pinto case of the 1970s is a classic example of an innocent firm paying to settle chargers rather than risking far greater expense in a court battle. This is fully explained by Paul Weaver in his book, *The Suicidal Corporation*. The media headline story: "After several fatal accidents it was eventually revealed that these particular fatalities could probably have been avoided if Ford had spent about $11 per vehicle to reposition the gasoline tank so that fire would have been less likely to erupt when the car was hit too hard from the rear." However, Weaver points out that the government's own data indicated that there were over 100 other safety improvements that could have been made for about $11 each that would each have saved more lives than repositioning the gas tank. For example, installing an extra support bar on the roof would have prevented deaths that occurred when deer or other animals fell on the car. Fatalities from falling deer are rare but still more numerous than deaths from the Pinto gas tank catching fire (Weaver, 1989).

The Pinto was a subcompact automobile that sold for about $3,000 at the time. If Ford had chosen to implement each of these "cheap" improvements that would have saved more lives than would strengthening the gas tank, it would have driven the price of the vehicle up to over $4,000, or an increase of over one-third of its original price. In fact, Ford sold other vehicles around that higher price with those very safety features. Basically, if you wanted to spend more you could get a larger, heavier, safer car than the Pinto. Duh. If you wanted to spend far less you could have sacrificed some safety and bought a motorcycle instead of a Pinto. Crucially, the Pinto's overall government safety record was slightly above average when compared to other subcompact cars in its market. There was absolutely nothing sinister in this case; we all know that high speed vehicle collisions are always dangerous, and become more dangerous in smaller, lighter vehicles. Weaver expressed dismay that Ford did not aggressively and persistently make its case, since the government's own data completely vindicated Ford. But settlements of this sort are the norm in our litigious and biased world (Weaver, 1989).

## THE VESTED INTEREST OF REGULATORS

It is also important to remember the obvious bias inherent in government regulatory agencies. Every regulatory bureaucracy has to find substantial business misbehavior to justify its very existence. If the department of toothpick regulation admits that toothpick quality and safety is just fine then those toothpick regulators know that their bureaucracy is likely headed for big budget cuts and downsizing. It is in the direct financial interests of every regulator on the planet to exaggerate, possibly even invent wrongdoing, as much as they possibly can. In the world of politics, piling up settlements in a legal system stacked in their favor is the most reliable way for regulators to slash off the business scalps they need to maintain and increase their funding. In fact, sometimes the fines, or sizeable portions of them, are paid directly to the regulatory agencies that force companies to settle (Shen, 2016; *The Economist*, 2014b). We can hope honesty is sometimes a mitigating factor but it would be unwise to count on the integrity of regulators to systematically trump their own self-interest.

The bottom line here is clear: The justice motto "assume innocence until guilt is proven" particularly applies to business behavior. When a business agrees to pay some fine for alleged crimes rather than fight it out in court, this is not a reliable sign of guilt. Rest assured, if we had a government bureaucracy charged with prohibiting firms from hiring extraterrestrials, in the present legal system, that agency would get some firms to pay fines rather than going to court to prove that all their employees were earthlings.

## Reform?

How can we give innocent firms incentive to consistently take on their powerful regulator masters in court? It would take a radical change. Suppose, upon receiving the not guilty verdict a company would receive compensation from government to make them *whole*. That is, the company would receive compensation for all legal costs, lost revenues, general harm to their reputation, and any other harm that befell them as a result of the false charges brought. This would be a sizeable sum, yet still would often not be enough. The problem is that losing this kind of court battle will frequently be catastrophic, perhaps even spell the end of the firm's existence. Indeed, just being formally indicted often means doom for a company. No financial company, for example, has survived just being indicted (The Economist, 2014a).

Suppose an innocent firm estimates there is a 95% chance the judge or jury will wisely reject the regulators' bogus accusations. But a mistaken guilty verdict would spell the end of company. Thus, there is a 95% chance the company will essentially break even, receive compensation for all the damages they incur in fending off the legal attack, but a 5% chance they will cease to exist. Odds are this firm would still prefer to settle and pay a fine. Suppose we raised the compensation to triple the total damages. Now the firm has a great chance of doing much better than breaking even; vindication in court will bring them a windfall. Yet, there is still a 5% chance that a court battle ends in the death of the company. If the regulators throw in potential felony charges for the CEO who refuses to settle, with say, also a 5% chance of conviction, the firm's leader faces both professional and personal catastrophe. This seems likely to motivate a lot of settlements.

Still, not every firm faces complete destruction if they go to trial; it stands to reason that a policy that compensates innocent firms who win in court with triple damages would have some impact. After all, even in the current system blameless firms occasionally refuse to surrender the payoff regulators demand for a settlement. Around 3% of such civil cases ultimately are decided by trial (Barkai, 2006). Compensating vindicated firms with triple damages is bound to increase that number and at least slightly rein in regulatory abuses. More thorough analysis of this or other possible reforms is beyond our scope, and probably not worth the time in the modern political environment. It is difficult to imagine government embracing such a reform, or any reform that substantially checks their massive regulatory power. It would probably take an uprising from voters and the media to drag regulators, kicking and screaming, into a system where there are more effective checks and balances against wrongdoing by regulators. Perhaps one day voters and reporters will be well informed enough to demand reforms, but that day is not yet in sight.

## CONCLUSION

Corruption is a problem in all human activity, from marriage to government to television news to churches to businesses and everything else involving people. However, profit maximization, as long as it is channeled through voluntary trade, generally motivates good behavior, not bad. Chasing profits motivates sellers to give buyers what they want, not just what the seller feels like making. Firms focused on the bottom line are driven to set aside their own biases and even battle discrimination in society, as we saw in South Africa. But we need more than just the invisible hand; most economists would agree that government has an important role to play in insuring that voluntary trades are truthfully fulfilled, through efficient liability laws as well as laws against fraud and theft.

When something goes wrong in the U.S. economy there often seems to be an automatic assumption that the failure stems from a lack of appropriate regulation. This probably relates to the common notion that the United States is a sort of bastion of free enterprise. However, high-tax Sweden is, apart from those high taxes, generally more a bastion of free enterprise, less regulated, than the United States. In fact, many problems in U.S. business stem directly from flawed government regulation, as is the case with all banking crises since at least 1933. In the banking industry the federal government heavily subsidizes and encourages excessive risk-taking by socializing all losses to bank depositors, through federal deposit insurance. Logically, funds in government insured accounts should, by regulation, only be lent to the federal government, not higher risk private borrowers. Instead, we have the ongoing financial paradox where depositors drive banks to make riskier loans to generate higher returns for those depositors who are oblivious to the risk since any losses fall on taxpayers. This culminates in problems such as the 2008 financial crisis.

Since the economy is a complex, interrelated system, many problems have their roots in seemingly unrelated government policy errors. Thus, World War II wage controls lead to a bizarre mutation of health insurance into the employer-sponsored quasi-socialist fiasco we have today. The resultant government subsidy for low deductible, high administration cost systems has plagued us for about eight decades. Our political system, in all that time, has been unable to end the subsidy for an insurance structure that leads to constant insurance claims for minor, often predictable health costs. Health insurance is so bizarre compared to homeowners or auto insurance only because of the bizarre government subsidy that we stumbled into long ago. More broadly, it's a little silly to think of U.S. health care as a fundamentally private system when government directly pays over 73% of the costs and patients pay less than 7% themselves.

Perhaps the area of the economy least understood by most people in our culture is the labor market. It is often assumed that a host of bad behaviors—such as discrimination and arbitrary firings—are profit-maximizing strategies. They are certainly not. Firing a good worker unnecessarily means the employer, at minimum, must incur the costs of recruiting, hiring, and training a replacement. In fact, such capriciousness is likely to cause a wave of future resignations as many workers move to a more trustworthy, reliable employer. Employer discrimination is foolish and *always* conflicts with profits. While it is true that hiring women at wages lower than men will cut costs, the implication of this is that profit seekers would hire only women. If a man insists on receiving $100,000 to take a given job, but an equally productive woman is available at $82,000, then only a fool would overpay and choose the man. Instead, profit maximizers would hire the woman every time and thereby bid women's wages up, even as they shy away from hiring the overpriced males, which bids their wages down.

Discrimination may take other forms but it is always financially damaging to employers. Reported wage gaps do not prove the extent of discrimination since comparisons of all men and women lumped together are apples and oranges comparisons. Higher average wages for men at a hospital, for example, are simply reflecting the current reality that most doctors are male while most nurses are female. Doctors earn more than nurses; ergo, men at the hospital tend to earn more than women. It seems the view which imagines rampant discrimination assumes biased employers are somehow evil financial geniuses; in fact, a discriminating employer is a fool, harming themselves financially. To measure the true magnitude of discrimination we need very precise data that we don't have. But one thing is certain, any discriminating employer out there is foolishly sacrificing profits.

Various human biases, including the availability heuristic help, lead to a distorted, overly negative cultural view of free enterprise. This bias is reflected both in current media and in many historical accounts. Amplifying this slanted perceptive is the reality that innocent firms routinely pay fines to settle charges and end bad publicity rather than incurring the massive costs of a protracted court fight with deep pocketed prosecutors. The tendency to pay fines to settle false charges is exacerbated by the modern tendency to sometimes threaten executives with felony charges if they don't settle. Finally, there is the natural bias of regulators whose personal financial interests are in jeopardy if there isn't enough business evildoing to go around.

If a given regulatory body is unable to find enough wrongdoing to justify their current budget, can we count on them to honestly admit this and accept budget cuts and layoffs? It is a strong possibility that, instead, these regulators would abuse the power the system and culture gives them to shake down some innocent companies and extort some settlements to justify their full funding and perpetuate their existence. It seems many people do not factor in these considerations and unjustly assume businesses are guilty until proven innocent.

Of course, this is not to say that bad behavior in business is nonexistent. Humans have a tendency to abuse power whenever we get it. But, as we have seen, a business that must attract and keep labor in a free market and induce consumers to voluntarily buy their products is hardly in an all-powerful position. The real power is with politicians and their hired regulators, as we've seen in this chapter and in more detail on the chapters analyzing the FDA and taxi regulators. Ideally, highly informed voters would appropriately check this power, and hold government's feet to the fire the way consumers do with private businesses. But, obviously, we don't have anything remotely close to an ideal situation.

## NOTES

1. Deposit insurance, of course, is designed to prevent bank runs, where many depositors want to withdraw their funds at the same time triggering a liquidity crisis for their bank.

2. There were, of course, many other factors in the mortgage crisis and resultant recession (Taylor, 2009).

3. Such accounts would probably function like mutual stock funds, meaning the value of deposits would instantly fall if people learned some of the bank's borrowers would likely default. Thus, there would be no exaggerated incentive to quickly withdraw funds, no bank runs. Bank runs only happen when there are guaranteed returns but depositors realize some depositors will be too late to get their guaranteed funds.

4. To clarify, firms basically pass along the cost of health care to their employees through wages being lower than they otherwise would be. However, this is not done on an individual basis. Instead, if, say, the average cost of "employer paid" healthcare at a company is $14,000 then each salary ends up being $14,000 less than it otherwise would be. It is illegal to relate individual health costs and risk to individual salary. It is also generally illegal to fire an employee because of exorbitant health costs, though firms likely sometimes look for another excuse to let such people go or avoid hiring them in the first place.

5. Another problem with the theory that importing components or outsourcing jobs to foreigners is immoral is that it devalues the lives of poor people living in other countries. We hate to see workers in the United States suffer job loss but when firms move jobs to countries where wages are lower are they not creating jobs in an economy that needs the jobs even more desperately than we do? In comparative terms the United States is a fabulously rich country. Are we really so clearly on the side of the angels when we insist companies have a moral duty to keep jobs in our extremely wealthy country, rather than create new jobs in a very poor country? Of course, the fact that our overall economy always benefits from making products cheaper, the gains to consumers always outweigh the costs to workers, removes this dilemma. We help our economy and theirs when we allow free trade to cross borders, and the increased wealth makes it easier to help those who lose their jobs and need help in transition.

*Chapter 6*

# Is Air Travel *Too* Safe, and
# Need the TSA Screening Monopoly?

It actually is quite possible that air travel is "too safe," that we are pouring in so much money, time, and human resources into safety in this area that some of our expenditures are generating more costs than benefits.

> Increased delays and added costs at U.S. airports due to new security procedures provide incentive for many short-haul passengers to drive to their destination rather than flying, and, since driving is far riskier than air travel, the extra automobile traffic generated has been estimated to result in 500 or more extra road fatalities per year. (Mueller and Stewart, 2011, 42)

One tragic and very ironic cost, as mentioned in the above quote from Professors Mueller and Stewart, is that the time loss and unpleasantness, occasionally bordering on harassment, imposed by airport security sometimes spurs people to reluctantly travel by car, a veritable death trap compared to the safety of flying. The estimate of 500 more annual highway deaths caused by the harsh, time-consuming security at airports is based on an analysis that found for every 1 million reduction in enplanements an additional fifteen roadway deaths occurred (Blalock et al., 2009). Thus, our obsession with making flying ever safer may in reality be making us less safe overall.

A key point is that the TSA (Travel Safety Administration) makes no serious attempt to assure that its actions create more benefits than costs. The TSA itself should be estimating, among many other things, how many road deaths they are indirectly causing. In fact, they display no interest in any cost/benefit analysis, which has drawn heavy criticism from the Government Accountability Office, among others (U.S. Government Accountability Office, 2009; Mueller and Stewart, 2011). Furthermore, in the case of airport screening we will see that it is a virtual certainty that current costs exceed benefits, that

A airport screening makes us substantially less safe. Let us conduct that cost/benefit analysis that they fail to do, beginning with the cost side.

## TSA PASSENGER SCREENING COSTS

It is difficult to find a favorable view of the TSA, outside of the TSA itself.

> [TSA administrator Kip Hawley] wants us to trust that a 400-ml bottle of liquid is dangerous, but transferring it to four 100-ml bottles magically makes it safe. He wants us to trust that the butter knives given to first-class passengers are nevertheless too dangerous to be taken through a security checkpoint. . . . He wants us to trust that the deployment of expensive full-body scanners has nothing to do with the fact that the former secretary of homeland security . . . lobbies for one of the companies that makes them. He wants us to trust that there's a reason to confiscate a cupcake (Las Vegas) . . . a purse with an embroidered gun on it (Norfolk, VA) . . . and a plastic lightsaber that's really a flashlight with a long cone on top (Dallas/Fort Worth). Additionally, there's actual physical harm . . . and the mental harm suffered by both abuse survivors and children: the things screeners tell them as they touch their bodies are uncomfortably similar to what child molesters say. . . . In 2004, the average extra waiting time due to TSA procedures was 19.5 minutes per person. That's a total economic loss—in—America—of $10 billion per year, more than the TSA's entire budget.
>
> —Bruce Schneier, of Harvard's Berkman Center (Dobbs, 2012)

As well summarized in the above quote, airport screening policies impose major costs and sometimes seem to be pointless. Some of the worst instances of TSA insensitivity, bordering on cruel brutality, are summarized in *10 TSA Horror Stories of Pat-Downs Gone Wrong* (Goldman, 2010). However, as always, focusing on a relatively few worst cases can paint a misleading picture. Virtually all passengers find airport security annoying but, thankfully, truly traumatic experiences are unusual. For example, in an extensive passenger survey the main complaints by the vast majority of passengers were loss of time and other inconveniences. Only 9% of those surveyed said the worst aspect of airport security was getting patted down by TSA (Festa, 2016). Granted, 9% is not a trivial number, and we do want to include the unpleasantness of pat downs in our cost estimate; however, let us begin with more conventional costs.

This analysis largely extends the excellent work of Mark Stewart and John Mueller. First, consider the direct TSA expenditures for airline passenger screening, which totaled about $5.4 billion for the 2016 fiscal year (Stewart and Mueller, 2017). But, that's just the tip of the iceberg. There are several other costs to consider: time going through security, extra time at the airport to cover risk of abnormally long security lines, annoyance/pain, and suffering imposed by TSA screeners, costs of Pre-check and Global Entry used to reduce security costs imposed on passengers, economic losses from driving rather than flying, and, of course, the loss of lives from driving rather than flying.

## Costs of Passengers' Sacrificed Time

Actual time passing through the airport security line, much improved from 2004, averaged only about ten minutes in 2015, around twenty minutes for regular lanes and two minutes for the Pre-check lanes (Stewart and Mueller, 2017).[1] However, this doesn't include the time cushion passengers build into their airport arrival time to make reasonably sure they don't miss their flight. If passengers allowed themselves only ten minutes to pass through security they would miss their flights about half the time!

The official advice from both TSA and the airports is to arrive two hours early for domestic flights, three for international. But, that is somewhat conservative, intended to give enough time cushion for those who rarely fly and need some extra time to find their way. Also, some of that time goes to other purposes; for instance, it takes an average of about thirty minutes to check luggage for those who do so (Elliott, 2017). In an extensive customer survey at John Wayne International Airport, it was found that passengers arrived an average of one hour and forty minutes early (John Wayne International Airport, 2018). This seems roughly consistent with another survey, of 2000 passengers nationally, that found 59% planned to arrive at the airport at least two hours early (Festa, 2016).

Let us now consider how those 100 minutes (one hour and forty minutes) are allocated. Only about 43% of passengers in the U.S. check luggage. However, let's round that up to 50%, in part to allow for those who might wait in the airline check-in line for another reason such as seat assignment. So, since it takes thirty minutes on average to check luggage but half don't bother then that averages out to fifteen minutes checking in with the airline. Next, consider the average time it takes to get to the terminal from parking, since this is close to zero for the many passengers who get a ride and are dropped off at the airport it seems reasonable to allocate an average of, say, ten minutes for this. Then there is the time moving through the airport to security check-in, then, after that, the time moving to the gate from the security checkpoint. This varies widely, depending mainly on the size of the airport, but say, on average, this takes another ten minutes or so. Throw in another five minutes for miscellaneous stops. This, as shown in table 6.1, adds up to about forty minutes for essential activities other than dealing with airport security. This suggests that the average traveler allocates about an hour to deal with airport

**Table 6.1    Approximate Allocation of Passengers Time at the Airport**

| | |
|---|---|
| Moving from parking to terminal | 10 minutes |
| Checking baggage or other check-in | 15 minutes |
| Other movement/stops in the airport | 15 minutes |
| Waiting in security line | 10 minutes |
| Waiting at gate (security cushion) | 50 minutes |
| Total | 1 hour, 40 minute |

security, ten minutes in line on average with another fifty-minute time cushion once security is cleared.

The time cushion is to protect us from unusually packed security lines and procedures. Returning to the passenger survey data, 54% reported being caught at least once in a long security line in the year prior to the survey that stressed them out about potentially missing their flight, while 7% of passengers actually did miss their flight because of security delays (Festa, 2016). There is no other activity at the airport with such a downside potential. There may be long lines at airline check-in lines, but any risk of missing a flight is generally mitigated there by airline procedures that move passengers desperately short on time toward the front of the line.

However, waiting in the security line for the average ten minutes is surely a worse waste of time then waiting in the gate area an average of fifty minutes after we've survived the security gauntlet. Once there, we may kill time eating, working on a laptop, or whatever. It is likely we would generally prefer to spend those fifty minutes somewhere other than near our departure gate, but those minutes are not as thoroughly wasted. I know of no formal survey data or anything else that might provide grist for a more formal estimate so let us simply guesstimate a reasonable possible range. It seems likely that leisure travelers, especially those who seldom fly, would have the greatest sense that they are wasting their time waiting around for their flight rather than being with loved ones a bit longer or enjoying the sights.

But even in the worst case they can make some better use of their time than waiting in the security line. Perhaps time at the gate could be no worse than 15% as valuable as truly free time. This means 85% of that time is wasted. On the other hand, maybe the time is much more useful than that—a chance to eat, stretch your legs, or run the kids around a bit to burn off energy before getting on the plane. However, all those things can be better done somewhere else, so this time value must still be well below 100% on average, perhaps the maximum is about 70%, meaning only 30% of the time is wasted.

Business travelers may generally get some work done on their computers or in phone conversations but the more distracting environment and lack of privacy are bound to reduce average productivity somewhat. Perhaps the worst case here is that the average business traveler values the time about half as much, 50%, as completely free time they could have spent anywhere, like working more privately and efficiently in their hotel room. The best case scenario is likely very close to 100%; one can picture seasoned road warriors learning to use that airport time extremely efficiently. Thus, the upper bound might be, say, 98%.

So, our guesstimate is that leisure travelers value that airport wait time somewhere between 15–70% of truly free time that might be spent anywhere while business travelers value the time in the 50%–98% range. Leisure travel comprised about 69% of enplanements in 2015, business about 31%. Thus, weighing the preferences by these percentages yields a range of average gate time valuation from 25% to 80%, meaning wasted time is at least 20% (100–80) and could be as high as 75% (100–25) of the average fifty minutes spent waiting at the gate. Net wasted time at the gate, then, is estimated to be at least ten minutes (20% of 50) and could be as high as thirty-eight minutes (75% of 50) which needs to be added to the average time spent, ten minutes, actually in the security line. Thus, total time lost to security procedures is estimated to be at least twenty-five minutes and could be as high as forty-eight minutes.

Stewart and Mueller assign a value of the average time of airline passengers of $32.70 per hour based on calculations from survey data (Landau et al., 2015). Thus, using only the average ten minutes spent in line, they calculate the 708 million passengers flying in 2015 spent 118 million hours going through security, yielding a total opportunity cost of $3.85 billion in 2016 dollars for those passengers (Stewart and Mueller, 2017). Bringing in the value of time lost waiting at the gate will at least double these figures and could make them almost five times as high. This raises the estimated opportunity cost of passengers' time to somewhere in the range of $7.7 billion to $18.48 billion.

## Considering the Pain and Occasional Suffering Imposed by TSA Security

Next, we need to account for the annoyance, "pain, and suffering" passengers incur going through security. Although most of us are probably familiar with some of the worst cases of TSA rudeness and even brutality, these are, happily, not at all the norm.[2] Some children end up in tearful abject misery, and some adults feel they have been basically sexually assaulted by TSA groping but these are not typical experiences. Virtually all air travelers find airport security irritating, at the top of the air travelers complaint list, or near it, in several surveys (Martín, 2011; Yamanouchi, 2017) but very few are actually terrorized by airport security. In a survey where passengers name the worst aspect of TSA security the vast majority, about 85% listed the lost time or various inconveniences, such as taking off shoes. Only 9% said the worst aspect of airport security was getting patted down by TSA, while 6% hated the full-body scan the most (Festa, 2016). Thus, only about 15% of passengers were primarily bothered by anything other than lost time and basic inconveniences.

Of course, the pain and suffering imposed by airport security can be minimized through programs like TSA Pre-check and Global Entry. Pre-check members can generally leave shoes on, leave laptops packed, and go through metal detectors rather than full-body scanners. TSA Pre-check costs $85 plus some time. Filling out the application takes maybe about ten minutes, visiting a TSA enrollment center for an interview and fingerprinting about another fifteen minutes. The time of travel to the enrollment center varies tremendously depending on where one lives. It happens to be about eighty-minute roundtrip from my smallish central Florida town; it's likely far less in larger towns and many airports have enrollment centers. If we assume the average time to an enrollment center is only thirty-five minutes round trip, then that gives us a total time of one hour required by each Pre-check enrollee. Using Stewart and Mueller's figure for the value of the average time of airline passengers of $32.70 per hour, this means the Pre-check enrollment cost is $85 cash plus $32.70, a total of $117.70. It lasts for five years, so annual cost is $23.54 per passenger.

Global Entry includes TSA Pre-check and provides some additional benefits for moving through customs more quickly; the cost is higher, $100 per year. To estimate how much of that security cost let us simply use the $85 figure from Pre-check, since this includes Pre-check in its price. Time costs are also greater, mainly because there are far fewer Global Entry enrollment centers, for example, only seven in all of Florida. Allowing an extra twenty minutes travel each way to the figures we used for Pre-check brings total time costs to one hour and forty minutes, making the time costs about $54.61. As with the cash price, let us estimate the portion of this that is security cost by taking 85% of that $54.61, giving us a figure of $46.42.

Total passengers in Pre-check in 2015 were about 21.1 million while Global Entry had about 14.43 million.[3] So, multiplying these figures by the per passenger costs above give us added security costs of $496.7 million for Pre-check and $669.84 million for Global Entry. Totaling the two give us an added security cost of about $1.167 billion. Most of this expenditure is probably motivated by saving time, but some can be to reduce pain and suffering, since, for example, passengers in these programs are less likely to be patted down. We don't need to distinguish the two; we simply need to estimate any remaining pain and suffering.

For passengers going through Pre-check lines pain and suffering will generally be very minor—again, no need to take off shoes, go through body scanners, unpack laptops, and so on. Still, there is a little annoyance in going through this more moderate security, with maybe some tension that some sort of problem will arise. The worst case would be for those who are very tense about the slight chance of a pat down occurring, and truly miserable if it actually happens. Only 9% of all passengers are highly concerned about this, though it makes sense this group is especially likely to be in Pre-check, so the percentage in this group could be higher. On the other hand, those truly terrified would likely fly seldom or never—leading to a different kind of pain we'll discuss later. Given the rarity of serious pain here, perhaps average pain and suffering could range from one to three dollars per passenger. In 2015, 45% of all 708 million passengers went through the Pre-check lines (Stewart and Mueller, 2018). So, for those 318.6 million enplanements our total estimate for pain and suffering would be between $318.6 million to $955.8 million.

For the 55% of passengers who go through the full TSA gauntlet, shoeless and hassled, pain and annoyance/suffering will be greater but still not huge. After all, if it was more than $23.54 per year, the total annual cost of Pre-check, they could avoid most of that annoyance. On the other hand, this group likely travels much less than the Pre-checkers, meaning their pain and suffering per trip could feasibly be much more substantial. About 31% of passengers made only one round trip (two enplanements) in 2015, another, 20% made two round trips, and 10% made three round trips (Heimlich, 2016). If we assume virtually all of the one trippers and two trippers were non-Pre-check, with the remaining non-Pre in the three tripper group, then the average non-Pre made about 3.1 enplanements. Dividing this into the $23.54 gives us $7.59 for the upper bound estimate of pain and suffering. However, it seems unlikely that every person would be right at this upper bound, so let's round it off to $7.

That leaves us with the lower range to consider. What is the minimum an average person would pay, time concerns aside, for the convenience of leaving their shoes on, not having to unpack, avoiding risk of a pat down and skipping the body scanning? Based on the annoyance commonly expressed let's go with a minimum average of $4. So, with a range of $4–$7, for the 389.4 million non-Pre-check enplanements, total pain and suffering for this group would be estimated to be in the range of $1.6 to $2.73 billion.

## Costs of TSA Screening Shifting Travelers to Cars

Previous studies have focused on driving deaths, the worst aspect of the TSA procedures displacing passengers back to their cars. The estimated loss of 500 lives follows from about 14 million less enplanements, a bit less than a 2% reduction in passengers, as people shift to driving (Blalock et al., 2009; Stewart and Mueller, 2018). However, you don't have to have an accident to find driving less than ideal. By definition, every single person induced to *not* fly by the TSA suffers some economic loss; TSA is forcing them into an otherwise less preferred transportation mode.

There does not appear to be any survey data or anything else readily available as a foundation for estimating this loss of traveler welfare; however, let us cover some related points that can help us hazard an educated guess of the feasible range of loss. First, let us consider the low end of the range, the minimum average loss travelers incur when forced out of air travel by TSA procedures. Ken Button estimates the cross price elasticity between airline prices and driving, finding that for every 1% increase in air fares there is a 0.3% increase in driving (Button, 2005). Using that figure, to shift 2% of erstwhile air travelers to their cars, the airlines' average price would have to rise about 6.7%. The average roundtrip fare in 2015 was $364.05 as reported in the U.S. DOT Passenger Airline Origin and Destination Survey (Airlines for America, 2018). Taking 6.7% of that $364.05 gives us $24.39, so an increase in average fare of that amount would prod enough people into their cars to cause the 500 annual highway deaths we've discussed. The $24.39 is roundtrip, cutting that in half gives us about $12.19 per enplanement.

However, this is not our estimate of minimal loss for the flyers-cum-drivers. This is the estimate of what it takes to induce driving but the net loss from driving could be less. For example, consider a traveler who initially is almost indifferent between flying and driving on their trip such that flying is more valued by just $1. When cost goes up $12.19 one way they shift to driving but the loss is just that $1. On the other hand, a traveler who initially prefers flying by a value of $12.18 suffers a loss of that amount when they shift to driving. If passengers are about evenly distributed along that spectrum of losing $1 to $12.18, then the average net loss is the average of those figures, about $6.60. This $6.60 then is our rough estimate of the minimal average loss from induced driving.

The high end of possible loss is an entirely different matter. Recall, for example, that while most air travelers complain primarily about the time wasted going through security, 9% of surveyed passengers listed being patted down by TSA agents as their worst security suffering and another 6% listed the body scan as the worst aspect (Festa, 2016). It does not seem reasonable that passengers focused on time would often switch to driving which, of course, will still generally take much longer than flying. People who drive to avoid trauma or to avoid a perceived health risk may have much preferred to fly; thus their loss could be far in excess of the relatively trivial $6.60 we came up with as a minimal estimate. Incidentally, the U.S. government estimates the risk of getting cancer from one body scan to be 1 in 60 million, while the probability of a passenger being killed by terrorism on one flight is far less, only 1 in 110 million (Stewart and Mueller, 2017).

Unfortunately, it is difficult to extend this reasoning to come up with a numerical estimate. The loss from induced driving could be great but how great? To rephrase, what is the upper estimate of how much these drivers would be willing to pay to be allowed to fly without the TSA interference they dread, in order to avoid driving? Let's go with $20, so we have a guess-timated range of loss of $6.60 to $20 per passenger. Multiplying that by the number of 2015 passengers-cum-drivers, 14 million, gives us total induced driving costs of $92.4 million to $280 million.

If somehow none of these drivers had traffic accidents this would be the end of the story. Of course, tragically that is not ever going to be the case. So, let us consider more carefully the total costs associated with the 500 people per year who die on the highway only because they drive to avoid the hassles and delays imposed by TSA security screening (Blalock et al., 2009; Stewart and Mueller, 2017). Stewart and Mueller incorporate the cost of those fatalities in terms of the "value of a statistical life" but, since their analysis focuses on other points, do not delve into the full costs of highway accidents. In a given accident with at least one traffic death there are often medical costs and a reduced quality of life for survivors, forgone earnings, and damage to property. A study of 2010 traffic accidents provides detailed estimates of all these costs (Miller et al., 2015). Unfortunately, such data is not available for 2015, our study year. So, let us extrapolate a bit from those 2010 statistics.

In 2010 there were 32,999 deaths from auto accidents with a total cost from all traffic accidents of $836 billion. The ratio of total accident costs to total deaths was then $25.33 million. It seems reasonable to assume that this ratio of total accident costs to total deaths would be roughly the same in 2015. Thus, if 500 people died as an indirect result of TSA security screening, that is, driving specifically because of the costs imposed by TSA, then 500 times $25.33 million give us an estimate of total costs of TSA generated auto accidents of $12.67 billion.

Table 6.2 summarizes estimates of the various costs of TSA airport screening. There is quite a range since some of the figures are, of necessity, just

**Table 6.2   2015 TSA Security Screening Costs in Millions (2016 dollars)**

| | |
|---|---|
| Federal Expenditures on TSA Screening | $5,436.1 |
| *Costs Imposed on Passengers* | |
| Time spend going through security | $3,850 |
| Time cushion/time wasted at the gate | $3,850–$14,730 |
| Cost of Pre-check (including app. time) | $497 |
| Cost of Pre-check portion of Global Entry (including app. time) | $670 |
| Additional/annoyance/pain and suffering of Pre-check/ Global Entry passengers | $319–$956 |
| Annoyance/pain and suffering of all other passengers | $1,600–$2,730 |
| Annoyance of driving when flying was preferred | $92.4–$280 |
| Increase in driving fatalities, injuries, and related costs | $12,670 |
| Total cost of TSA screening in millions | $28.980.5–$41.819.1 |

educated guesses. Even at the very lowest range of estimates we see total annual costs of nearly $30 billion, with a possibility that cost might total nearly $42 billion. It is a tall order to justify costs of this magnitude.

## BENEFITS OF TSA SECURITY SCREENING

Benefits from TSA screening are not obvious, as summarized in this quote:

> It was a job that had me patting down the crotches of children, the elderly, and even infants as part of the post-9/11 airport security show. I confiscated jars of homemade apple butter on the pretense that they could pose threats to national security. I was even required to confiscate nail clippers from airline pilots—the implied logic being that pilots could use the nail clippers to hijack the very planes they were flying. . . . We knew the full-body scanners didn't work before they were even installed. . . . The machines cost about $150,000 a pop.
>
> —Jason Harrington, *Confessions of a former TSA officer* (Harrington, 2015)

It is true that the United States has remained relatively safe from terrorism, and it may well be that other TSA activities have been helpful in that regard. But there is no sign that TSA airport screening itself can possibly justify its enormous cost. The clearest benefit would come from actually catching a terrorist who otherwise would have killed some airline passengers. In seventeen years and counting, as of this writing, this has not happened a single time. The closest the TSA has ever come was when they apprehended Kevin Brown at Orlando International Airport when he tried to check luggage containing material that could be used to make a pipe-bomb. Note there was no functional bomb and the materials were being checked so Brown could not have bombed the plane he sought to ride. He was caught mainly because he was obviously unstable. Although TSA officials have hinted that they might be keeping information about captured terrorists a secret this doesn't seem credible since the TSA has a reputation for loudly proclaiming anything remotely successful, as they did in the Brown case (Lapidos, 2010).

Over the years, TSA employees have confiscated a few firearms, a number of knives, and of course, a great many nail clippers and, in the earlier years, many tweezers but no one has been prosecuted for, let alone convicted of, any crime related to attempted highjacking. It appears the people with firearms and knives mainly forgot to remove these items from their bags.

One might assume that surely all this security has done some good, perhaps caused terrorists to abandon plans to attack airlines. But there are two problems with this line of reasoning.

Most fundamentally, it seems doubtful that TSA security screening is effective enough to seriously dissuade real terrorists. During an undercover test in 2015 Homeland security agents attempted to smuggle fake weapons through TSA security lines and succeeded 95% of the time (Inserra, 2017)! In more recent tests the failure rate was reportedly reduced to 80% or possibly even as low as 70%; actual test results were not released as, apparently, someone in authority realized it might be best not to publicly acknowledge such extremely high TSA failure rates (Goldstein, 2017). But a maximum success rate of possibly 30% is not impressive.

Numerous government congressional studies and GAO reports confirm the ineffectiveness of TSA screening (Edwards, 2016). But is this really surprising? Is there a more mind-numbing, boring job in the world than endlessly scanning passengers' belongings for weapons that are virtually never there? In the few cases where a weapon is found it seems, as already mentioned, merely an oversight by a nonthreatening passenger. It is possible, perhaps even likely, that not a single TSA screener has ever done much of anything directly useful to society in over seventeen years of operations. A young screener in their job until retirement might reasonably expect that over the course of their entire career at TSA, a real terrorist will sometime pop up somewhere at some U.S. airport. But the chances of that happening at your airport on your screening watch are about zero. If, against all odds, a terrorist does try to smuggle a weapon past you there is, based on government tests, something like a 70–95% chance that you will miss it. Maintaining constant vigilance in these circumstances is probably humanly impossible. No wonder undercover government testers get weapons past screeners so regularly.

Of course it is possible to have effective screening—the Israeli's do it and have prevented any successful attack on El Al airline for over fifty years. (Of course, Israel is hardly free of terrorism; terrorists may have simply switched to malls, buses, and other easier targets.) But this comes at tremendous cost since they interview every passenger and routinely search their luggage, rather than just trying to quickly scan it with x-ray machines. It is estimated that Israel spends about ten times as much on passenger screening as the U.S. per passenger (Stewart and Mueller, 2017, 90–91). Thankfully, there is no plan to emulate Israel's massively expensive program here, which would certainly not be worth it to us.

Realistically, as Bruce Schneier, prominent security technologist at Harvard and frequent TSA critic, details, all we can reasonably expect of TSA screeners is that they will catch the dumb or crazy terrorists. He explains, and demonstrates, how terrorists could easily evade no-fly rules, make convincing counterfeit boarding passes, and bring materials to easily make functioning knives once on the plane (Goldberg, 2008).

The other factor limiting any net benefits from tougher airport security is that, even effective, Israeli-style security is likely to just shift terrorism to different targets. Serious terrorists are unlikely to decide to just live peacefully because airport security is so tough. Instead, *determined terrorists will likely simply shift their attacks to more vulnerable targets such as schools, synagogues, churches, hotels, nightclubs, and other crowded places known to be without much in the way of armed guards, as seems to be exactly the U.S. experience.*

Indeed this has been clearly documented in a number of cases. For instance, the Colorado killer who randomly shot up a movie theater, leaving twelve dead and fifty-eight wounded, mentioned in his diary that he first thought of attacking people at an airport but decided security was too tough there. Likewise the shooter who attacked a Charleston church first targeted the College of Charleston but switched to the church when he realized the college had armed guards (Lott, 2015). Likewise, terrorist attacks in Moscow and Israel revealed, in video observed after the fact, each terrorist adjusting and moving to a less secure part of the airport and mall, respectively. These cases illustrate a common sense, well-established principle in counterterrorism—making a given target safer is of extremely limited value since it inherently makes other targets less safe (Mueller and Stewart, 2011).

The potential use of a hijacked aircraft as a weapon, the 9/11 scenario, could justify special attention at airports. Though, as we will see, factors other than airport passenger screening have proven effective at mitigating this risk.

Perhaps, the clearest benefit of current TSA screening is some value as *security theater*. The term was coined by Schneier and refers to activities that have little to no impact on security, but that gives an appearance of security improvement that may comfort some people who aren't thinking very carefully about the issue (Ijaz, 2017). Presumably, some airline passengers assume anything as painful as current airport security screening must surely be doing some good, rather like supposing any food that tastes extremely bad must certainly be healthy and nutritious.

## Could TSA Screening Ever Possibly Generate Benefits Greater than Costs?

With annual costs over $28 billion, maybe well over $41 billion, it is difficult to imagine how an activity that has proven approximately useless, actually far worse than useless, for seventeen years and counting could ever be a net benefit to society. The statistical chances of you or me ever being harmed by a terrorist are extremely remote. The U.S. State Department tracked *worldwide* deaths from terrorism for the period 1975–2003 and found deaths averaged 482 per year. A similar study with a longer time period, 1968–2006 found average annual deaths of 420. These *worldwide* deaths from terrorism are comparable to annual deaths in the *United States* caused by collisions with deer. In other words, deer wandering onto the road kill more Americans than terrorists! It turns out malfunctioning household appliances are even deadlier than deer. The annual risk in the United States of dying from an accident involving a home appliance is about 1/1,500,000 while death by terrorism poses a risk less than half of that, 1/3,500,000. Your blender is almost twice as likely to kill you as a terrorist (Mueller and Stewart, 2011, Chapter 2).

We are speaking of total terrorism risk; the risk of being attacked specifically while in a commercial aircraft is even lower. In fact, TSA is more dangerous to passengers than is the threat of terrorism on a flight. The probability of a passenger getting cancer form one trip through the full-body scanner is, according to U.S. nuclear regulators, 1 in 60 million. However, the probability of a passenger being killed by terrorism on one flight is only 1 in 110 million (Mueller and Stewart, 2017).

There simply isn't a serious enough threat of terrorism against airlines for even a magically perfect TSA screening system to justify the massive costs. Remember, since TSA screening indirectly kills at least 500 people a year who drive to avoid TSA costs, the agency screeners would have to save well over 500 people per year to justify their procedures.

Incidentally, the annual risk for the average U.S. resident of dying in a traffic accident is 1/8,200 about 427 times greater than the risk of death by terrorism. The U.S. risk for dying in a commercial aircraft crash, including any caused by terrorism, is about 1/2,300,000 (Mueller and Stewart, 2011, Chapter 2). So, the next time someone you know is nervous about the risks of flying just remind them to be careful during the really dangerous part of their journey—the drive to the airport.

## The Value of a Statistical Life (VLS) Approach

It may sound cold to assign a dollar value to a human life, but it is a practical necessity and is also not as materialistic as it may sound. Consider, for example, how taxes will indirectly cost lives. The less income governments allow us keep the fewer people, there will be who can afford items like new cars with anti-collision technology or state of the art home security or certain health care options.[4] This means policy makers will end up indirectly killing more people than they directly save if they adopt a policy of "we must spend as much as we possibly can if it means saving a single life." Also, as discussed earlier, no sane person wants to maximize safety to the point they spend every cent they can on more safety. Picking some dollar value on a life for decisions involving relatively small risks makes sense. For instance, suppose Jane is willing to spend eight dollars to eliminate a risk that has one chance in a million of killing her; this means she is placing a statistical value on her life of $8 million in that situation ($8 million x .000001 = $8).

Appraising a Value of a Statistical Life (VLS) is complex, estimates vary considerably. A figure commonly used by economists and others for the VLS is $7.5 million (Mueller and Stewart, 2017). The U.S. Transportation Department used a VLS of $8.6 million in 2015 (Blincoe et al., 2015). Let us apply the Transportation Department's figure to our estimates of the total cost of TSA screening. Our low estimate is $28.9805 billion, $41.8191 billion for the high possibility. Thus, dividing those figures by the VLS of $8.6 million, TSA's screening procedures must save somewhere between 3,370 and 4,863 people each year to even "break even" in terms of lives saved. Total deaths from the 9/11 attacks were well below that 3,370 minimum; there were 2,977 victims and 19 terrorists killed. *Even if TSA screeners prevented an attack as catastrophic as was 9/11 every single year they would not be creating enough benefits from lives saved alone to justify their costs!*[5]

## SECURITY LESSONS FROM 9/11

A reoccurrence of the 9/11 style hijackings would be virtually impossible even if there had been no government response or policy changes at all.

> Conventional wisdom says the terrorists exploited a weakness in airport security by smuggling aboard box-cutters. What they actually exploited was a weakness in our mindset—a set of presumptions based on the decades-long track record of hijackings. In years past, a takeover meant hostage negotiations and standoffs; crews were trained in the concept of "passive resistance." All of that changed forever the instant American Airlines Flight 11 collided with the north tower. . . . [Now] any hijacker would face a planeload of angry and frightened people ready to fight back. Say what you want of terrorists, they cannot afford to waste time and resources on schemes with a high probability of failure. And thus the September 11th template is all but useless to potential hijackers.
>
> —Patrick Smith, Airline Pilot (Kramer, 2004, 58;
> Mueller and Stewart, 2011, 140)

The proof of Mr. Smith's point was made on 9/11 by the "adjustment in policy" made by the brave passengers and crew on the fourth hijacked aircraft, United flight 93, who fought back when they learned of the three previous targeted crashes. Unfortunately, they could not prevent the aircraft from crashing but they did prevent the aircraft from being used as a weapon. It is almost certain that the crash would not have occurred if passengers and crew had fought to keep the terrorists from taking control of the aircraft in the first place. Since then passengers and crew members in other nations have subdued terrorists before they could cause significant harm on three different occasions: The attempted "shoe bomber" of 2001, on an Australian domestic flight in 2003, and the "Underwear bomber" of 2009. Passengers and crew have defended aircraft so well that the hardened cockpit doors installed after 9/11 haven't been tested, though they clearly present a major obstacle to any attempt to take over the aircraft. Armed pilots and, to a lesser extent, air marshals (because they are on so few flights) are another potent defense that hasn't come into play in the seventeen plus years since 9/11 (Mueller and Stewart, 2011).

Again, the key change is in attitude. Another potent weapon a pilot might use against terrorists is the aircraft itself. This was demonstrated by an El Al pilot during an attempted hijacking in 1970. Israel, of course, has always taken terrorism more seriously than most. The reinforced cockpit they already had established as standard back then was securely locked when two heavily armed terrorists took a crew member hostage and approached the cockpit, telling the pilot, Uri Bar-Lev, to open up or they would start killing hostages. Instead, Bar-Lev quickly told the armed crew member in the cockpit with him of his plan. He sent the aircraft into a steep dive, knocking the two terrorists off their feet. Then, Bar-Lev's armed colleague burst out of the cockpit and killed one terrorist; the other had passed out and was captured (Ginsburg, 2014).

After 9/11 it is likely that U.S. pilots and others would act similarly. The days of terrorists readily taking control of an aircraft are gone, which massively reduces the attractiveness of an aircraft as a target.

## WHY TSA WILL LIKELY NEVER BE EFFICIENT

There are political parallels between the TSA and the FDA.

> The political incentives here work only one way. A politician who supports more extravagant counterterrorism measures can never be proven wrong because an absence of attacks shows that the "measures have 'worked,'" and a new attack shows that we "must go farther still." Conversely, a politician seeking to limit expenditure "can never be proven 'right,'" and "any future attack will always and forever be that politician's 'fault.'"

> —James Fallows, Author and former speech-writer for President Carter
> (Fallows, 2010; Stewart and Mueller, 2017)

As James Fallows implies, to unengaged, rationally ignorant voters, "playing it safe" always sounds good. The politics of ignorance drives the FDA to endlessly retest lifesaving medicines while patients die for the lack of those medicines. Likewise, the politics of ignorance drives the TSA to waste money and indirectly kill people by prodding them to drive the dangerous highways rather than flying the safe skies.

The passenger screening division of the TSA is probably the most universally despised bureaucracy in the United States. In the panicked aftermath of 9/11 we desperately embraced a federal government takeover of airport screening. We imagined government screeners would be like the FBI at their best; instead we got a combination of the Post Office and the IRS at their worst. (Though, in fairness, even the FBI, the Marines or whoever could probably do little better in our system.) TSA is criticized harshly all across the political spectrum, from CNN (Schneier, 2015) to the Heritage Foundation (Inserra, 2017) to *Slate* (Lapidos, 2010) to *Forbes* (Goldstein, 2017). The concept of privatization of airport screening is also widely embraced. San Francisco, perhaps the most liberal city in the country, has privatized airport security screening. In all likelihood, the only reason privatization has not become widespread is because this limited version of privatization permitted still leaves the TSA in charge. Private screeners are required by the governing law to follow all TSA procedures. So, why doesn't Congress do something? Congress could have at least immediately stopped the silliest TSA shenanigans, like, say, confiscating cupcakes or pilots' nail clippers.

The reason, of course, is that, unlikely as it is, if a bomb is one day hidden in a child's cupcake, then all the politicians who supported the cupcake tolerance amendment will be in huge trouble. On the other hand, any political gain for supporting cupcake tolerance will be very slight. The political risk isn't worth the reward. Even support for a riskless change in security policy, such as allowing pilots to keep their nail clippers, entails political risk. That is, even though a pilot will never use nail clippers to highjack an aircraft they are already piloting, the big political picture to the least informed voters may be that Senator Foghorn voted to REDUCE TSA SECURITY! In the election following a terrorist attack the TV commercial run by Foghorn's opponent won't mention nail clippers, just that Foghorn was weak on national security.

Voters are not dumb but they are uninformed and otherwise occupied. Just as the voting mob unintentionally sabotages medicine innovation, they also inadvertently drive politicians to generally keep the worst aspects of TSA policy. Most voters probably would not, for example, readily process the idea that some slight reductions in airport security will save lives by getting people out of their cars and into airplanes. The explanation won't fit on a bumper sticker.

## POLITICS ASIDE, WHAT IS OPTIMAL AIRPORT SCREENING POLICY?

We need to first face reality. Despite massive increases in spending and inconvenience, airport security screening is about as effective now as it was in the old days before 9/11. Back then, security, controlled by airlines, could only be counted on to catch crazy or dumb terrorists, exactly where we are today. Fortunately, other factors, primarily an assertive mindset in passengers and crew, have improved so that flying remains extraordinarily safe, with little chance of terrorists being given control of an aircraft. Flying is safe, despite a system that has routinely failed to detect weapons in undercover testing for seventeen years. Driving, in comparison, is extremely dangerous. Our priority should logically *not* be to improve airport screening which has proven to be mainly irrelevant for these seventeen plus years. Instead, our priority should be to make airport screening far less inconvenient and less expensive so that we can make flying cheaper and more fun in order to get people flying more and driving less.

It is, to understate, difficult to imagine how the TSA could be success-fully reprogrammed to emphasize making flying more attractive. However, this is a natural impulse of the airlines themselves. Ideally, and ignoring the limitations of politics, we should return control of passenger screening to the airlines. The airlines themselves may well be resistant to this idea, though that might be overcome by shifting the right portion of TSA funding to them. Your first thought might be, "Oh, no! Sure airlines would be nicer and faster but they won't take security seriously." That's not true, as we will see, but even if it were, so what? TSA is not really serious itself. They are pushy, annoying, and extremely expensive but are mainly engaging in mere *security theater*, or as many have put it, *security farce*. As mentioned, we can expect them to catch only obvious terrorists, but virtually any system, including one run by the airlines, can do the same. But the airlines have incentive to do it better.

## THE LOGIC OF AIRLINE CONTROL OF AIRPORT SECURITY SCREENING

For starters, we need to remember that *all* the world has changed since 9/11. The new airline system that would emerge won't be identical to the system some of us can remember. Just as crew and passengers were routinely passive up to that fateful day in September so was the screening system. The new system will be more serious, though it is guaranteed to never go as berserk as the TSA has. Another key point is that airline-run security will still be largely driven by government, through liability law. Tort law is not likely to ever be perfect but stands well ahead of the TSA. We have not seen cupcakes and tweezers banned because of liability concerns.

With no TSA control, liability for errant security procedures guarantees that airlines will not just go through the motions. Concern for avoiding law-suits is an obviously powerful motivator for any business in any context. In fact, Jakubiak makes a strong case that it may be more efficient to motivate airline safety in general completely through liability rather than the current mix of liability and direct FAA regulation which, as with the TSA, can be more expensive and politicized (Jakubiak, 1997).

Also, in an airline-run system, airline management will be heavily influ-enced by consumers, insurers, financial stakeholders, and airline employees. Some who are especially afraid of terrorism might think, "Sure liability laws and market forces motivate safety but those are there regardless. Just to play it really safe why not keep TSA regulation, however imperfect, as well; we'll have the best of all safety worlds with full market incentives combined with incentives from TSA." This turns out to be impossible. Government regulation inevitably dampens market incentives, as we discussed before. We can't have our cake and eat it too; we have to make a choice.

All stakeholders will pay more attention when screening policies are free of TSA dictates. To begin with, any rogue airline that courts disaster with sloppy security is not appealing to stockholders or lenders. A firm that seems potentially negligent in this regard risks being penalized with a higher cost of capital—having to pay higher interest rates on loans and seeing its stock value tumble. Airline employees will constitute a sort of informal army of inspectors. Even those not in flight crews or directly employed in screening routinely fly often, since low cost flying is a valued fringe benefit. If employees see unwise compromises in safety they can readily report it or leak it to the press if management is not responsive. However, it is the airlines' insurers who are especially well placed and motivated to assure that screening procedures are efficient.

## The Role of Airline Insurers in a Private Security Screening System

The buck stops with insurers. They are the ones who will pay for most of any damage done by security lapses. After 9/11 the insurers for American and United airlines paid out, for example, $95 million to developers of the World Trade Center to settle claims that airline security lapses led planes to be hijacked (Associated Press, 2017).[6] You can bet that, with airlines free to set their own screening security polices, leaving their insurers on the hook for damages if something goes wrong, these insurers will take a strong interest in those screening policies. Note also that insurance underwriters, unlike politicians, have no interest in safety theater; only real risk reduction is valuable. Insurers' incentives are pretty much ideal. They want to stop all imprudent risk-taking but have no interest in tweezers being confiscated. Furthermore, any mistaken tendency by an insurer to be unduly risk averse, their bias if they have one, will result in the airline looking for a new insurance company. If an airline's insurer goes off the reservation a little and tries to insist that all nail clippers and cupcakes must indeed be confiscated, then the airline can look for a better policy elsewhere. Insurers need to be careful that the rules they impose on airline clients make sense or they can lose that client. There is no all-powerful government monopoly able to be as unreasonable as it chooses.[7]

## Replacing Voters with Consumers as the Ultimate Authority

In a broad sense, giving airlines control of airport screening replaces the TSA with insurers while the airlines kind of replace the politicians. Just as politicians ultimately are controlled by voters, airlines are ultimately controlled by their customers. Whatever security procedures airlines, with the advice and consent of their insurers, choose they have to satisfy air travelers—there's no point in flying off without them. Poorly informed voters are at the root of TSA's problems (and most government problems in general). But will consumers of air travel exert an influence that is any better? Will air travelers be any wiser than voters? Yes, in all likelihood they will.

For one thing, they aren't entirely the same people. Almost anyone over eighteen with a pulse can vote in political decisions. To "vote" in the market you have to buy an airline ticket, or at least be a potential buyer. In a 2001 poll there were 10% of U.S. adults who had never flown at all (Washington Post-ABC News, 2001). It seems likely that those who have never flown will tend to be less informed on airport security, especially about its costs, than those who have; therefore, it's good to remove their influence by shifting control from voters to consumers. Perhaps more importantly, in politics the least informed voters have exactly the same influence per vote as the most informed voters. On the other hand, the more often a consumer buys tickets and flies the greater their influence on the airlines. In the consumer realm dollars spent are basically "votes." If, as seems reasonable, more experienced travelers tend to be better informed about security issues and trade-offs, than those who seldom or never fly, then the wisdom of the average "vote" by passenger purchases will vastly exceed the wisdom of conventional political voting.

More fundamentally, the consumer-voter has much greater incentive to be informed because their vote always determines an outcome: You decide whether to fly or not. As safety emerges as a competitive potential issue you decide which airline to fly. In contrast, your political vote is morally/symbolically important, but a single vote is likely meaningless in determining an outcome—the root cause of rational political ignorance. Voters have some tendency, since there is usually little analysis underlying their opinions to be wildly risk averse. Passengers on the other hand inherently see trade-offs and can more readily recognize those security procedures that, upon reflection, may not be worthwhile, at least not worth the cost. All in all, the consumer vote is likely to be far better informed than the political vote.

Ideally, each airline should run their own security screening as much as possible, basically have their own security line, usually side by side with other airlines at a given airport. When an airline has too few passengers to cost efficiently run their own security they could contract with another airline, as is sometimes done with maintenance or other functions currently.

With airlines generally running their own security this becomes part of their product, a component of their brand name reputation. One clear advantage of this is better customer service in terms of making sure passengers make it to their flight on time. TSA generally does not care in the least if you miss your flight. The airlines will prioritize passengers on tighter schedules. More broadly, the airlines have incentives to minimize unpleasantness as much as possible, to balance security concerns with common sense and customer service. They may not limit your liquids at all, but if they do hold you to 3 ounces it's likely they'll let you pour out 1 of your 4 ounces rather than obnoxiously trashing the whole 4 ounces TSA style. All of this will help get some people out of their cars for road trips and back into airline seats—lifesaving—and highly important to the airlines.

At the same time, neither insurers nor air travelers themselves (and maybe other stakeholders) will let the airlines get away with just rushing all their passengers through the security line. *A balancing act must be maintained, as is the case with optimizing activity in every area of life.* This is the fundamental flaw with the TSA, they have little incentive to worry about the cost of their actions. From their viewpoint, it doesn't matter that the radiation damage done by body scanners is less than the benefit of increased security. It doesn't matter that TSA's obnoxiousness and waste of travelers' time indirectly kills people by prodding them away from the airlines and into their cars.

It seems likely, especially initially, that the quality of security is likely to be about the same as TSA's, which of course, is not so great but will catch obvious threats. But better customer service, with a priority of avoiding missed flights will probably save the vast majority of those 500 lives lost annually to highway deaths. Less lost time and reduced annoyance/pain and suffering will also add to the substantial benefits from booting out TSA screeners.

An intriguing possibility is that security might eventually improve greatly under airline management. Right now there are basically two types of known airport screening in the world. There is the minimally effective TSA-style screening with lots of safety theater, and there is the El Al-style security which is effective but exorbitantly expensive, clearly not cost effective for the United States. If it is possible to meaningfully improve security at a reasonable cost, then a decentralized, competitive system with each airline free to creatively innovate offers us the best chance of discovering this. Remember, the history of safety improvements is mainly a history of discovering wonderful new things rather than a history of using regulation to compel safer procedures with static technology.

Perhaps such an innovation would be new machinery with an entirely new technology or a multitude of better trained dogs to sniff out all weapons. Maybe the airlines would move virtually everyone eligible into Pre-check status, perhaps by making it free, and doing the fingerprinting, interviewing, and everything else while passengers are in the airport on a layover or possibly even while passengers are on a long flight. Or maybe existing technology with more unique incentives would work well. Suppose there routinely was something actually important for screeners to detect, such as fake weapons turning up several times per day. Screeners' base pay might be reduced substantially but with bonuses making up the difference. Bonuses would be awarded only to those who detected the fake weapons. Whatever innovation might be waiting to be invented it is unlikely that TSA would find it and properly implement it any time soon. But with a diverse group of airlines freely competing to be the first to find the answer there is some hope.

There would be other details to work out in this system, including how much funding should be continued by government and provided to airlines. However, the ideas we've sketched are probably sufficient to illustrate the thrust of the approach. Remember, we have ignored political reality in this section in order to outline an optimal system. But, returning to that reality, we know politicians are generally too intimidated by politics driven by uninformed voters to properly reign in the TSA's worse excesses. After all, they didn't immediately end the confiscation of pilots' nail clippers or a child's cupcake. Politicians who do not trust voters to reliably handle those simple reforms are not going to abolish TSA screening and turn it over to airlines in a free entrepreneurial system anytime soon. We need to come up with a baby step our government system, including our easily stampeded voters, might be able to handle.

## DECENTRALIZATION AND DIVERSITY: ENDING THE TSA MONOPOLY

There is no apparent justification for a TSA monopoly in airport screening; the United States is virtually alone in this centralized monopoly approach.

> If you go to Canada or any of the major EU countries . . . actual airport screening is carried out either by the airport itself or by a government-certified private security firm. Legally, in Europe airport security is the responsibility of the airport operator. Whether the screening is carried out by the airport or a security company varies from country to country, but in no case is it carried out directly by the national government aviation security agency (TSA equivalent).
>
> —Robert W. Poole, Jr., Testimony before the House Subcommittee on Transportation Security (Poole, 2012)

We are a long way from allowing competing security screening systems within an airport but we might be able to handle moving controlling authority from the federal government to the city or other local government in charge of the airport. Thus, we could get a little diversity and competition between airports. This is widely favored by security analysts, and as explained by Poole above is actually the norm outside of the United States (Poole, 2012).

The federal legislation to start this process could simply allow these local governments to opt out of TSA control and establish their own approach. Our national politicians would basically offer the responsibility to local governments but not compel them to take it, which is less politically risky then taking a clear political stand to abolish TSA screening. To facilitate the handoff, federal funding could be shifted from TSA screeners to the local controlling government, who would be free to keep or fire current TSA screeners. Other TSA personnel in the system, such as air marshals, would not be affected.[8]

Government airport authorities are likely to be far less efficient and innovative than the airlines would be—they are government operations not nimble entrepreneurs facing intense competition who can personally get rich if they invent a superior security system. But there is some competition between airports, though it is not nearly as intense as between airlines. Airports do have some incentive to weigh costs and benefits of their security procedures. We would also have a more diversified approach, where best practices developed at one airport could be duplicated by another. This decentralized, non-monopoly system is bound to be superior to the TSA dictatorial monopoly. Giving government airport authorities the chance to improve security would indeed be a useful first step.

## CONCLUSION: ENDING THE TSA SECURITY SCREENING DICTATORSHIP

There are two overwhelming flaws to the TSA approach. One, they are simply not effective, not capable of reliably catching would-be terrorists. Two, it seems there is not enough of a terrorist threat, due to other factors, to justify the entire TSA approach, mindset, and massive expenditures. The total costs of TSA screening are astronomical, somewhere well over $28 billion, possibly even well over $41 billion annually in our case study year of 2015.[9] Perhaps the worst cost comes from TSA screening procedures spurring people out of airports and into their comparatively highly dangerous cars, resulting in about 500 annual highway deaths. Totaling those deaths for the past seventeen plus years implies TSA screening has indirectly killed over 8,500 people in the 2001–18 period, nearly three times as many deaths as those suffered in the terrorism of 9/11. Yet, it is not clear that there is any significant benefit from these enormous costs. In undercover tests the TSA routinely fails to detect weapons in the vast majority of cases, with a failure rate frequently over 95% and never reportedly below 70% at the very best.

Essentially, the technique of having agents staring at x-ray monitors all day simply does not work. Regardless of how we structure the job with frequent breaks or anything else, the interaction of the technology with human minds has not been effective. Apparently this work is just too mind-numbingly dull to be done effectively, worse than looking endlessly for the needle in the haystack because there generally isn't any real needle there!

It seems the TSA has never caught a single would-be hijacker—how would they since they routinely fail to catch undercover agents smuggling in pseudo-weapons? Furthermore, TSA's high failure rate is well known; it is unlikely that their security theater is frightening away terrorists. More likely, airlines stopped being likely targets as it became apparent, even on the fourth hijacked aircraft of 9/11, that passengers and crew would no longer passively let terrorists take control of the aircraft. Indeed, three attempted hijackings elsewhere in the world since 9/11 have been thwarted by passengers and crew. Even if well-armed terrorists get on a plane, they have no guarantee they can gain control of the plane, with Israeli-style hardened cockpits the norm as well as the threat of armed pilots. Pilots would also likely employ aggressively destabilizing flying as did the Israeli pilot in the last attempted hijacking of El Al.

Given the possibility of armed pilots and general resistance from crew and passengers it seems terrorists have no special reason to target airlines or airports. We have seen terror attacks in the United States and elsewhere shift to hotels, movie theaters, nightclubs, schools, synagogues, churches, and other places where powerful resistance is less likely. Looking at long-term data that fully includes the 9/11 attacks, the risk of terror is miniscule. The probability of being killed in the United States by any sort of terrorism is much lower than is the probability of dying in a traffic collision with a wandering deer or being electrocuted by a household appliance. An airline passenger is more likely to die from cancer triggered by the TSA body scanner than to die on their flight from a terrorist attack.

So, TSA screening is incapable of reliably thwarting airline terrorism, even if there was some threat to thwart—but there isn't! Despite the spectacular, and inadvertently deadly failures of the TSA serious reform is nowhere in sight. TSA is a creature of politics, precisely the reason for both its failures and the difficulty of achieving ideal reform. Earlier we saw how politics drives the FDA to endlessly test medicines even when it is obvious dying people would be saved by those medicines if only the FDA would let them. There is a similar dynamic corrupting airport screening. Politicians fear to even legalize a pilot's nail clippers since this may ultimately come across as being weak on security to voters who are paying so little attention, especially if a terrorist attack occurs anywhere near in time to a "relaxing of security standards." Absurd TSA policies and frequent rudeness are not reliably reined in by these timid politicians

The ideal solution is to return airport security screening to the airlines, which returns power to consumers, taking it away from voters who have proven to be so utterly inept. Such a system would be very different from its previous incarnation in pre-9/11 times—though even if it wasn't it would be as directly safe as the TSA and far cheaper and more convenient, saving billions in expense and saving many lives otherwise lost on deadly roadways. Government would exert a useful influence through liability law while market forces, especially from the airlines' insurers would also help keep airline passenger screening procedures efficient. Ultimately, consumers would largely drive the system where safety innovation would be facilitated in a decentralized, diversified system where safety is a competitive variable, a key aspect of the airline product. Consumers would be a better informed driving force than voters, partly because some voters never fly and many fly very seldom. More fundamentally, each consumer would choose their own airline with attendant security procedures. A voter typically doesn't choose anything, merely casting a single vote that doesn't determine any outcome and is therefore not worth researching much.

However, current politics makes the ideal solution impossible. Even so, we can take a small but key step by denationalizing airport security, by taking passenger screening away from the TSA and giving it back to the local government bodies in charge of airports. This is standard procedure most everywhere outside of the United States; our national monopoly of airport security screening is a rather unique mistake. Competition between airports is minor compared to competition between airlines but at least there is some competition. With a diversified approach any useful innovation at one airport could be copied by others. Local government airport authorities are bound to be superior to the current TSA monopoly, a very useful first step.

## NOTES

1. This was for our study year, 2015. Wait times have since generally increased since then. In early 2019, for example, average waits in the prechecked lines were close to ten minutes (Ogg, 2019).

2. Some of these horrible worst TSA cases have been captured on video. To see these, go to YouTube and search "TSA brutality."

3. This is based on passenger survey data (Heimlich, 2016) and U.S. Census data (National KIDS COUNT, 2018).

4. Of course the taxes, presumably, pay for beneficial government programs that can save lives. Hopefully, lives saved from spending will be greater than lives lost from taxes, though this seems impossible in the case of TSA airport screening expenditures.

5. Of course there were also significant injuries and property damage, and there are probably psychological impacts to consider as well.

6. It is difficult to find total payments by the airlines' insurers since some settlements were confidential and government compensation was also in the mix.

7. Robert Poole, Jr. makes a similar case for basically allowing insurance underwriters to replace politicians in a privatized system that would replace politics and the FAA with cost/benefit analysis by insurers with a vested interest in maintaining airline safety (Poole, 1982b).

8. It is beyond our scope but there is some question as to whether money spent on air marshals is worth it (Stewart and Mueller, 2017).

9. In their more basic, less speculative estimation, Stewart and Mueller consider only the ten minutes actually spent waiting in the security line, highway deaths, and direct TSA screening expenditures. Thus, they leave out other accident costs associated with those 500 highway deaths, other losses from driving rather than the preferred flying, extra time waiting at the airport (a time cushion to assure flights aren't missed while stuck in security), and other costs such as annoyance and pain/suffering from airport screening. Still, the costs they do cite total over $13 billion, far in excess of any conceivable benefit (Stewart and Mueller, 2017).

*Chapter 7*

# Toward More Safety, More Choices, and Better Prices

## WHEN DOES GOVERNMENT REGULATION WORK?

Consumers benefit from more choices but government regulation often tends to suppress choice.

> Government is not reason; it is not eloquent; it is force. Like fire, it is a dangerous servant and a fearful master. Never for a moment should it be left to irresponsible action.
>
> —George Washington (Eddy, 1902)

Of course, some actions clearly should be suppressed. Regulations to control pollution and reduce murder are examples of successful regulation, though very imperfect, that have created more benefits than costs. But, as we've seen, there are also cases where regulation has made things worse, sometimes much worse. *Note that the problems we've examined do not relate to "liberal" or "conservative" viewpoints.* It may be that conservatives tend to be more supportive of tough counterterrorism policies, but what informed conservative favors pointless TSA safety theater that actually costs lives rather than saves them? Likewise, it may be that liberals more strongly favor regulation of business, but what informed liberal supports an FDA policy that continues with years of needless testing, leaving certain cancer patients to die when it's obvious to everyone that Gleevec could save them? The problem with the various regulatory failures we've exposed in this book is not that policies are too liberal or too conservative; they are simply illogical and incoherent. We have, in the words of George Washington, left dangerous bureaucracies to "irresponsible action."

The common thread in murder and pollution is that they both involve *external costs*, costs imposed on victims without their consent. The steel company that builds a plant nearby and pollutes the air without compensating you is in effect stealing clean air. A murderer is, of course, stealing your life. Unlike any sort of business transaction there is no negotiation or chance to shop around for a more favorable agreement in these situations, the perpetrators physically force external costs on their victims. We don't get an opportunity to reason with the attacking murderer or the stealthy thief. In circumstances of this ilk, it is often optimal to meet aggressive brute force, or its sneaky equivalents, with the brute force of government. This is the job government was born for. As the father of our country eloquently summarized, government is force.

## REGULATION THAT HOLDS WRONGDOERS ACCOUNTABLE OUTDOES PREEMPTIVE REGULATION

Another area where consumer protection regulation, though far from perfect, is often successful in generating net benefits, is liability law. Laws against fraud are similarly effective. What makes these regulations workable is that they usually do not directly interfere with any voluntary trade before the fact.[1] Think of it this way: Government consumer protection is like a not very bright, giant gorilla—King Kong size. With the protection afforded by fraud and liability laws, King Kong is your body guard, but he stands behind you, pounding his giant fists together and glowering at the business from which you are about to buy something. The business knows if they can make a satisfied customer out of you, then you may provide future business yourself and also perhaps through referrals. And you will not set King Kong against them!

On the other hand, when a regulatory body is authorized to preempt your decisions the wild and crazy King Kong now stands in front of you, face to face with the business that could help you. The FDA version of Kong requires the inventor to wait seven or eight years and pay about $2.6 billion before he can bring a new medicine to you. In many cases the would-be inventor just gives up. Sometimes the inventor perseveres, jacks up the price to cover the FDA-generated costs, and you eventually get the medicine, unless of course you die in the interim—not Kong's problem. The TSA King Kong is even nuttier; jumping up and down frightening children; stealing shiny objects like tweezers, nail clippers and liquids; and generally scaring a lot of people out of the airport and into their cars—which is fine with Kong, fewer suspected terrorists to deal with.

Thus, in situations where we are free to reason, negotiate, and make our own choices, the brute force of the government gorilla usually has little chance of making things better for us. It is in fact is very likely to make things worse. However, the gorilla standing behind you, more or less staying out of your way, is much less dangerous and can generally add incentives for the seller to deal fairly with you.

Washington's more dignified fire analogy is also apt. A controlled burn is a useful tool, but it would be absurd and disastrous to impulsively set fire to every single obstacle we encounter. Even where controlled burns are appropriate, we need to plan carefully, and alertly monitor that fire, standing ready to fight the fire if it escapes the constraints of the firewall we prepared. In letting politicians and bureaucrats usurp our choices, often blindly trusting them to act in our interests, we have unleashed an inferno. We assumed, in, perhaps, the worst miscalculation in history, that the process of voting itself would somehow magically force the politicians to act in the public interest. Even when the public interest is too complex for busy voters to discern, or where "the public interest" is immaterial or undefined because individual concerns of patients or other consumers are paramount.

## POWER CORRUPTS AND ABSOLUTE
## POWER CORRUPTS ABSOLUTELY

The above subtitle on corrupting power, a quote from Lord Acton, nicely summarizes the state of current consumer protection regulation. It is consistently corrupt and the greater the scope of regulators' power the more corrupt they are. Often, the corruption is ultimately driven by ill-informed voters who know just enough to be concerned about the area of regulation, though nowhere near enough to understand how the regulation should be structured, or how easily well intentioned regulations can backfire.

Voters aren't dumb but we're very busy and distracted. Each voter does know, on some level, that one informed voter is not likely to change a thing. So, why spend a lot of time analyzing these issues when a single vote, though morally and symbolically important, is virtually certain to have no impact on political outcomes? This is the problem of *rational political ignorance*. It's rational, in the sense of narrow self-interest, to spend more time researching which car to buy than who to vote for in a presidential election, or what optimal FDA polices would be. You actually get whatever car you choose but your vote doesn't determine who becomes president or how the FDA behaves.

### Death by FDA Delays

In the case of the FDA, we, the voters, are paying just enough attention to be very concerned about "bad" medicines being approved. A host of biases, as discussed in chapter 2, tend to draw us to mistakenly over-emphasize the avoidance of *bad* things, when it is actually the more rapid development of *good* things that is fundamental to improving our safety. In this instance it is especially foolhardy to focus on the negative *since there is never any direct harm from FDA approval of any medicine*. The FDA is merely a problematic first step; next, each doctor sits down with each patient and considers if a given treatment is best for that patient. FDA approval forces no patient to take any drug. However, when the FDA holds new medicines hostage to years and years of testing, this does force some patients to stick with old treatments that fail to save their lives or restore their quality of life. This regulation by timid hesitancy, induced by voters, forces these patients to suffer and die while the FDA forcibly deprives them of the medicine that would save them.

We estimated the total deaths caused by the FDA at 3,360 to 19,200 annually in the 1970s and 1980s, when comparisons with Europe more readily supported the calculation of such estimates. The number of deaths by the FDA today is, given the exponential growth in technology and potential medicines, likely far, far higher. FDA delay and suppression of new medicines jumped dramatically when they expanded from testing only safety to testing safety and *effectiveness*. However, our extensive experience with *off-label* medicines, which are *not* FDA tested for effectiveness, strongly indicates that there is no medical benefit at all to government effectiveness testing. Private doctors and researchers verify effectiveness just as well as the FDA, but much, much faster.

## Death by the TSA

In chapter 3 we discussed how the procedures of TSA airport screeners cause millions of travelers to drive rather than fly. Since driving is far more dangerous than flying this results in about 500 deaths or more per year. Also, the various costs of TSA screening totaled about $30–42 billion annually in 2016 and created negligible benefits.

## Death by Government Sponsored Taxi Cartels

Corrupt taxi regulation is far less deadly than the FDA, though decades of technology suppression caused more than a few deaths, with taxi driving consistently being the most murdered profession. The potential for one-on-one isolation was also dangerous for passengers; cab driving has been the chosen profession of at least a few serial killers who murdered on the job. More commonly, assaults against female customers have always been a frequent problem. With occupational licensing stifling new entry, under the ironic pretense of consumer protection, the taxi industry cartel did virtually nothing to make the profession and product safer. They ignored new technologies, including, eventually, even smart phones. Rather than quickly emulating Uber's technology, with constant electronic paper trails and prescreening of both customers and drivers, the cartel deployed government enforcers to suppress Uber and that technology. Regulators' contribution was to arrest the people that brought safety, superior service, and generally lower prices. So much for government consumer protection.

## GOVERNMENT IS MOST DANGEROUS WHEN DRIVEN BY FEAR

Although FDR was speaking in a different context, here is a bull's-eye summary of the roots of government failure in consumer protection:

> The only thing we have to fear is fear itself—nameless, unreasoning, unjustified terror which paralyzes needed efforts to convert retreat into advance.

> —Franklin D. Roosevelt (Roosevelt, 1933)

In the case of both the FDA and TSA we see a massive, ultimately deadly, overreaction to a horrible but anomalous event. The FDA's very existence as a medicine regulator is arguably an overreaction to the 1938 Elixir Sulfanilamide tragedy. The FDA has never prevented a reoccurrence of this sort of incident, probably because private companies learned from this deadly, costly and flukiest of blunders. But it was the panicky response to 1962's thalidomide disaster that gave us today's oppressive FDA, resulting in many thousands of deaths each year. Again, the FDA has not prevented any disaster of thalidomide proportions, because everyone quickly learned from that experience to be very careful prescribing new drugs to pregnant women. This is a running theme; unless government massively distorts incentives, companies will not repeat catastrophic mistakes. Such disasters are always financial disasters as well. Thalidomide happened simply because our knowledge, inside government and out, was (by today's standards) so shockingly primitive that no one knew unborn babies were especially sensitive to medicines. *That knowledge, once gained, immediately eliminated the possibility of a repeat of a thalidomide type of incident.* No regulatory change was at all necessary. You can't win customers selling medicines that harm babies or make money by generating millions, even billions of liability losses.

Like foolish generals in an age with rifles concocting strategies to win the last war fought with swords, our regulators often aim backwards, casting about wildly to avoid particular errors that have no chance of being duplicated anyway. The tragically mistaken changes in FDA policy motivated by one event have over time taken the lives of over a hundred thousand people, perhaps many hundreds of thousands.

The story of TSA airport security screeners is strikingly similar but perhaps even more depressing. Like the FDA, TSA has, over time, killed many more people, about 8,500 as of this writing, than died in the vicious 9/11 attacks that stampeded us into TSA airport security screening in the first place. One can imagine gleeful terrorists and their sympathizers cackling in delight, if they're economically sophisticated enough to understand the highway deaths triggered by TSA. Even the unsophisticated terrorists must rejoice at all the billions wasted, savoring every report of TSA frightening children with aggressive pat downs, snatching pilots' nail clippers and all the other absurdities of the TSA safety theater. All this commotion, and yet tests confirm the TSA screeners cannot reliably detect weapons. Fortunately, it doesn't matter that our screeners can't catch airline terrorists since it appears there haven't been any to catch! We know the 9/11 tactics can't be repeated, and terrorists seem to also know, because those techniques actually became obsolete later on 9/11. On the fateful United flight 93 that day the courageous crew and passengers fought back when they realized it no longer made sense to give terrorists control of the airplane. Readiness to fight back is the new normal forevermore.

The moral of the story is that it never makes sense to enact a rigid, knee-jerk response to a horrible cataclysm while we are still emotionally reeling. A temporary, stop-gap response can be worthwhile, as in 9/11 when airlines grounded their flights not long before the FAA also issued orders grounding all flights. In hindsight, that grounding appears to have been completely unproductive, not nearly worth the costs, but given the high stakes and uncertainty at the time it seems a reasonable precaution. However, our panicked creation of a national monopoly of airport screeners was an unwise idea from the start. We frantically grasped for the TSA, picturing an FBI-style operation at its best and instead got an amalgamation of the IRS, the post office and the keystone cops at their worst.

However, not all of our poor ideas are spawned by crisis. The less extreme, though, as we've seen quite exaggerated, fear of private businesses leads us to blindly trust occupational licensing. In the absence of panicky demands by voters corrupting the political process one might hope politicians would succeed. Dream on! When general voters aren't pressuring politicians in the wrong direction it is likely that businesses will do so instead. It was the desire of businesses to harness regulation to stop competition that produced a corrupt taxi cartel run by regulators. So, we got sky-high prices, poor service, and procedures safe for neither passengers nor drivers for decades, until Uber saved the day.

## A BETTER PATH FORWARD INTO THE SUNSET

Panicked responses to tragedies, given political reality, are probably unavoidable. When voters are riled up, with flames fueled by a press giddy with the excited attention given them and their reporting in a crisis, it is difficult to imagine a majority of politicians emerging with the integrity to say, "Stop. Yes, 9–11 was horrible but we've all learned not to surrender the plane to terrorists. We need to remember we're more likely to die in collisions with deer than to be killed by terrorists. If we make it less convenient to fly then we'll drive more and that's really dangerous. If we panic now the terrorists win." Likewise, regarding the FDA, how many politicians would step up and say, "The FDA can't protect you from bad drugs without simultaneously denying you good ones; regulation is too blunt an instrument. More crucially, medical treatments need to be tailored to each individual. All medicines have side effects and risks that you need to weigh and discuss with your doctor; a group decision for everyone is absurd." It's fun to deride politicians, but the reality is that any government official that spoke truth like this would likely be shouted down as being a tool of the airlines or the big drug companies. The reward for such political heroism would likely be scorn by the media and, in short time, rejection by the voters.

Accordingly, it's virtually certain that we'll pass more bad laws in the next crisis and every one after that. However, panicky legislation could contain a seed or two of future rationality. One simple approach would be to include a "sunset provision" where the law exists only for a set period, then must be periodically renewed. If we're lucky, cooler heads will sometimes prevail in one of those future votes to renew the law.[2]

## TWO LESSONS FROM UBER

While Uber's civil disobedience approach to corrupt regulation is amazing and, at least to some, inspiring, it is difficult to imagine that approach being commonly duplicated. But what can we learn from this rare success story?

### Avoid Regulatory Monopoly

It is not a coincidence that Uber faced mainly corrupt local governments and regulators, rather than massive, national monopolies like the FDA or the TSA. It allowed Uber to fight one smaller battle at a time and get revenues in the cities where they won to use to challenge the next corrupt city regulatory body. If we had national taxi regulation it is very likely that Uber wouldn't even have entered the fray, let alone prevailed against such colossal power. Moreover, not every city fought that hard and some even readily tolerated Uber. With decentralization of regulation we inherently get some diversity and a chance that some regulators will get it right, or at least less wrong.

Some government roles may need to be largely national—anti-terrorist intelligence gathering or military strikes, for example. But many other activities, like airport screening, can be localized. This, as mentioned earlier, can be the first step away from the appalling airport screening policies of the federal government. We need to allow local government airport authorities to take over screening, as is done virtually everywhere else in the world. More broadly, we need to avoid the shackles of national regulatory monopolies as much as possible. Federal regulation is necessary at times, but federal regulation of anything should be our absolutely last resort, not our first.

## Modern Tech Enables Stronger Private Regulation and Reputation Effects

The technological revolution brought forward by Uber and others, such as Airbnb, has brought "small town reputation effects" to large, modern markets. It is a remarkable thing that it has become common for us to routinely jump into cars with people we have never met. Uber constantly monitors their driver-partners electronically, and in terms of background checks and such is often more strict than taxi companies, but it is the online reputation effects that Uber facilitates that seal the deal. That Uber driver is not really a stranger, we can see a crucial summary of their history before we hail them. Likewise, the driver "knows" prospective passengers. Similarly, Airbnb has us comfortably staying with people we've never met or letting them stay with us. Again, thanks to online information and reputations these people aren't really strangers (Stone, 2017). Of course, government also facilitates these high-tech transactions through liability laws and also criminal laws that help protect us from fraud or assault.

More broadly, our experience with Uber and Airbnb is grounds for considering a broader deregulation movement. We have seen that reputation effects work fine, along with liability and all that, to make sure Joe Kumquat acts reasonably in renting a bedroom in his house through Airbnb. Do we really need a lot of regulation of Holiday Inn or Hilton Hotels? These businesses, with their massive assets and well-known brand names, have much greater incentive to maintain quality and a solid reputation than our friend Joe Kumquat who rents out a single bedroom once in a while. Regulations always impose costs; if benefits are negligible then we should get rid of them. *Less regulation reliably translates into lower prices and more diverse offerings.*

## Government as an Advisor rather than a Dictator

Our long experience with off-label medicines, as mentioned, demonstrates that the massive costs, in lost lives and money, of FDA effectiveness testing generates essentially no medical benefits. Politically, scaling the FDA back to merely testing for safety might be the way to begin. But, ideally, we've seen that a strong case can be made that the FDA should have only an advisory role. They could advise people to wait for more tests but could not stop doctors from prescribing developmental drugs for their desperate patients that have no better option. This is really the only way to stop regulators from leaving some people to suffer and die when the most cutting-edge medicines could save them. If the FDA merely gave recommendations they might still do some slight harm if the advice is flawed enough. But as long as patients can get a second opinion and make their own decision, the FDA would essentially be defanged, no longer a deadly dictator.

In the long run there would be two possible results of converting the FDA to an advisor. One, if they don't change, just constantly sing the same song they force us to listen to now, "wait for more testing," most people will likely come to ignore them, relying instead on information from their own chosen health care professionals. Possibility two, deprived of dictatorial power, the FDA staff may learn to offer, more nuanced, valuable advice on trade-offs, risk levels for different patients, and so on. In either case, removing today's extremist FDA as an entry barrier would unleash the full potential of modern technology. Development costs would plunge from the absurd current level of $2.6 billion, investment would pour in, prices for patients would plummet, and the number of new medicines would surge, especially in the "orphan" drug category. Today's trickle of new medications, less than 35 per year, would morph into a tidal wave of new treatments, probably well over 100 annually. *Thousands, most likely tens of thousands, maybe even hundreds of thousands of lives would be saved each year.*

Occupational licensing is another category of corrupt regulation in desperate need of being reformed to advisory status. The safety revolution in ride services ushered in by Uber would have happened much faster, virtually overnight and would have been universal if occupational licensing didn't exist. If government had merely advised people to stick with antique taxi service, with all its dangers, inconveniences, and high prices, then the advice would have been widely ignored. No drivers would have been arrested or fined, most cabbies would have converted to ride share-drivers, and riding with unknown and sometimes unsafe strangers would have quickly wound down. Uber's guerilla civil disobedience approach to business would have been unnecessary. Companies less assertive than Uber, understandably reluctant to rebel against corrupt government, would have had nothing to fear. Numerous ride share companies would have popped up in markets all over, speeding the transition to safer, cheaper, and superior service.

Pretty much every occupational licensing regulatory board ends up mainly operating a competition-stifling cartel similar to the taxi lobby. Giving consumers the option to either heed politicians'/bureaucrats' advice with no questions asked, or investigate for themselves will ultimately break up all these cartels. If unlicensed lawyers, carpenters, and the unlicensed in every other profession have to let customers know that government doesn't endorse them it will often hamper them at first. But that's much better than being arrested. The unlicensed will be free to make their case. If they are truly qualified, merely victims of crooked politics, the truth will come out. The information age of online reputations will help facilitate that, just as it did with Uber. Once the truth is fully revealed people will come to ignore the licensing board hoopla. Of course, again, there is the possibility that today's occupational licensers-cum-cartel enforcers might improve once they lose the power to bully people with the brute force of law. They might start offering some useful advice rather than just their standard drumbeat of "these new competitors aren't licensed, aren't approved, pose great dangers, have no respect for authority, are probably communists, blah, blah, blah."

In the same spirit of less government dictatorship and more consumer choice, the eventual ideal alternative to the TSA screeners would be to turn over airport screening to the airlines. Government's role would be to get the liability law right and handle other aspects of terrorist risk such as intelligence gathering and military strikes. But basic airline security and passenger screening should really be part of each airline's product. With each airline choosing their particular security procedures (though smaller ones may contract to use other airlines' screeners) we make security a competitive variable. Competition between airlines is much more intense than competition between airports. Local governments would be better positioned than the TSA, but only airlines, constrained by their insurers and others, have the right incentives to balance security and convenience, and the full freedom to innovate.

Some would fear the airlines might handle security screening no better than they did in the old days. Highly unlikely, but a return to those days would actually be superior to where we are now with the TSA. Today we have some pointless safety theater where the TSA routinely fails to detect weapons in undercover testing. They massively increase costs yet are no better in keeping airlines safe than the airlines were in those relaxed, more innocent days before 9/11. The priority needs to be ending the rude, expensive safety theater so that we get people back on airplanes more and off the deadly highways. It's absurd to continue with current procedures where radiation from TSA body scanners poses a greater risk than actual terrorism.

It's probable that airline-managed screening would look very similar to TSA Pre-check, at least in the beginning. It might well stay that way for some time, given that terrorism risks are so extremely low here that it would be silly to go to the massive expense of duplicating Israeli-style screening. Of course, over time, creative airlines in a competitive system might come up with better security without an explosion of costs and inconvenience. Maybe supertrained dogs to sniff out all weapons without any passenger inconvenience, or better automated technology to replace bored agents staring at electronic screens are the answers. Innovation is hard to forecast, but it's not hard to forecast that innovation will be about zero as long as TSA is in charge. For them a major advance is something like letting pilots keep their nail clippers.

## WE NEED LESS FEAR-DRIVEN REGULATION
## AND MORE SAFETY INNOVATION

*In politics, it seems we can't recognize that expanding regulation inherently means stifling innovation.* We tend to erroneously think that the key to better safety is to look backwards and design more rigid regulations to try to make sure bad things never happen. Worse, when something really bad happens we immediately pass new regulations with no clear notion of either their costs or benefits, since uninformed voters figure, after a calamity, regulating something more must always be better than doing nothing. Hence, after 9/11 we scrabbled together the appalling TSA screening procedures that indirectly have now killed far more people than the terrorists. Likewise, our panicked response to the thalidomide disaster strangled innovation, indirectly killing and injuring far more people than in all of the combined negative side effects in all of history. We keep coming up with regulatory "cures" more deadly than the tragedies that panic us.

It is, naturally, worth devoting some resources toward avoiding fearful events; however, when we completely obsess about old risks we poison the wellspring of new cures. We seem unable to recognize the deadly trade-off, that regulating innovation to make sure new bad things don't happen will inevitably prevent or fatally delay many new wonderful things from happening. Government regulators the world over have proved it is impossible to get politicians to fully embrace and foster innovation and hope. Approving something hurtful that kills 100 people is more harmful to a politician's or bureaucrat's career than *not* approving an innovation which results in 100,000 deaths. To distracted voters, excessive testing and caution just seem prudent. Even when clearly proven harmful, a desire to pedantically verify safety seems pure hearted; any mistake seems well intentioned and understandable.

However, approval of innovation that turns out to have a substantial downside, even, as we have seen, if it's less than the upside, seems more sinister. "Aha! The regulator, probably after taking a bribe, approved this dangerous pain medicine just so some company could make a buck! We need another regulator to regulate the first regulator. Safety redundancy, yeah, that's the ticket!"

## WHY CONSUMERS ARE NOT AS
## CLUELESS AS VOTERS

Every consumer actually makes a choice, deciding whether or not to buy a product for themselves. Not many elections are decided by one vote; a vote is morally significant but mostly symbolic. You can choose what medicine to take if the FDA will let you but you can't choose the president. It makes sense to research alternatives when you have a real choice to make, not so much when you don't. Also, researching a purchase is usually much less complex than researching how you should vote. Any friend can be a valuable information resource for consumer purchase decisions. But if you're a committed liberal you might not be interested in your conservative friend's advice, nor they in yours, on how to vote.

Even a lazy consumer who does no research is frequently protected by the knowledge of other consumers. This can be true even if the majority of customers are uninformed. If, for example, 20% of consumers come to realize a product with surface appeal is actually a poor deal, then that 20% drop in demand will often be enough to get the firm to drop it from production. In contrast, the minority of voters who are better informed can't protect the uninformed majority. If 49% know enough to vote against Hitler, it doesn't accomplish anything at all if the other 51% vote for him.

More fundamentally, a consumer choice has a narrow scope, it's just that individual's decision. A severe arthritis patient speaking with her doctor, deciding whether or not to take Vioxx, has only to consider this: Is a 1% increased risk of a heart attack worth it to reduce her pain? There's no need to research how much pain she's in since that's apparent. If other less risky drugs have been tried and all failed, there's no analysis needed in that area. She can ask for others' advice if she feels like it but there is no real need to consider others' preference since this decision is just for her.

In contrast, when regulators who are controlled by politicians make a decision they are buffeted by voters who have only the shallowest understanding of the issue. Except for those relatively few voters who were knowledgeable health care professionals, had severe arthritis themselves, or knew someone who did, those voters had only a vague notion of what they were doing. Those voters generally favored forcing Vioxx off the market as soon as they heard it increased the risk of heart attack. The uninformed majority got their way; that's who politicians cater to, and regulators cater to the politicians. It didn't matter that doctors disagreed; it didn't matter that a million or so patients disagreed and were forced by the uninformed majority to live a life racked with pain.

We can do much better. We don't have to endure all this death and suffering by regulation. Government advice is fine, and sensible liability rules are useful. But it will be a much better and safer world if we let patients, and all consumers, choose for themselves.

## NOTES

1. Of course, extremely harsh, unreasonable liability or fraud laws can motivate the withdrawal of products that would otherwise be offered. If, for example, you're in my age range you might vaguely remember how virtually every public swimming pool had a diving board in those ancient times before tort law got to the point it essentially made diving boards illegal.

2. For a fuller discussion of sunset provisions, see these authors: (Davis, 1981; McKinley, 1995).

# Bibliography

Akst, Jef. "When Biomedical Research Fails." *Psychology Today*. Last modified April 8, 2017. https://www.psychologytoday.com/us/blog/diy-medicine/201704/when-biomedical-research-fails.

"Are Rideshares Really Safe? A Study of Rideshares vs Taxi in San Francisco." *Zendrive*. Accessed November 4, 2018. https://www.zendrive.com/references/taxi-rideshare-12-2014/.

Associated Press. "Airline Defendants to Pay $95 million in 9/11 Settlement." *Chicago Tribune*. Last modified November 22, 2017. https://www.chicagotribune.com/business/ct-biz-airline-insurance-911-settlement-20171122-story.html.

Bailey, Ronald. "The Evolution of Liberty." *CATO Unbound*. Last modified September 12, 2011. https://www.cato-unbound.org/2011/09/12/ronald-bailey/evolution-liberty.

Barberis, Nicholas C. "Thirty Years of Prospect Theory in Economics: A Review and Assessment." *Journal of Economic Perspectives* 27, no. 1 (2013): 173–196. https://doi.org/10.1257/jep.27.1.173.

Barkai, John, Elizabeth Kent, and Pamela Martin. "A Profile of Settlement." *The Journal of the American Judges Association* 42, nos. 3–4 (2006): 33–39. http://digitalcommons.unl.edu/cgi/viewcontent.cgi?article=1024&context=ajacourtreview.

Bender, Andrew. "Uber's Astounding Rise: Overtaking Taxis in Key Markets." *Forbes*. Last modified April 10, 2015. https://www.forbes.com/sites/andrewbender/2015/04/10/ubers-astounding-rise-overtaking-taxis-in-key-markets/#58fbc3e243d8.

Benson, Bruce L. *The Enterprise of Law: Justice Without the State*. California: Independent Institute, 2011.

Berenson, Alex, Gardner Harris, Barry Meier, and Andrew Pollack. "Despite Warnings, Drug Giant Took Long Path to Vioxx Recall." *New York Times*. Last modified November 14, 2004. https://www.nytimes.com/2004/11/14/business/despite-warnings-drug-giant-took-long-path-to-vioxx-recall.html.

Berkrot, Bill. "Success Rates for Experimental Drugs Falls: Study." *Reuters*. Last modified February 14, 2011. https://www.reuters.com/article/us-pharmaceuticals -success/success-rates-for-experimental-drugs-falls-studyidUSTRE71D2U920110 214.

Birkland, Thomas A. and Radhika Nath. "Business and Political Dimensions in Disaster Management." *Journal of Public Policy* 20, no. 3 (2000): 275–303. https:// doi.org/10.1017/s0143814x00000854.

Blalock, Garrick, Vrinda Kadiyali, and Daniel H. Simon. "Driving Fatalities after 9/11: A Hidden Cost of Terrorism." *Applied Economics* 41, no. 14 (2009): 1717–1729. https://doi.org/10.1080/00036840601069757.

Blalock, Garrick, Vrinda Kadiyali, and Daniel H. Simon. *The Impact of Post 9/11 Airport Security Measures on the Demand for Air Travel*. SSRN Electronic Journal, 2005. https://doi.org/10.2139/ssrn.677563.

Blincoe, Lawrence, Ted R. Miller, Eduard Zaloshnja, and Bruce Lawrence. *The Economic and Societal Impact of Motor Vehicle Crashes, 2010 (Revised)*. National Highway Traffic Safety Administration, May 2015. https://crashstats.nhtsa.dot. gov/Api/Public/ViewPublication/812013.pdf.

Boroyan, Nate. "Boston Police Have Ticketed Multiple UberX Drivers." *Bostinno*. Last modified May 29, 2014. https://www.americaninno.com/boston/how-many-boston-uberx-drivers-have-been-ticketed-by-boston-police/.

Boudreaux, Donald J. "The State Is the Source of Rights?" *Foundation for Economic Education*. Last modified December 1, 2003. https://fee.org/articles/the-state-is-the-source-of-rights/.

Bradley, Robert L., Jr. "Oil Company Earnings: Reality Over Rhetoric." *Forbes*. Last modified May 10, 2011. https://www.forbes.com/2011/05/10/oil-company-earn ings.html.

Brard, Caroline, Gwénaël Le Teuff, Marie-Cécile Le Deley, and Lisa V. Hampson. "Bayesian Survival Analysis in Clinical Trials: What Methods are used in Practice?" *Clinical Trials* 14, no. 1 (2017): 78–87. https://doi.org/10.1177/174077 4516673362.

Brazil, Noli and David Kirk. "Uber and Metropolitan Traffic Fatalities in the United States." *American Journal of Epidemiology* 184, no. 3 (2016): 192–198. https://doi. org/10.1093/aje/kww062.

Brons, Martijn, Eric Pels, Peter Nijkamp, and Piet Rietveld. "Price Elasticities of Demand for Passenger Air Travel: A Meta-analysis." *Journal of Air Transport Management* 8, no. 3 (May 2002): 165–175. https://doi.org/10.1016/s0969-6997 (01)00050-3.

Brown, Jonathan. "Killer Derrick Bird Sought Revenge on Taxi-rank Bullies." *The Independent*. Accessed November 4, 2018. https://www.independent.co.uk/news/ uk/crime/killer-derrick-bird-sought-revenge-on-taxi-rank-bullies-2231808.html.

Buchmueller, Thomas C. and Alan C. Monheit. "Employer-Sponsored Health Insurance and the Promise of Health Insurance Reform." *Inquiry Journal* 46 (2009): 187–188. Accessed September 6, 2018. http://journals.sagepub.com/doi/pdf/10.5 034/inquiryjrnl_46.02.187.

Buhr, Sarah. "Regulators Should Favor Lyft And Uber, Not Taxis For Safety Reasons." *Techcrunch*. Last modified 2016. https://techcrunch.com/2016/01/16/regula
tors-should-favor-lyft-and-uber-not-taxis-for-safety-reasons/.

Burke, Jason. "Violence Erupts between Taxi and Uber Drivers in Johannesburg."
*The Guardian*. Last modified September 8, 2017. https://www.theguardian.com/
world/2017/sep/08/violence-erupts-taxi-uber-drivers-johannesburg.

Byrne, John Aidan. "139 Taxi Medallions will be Offered at Bankruptcy Auction."
*New York Post*. Last modified June 9, 2018. https://nypost.com/2018/06/09/139-
taxi-medallions-will-be-offered-at-bankruptcy-auction/.

Campbell, Harry. "How to Deal With Drunk Passengers." *The Rideshare Guy*. Last
modified July 16, 2014. https://therideshareguy.com/how-to-deal-with-drunk-pass
engers/.

Campbell, Harry. "2018 Uber and Lyft Driver Survey Results." *The Rideshare Guy*.
Last modified February 26, 2018. https://therideshareguy.com/2018-uber-and-lyft
-driver-survey-results-the-rideshare-guy/.

Cannon, Michael F. "New Kaiser Survey Suggests ObamaCare Is Killing Jobs."
*Forbes*. Last modified September 16, 2016. https://www.forbes.com/sites/michae
lcannon/2016/09/16/new-survey-suggests-obamacare-killing-jobs/#1fcc13277654.

Canon, Scott. "Most Kansas City Taxis to Operate Like Uber and Lyft in Wake of
New State Law." *The Kansas City Star*. Last modified April 25, 2017. https://www
.kansascity.com/news/business/technology/article146776314.html.

Caplan, Arthur. "Medical Ethicist Arthur Caplan Explains Why He Opposes 'Right-
to-Try' Laws." *Oncology Journal* 30, no. 1 (2016). https://www.cancernetwork
.com/oncology-journal/medical-ethicist-arthur-caplan-explains-why-he-opposes
-right-try-laws.

Chamberlain, John. *The Enterprising Americans: A Business History of the United
States*. Texas: Institute for Christian Economics, 1991.

*Child Wellbeing Indicators & Data | KIDS COUNT Data Center*. KIDS COUNT
Data Center. https://datacenter.kidscount.org/data#USA/1/0/char/0.

Comptroller General. *FDA Drug Approval—A Lengthy Process that Delays the
Availability of Important New Drugs*. United States General Accounting Office.
Accessed October 9, 2018. https://www.gao.gov/assets/130/129558.pdf.

Corbett, Christianne and Catherine Hill. *Graduating to a Pay Gap: The Earnings of
Women and Men One Year after College Graduation*. Washington, DC: American
Association of University Women, 2012. https://www.aauw.org/files/2013/02/
graduating-to-a-pay-gap-the-earnings-of-women-and-men-one-year-after-college
-graduation.pdf.

Cuzzolin, Laura, Alessandra Atzei, and Vassilios Fanos. "Off-label and Unlicensed
Prescribing for Newborns and Children in Different Settings: A Review of the Literature and a Consideration about Drug Safety." *Expert Opinion on Drug Safety* 5,
no. 5 (2006): 703–718. https://doi.org/10.1517/14740338.5.5.703.

Davis, Lewis Anthony. "Review Procedures and Public Accountability in Sunset
Legislation: An Analysis and Proposal for Reform." *Administrative Law Review*
33, no. 4 (1981): 393–413. https://www.jstor.org/stable/40709182.

Daysog, Rick. "To Beat Uber and Lyft, Some Taxi Companies Are Trying to Become Them." *Hawaii News Now*. Last modified September 23, 2018. http://www.hawa iinewsnow.com/story/39016360/to-beat-uber-and-lyft-some-taxi-companies-are-trying-to-become-them/.

"Deaths from Liposuction Too High, Study Shows." *WebMD*. Last modified January 21, 2000. https://www.webmd.com/beauty/news/20000121/deaths-from-liposuctio n-too-high-study-shows#1.

Dills, Angela K. and Sean E. Mulholland. "Ride-Sharing, Fatal Crashes, and Crime." *Southern Economic Journal* 84, no. 4 (2017): 965–991. http://dx.doi.org/10.2139/ ssrn.2783797.

DiLorenzo, Thomas J. "Regulatory Extortion." *Foundation for Economic Education*. Last modified March 1, 2000. https://fee.org/articles/regulatory-extortion/.

DiMasi, Joseph A., Henry G. Grabowski, and Ronald W. Hansen. "Innovation in the Pharmaceutical Industry: New Estimates of R&D Costs." *Journal of Health Economics* 47 (2016): 20–33. https://doi.org/10.1016/j.jhealeco.2016.01.012.

DiMasi, Joseph A., Jeffery S. Brown, and Louis Lasagna. "An Analysis of Regulatory Review Times of Supplemental Indications for Already-Approved Drugs: 1989–1994." *Therapeutic Innovation & Regulatory Science* 30, no. 2 (1996): 315–337. https://doi.org/10.1177%2F009286159603000201.

Dobbs, David. "Is Airport Security Killing 500 People a Year?" *Wired*. Last modified April 5, 2012. https://www.wired.com/2012/04/is-airport-security-killing-500-peo ple-a-year/.

"Domestic Round-Trip Fares and Fees." *Airlines For America*. http://airlines.org/ dataset/annual-round-trip-fares-and-fees-domestic/.

Dreifus, Claudia. "Researcher Behind the Drug Gleevec." *The New York Times*. Last modified November 2, 2009. https://www.nytimes.com/2009/11/03/science/03 conv.html.

Durden, Tyler. "Argentine Judge Orders Arrest of Local Uber Executives, Shut Down of Uber Mobile App." *ZeroHedge*. Last modified January 30, 2017. https://ww w.zerohedge.com/news/2017-01-30/argentine-judge-orders-arrest-local-uber-ex ecutives-shut-down-uber-mobile-app.

"Economic News Release." *U.S. Department of Labor, Bureau of Labor Statistics*. Last modified December 18, 2018. https://www.bls.gov/news.release/cfoi.t01.htm.

Eddy, Mary Baker. "Liberty and Government." *The Christian Science Journal* 10, no. 8 (1902): 465. https://izquotes.com/quote/george-washington/government -is-not-reason-it-is-not-eloquent-it-is-force-like-fire-it-is-a-dangerous-servant-and -193683.

Edwards, Chris. "Options for Federal Privatization and Reform Lessons from Abroad." *Cato Institute*. Last modified June 28, 2016. https://www.cato.org/publ ications/policy-analysis/options-federal-privatization-reform-lessons-abroad.

Eidelson, Josh. "Uber-Union Proposal on Benefits Met With Skepticism From Labor." *Bloomberg*. Last modified January 25, 2018. https://www.bloomberg.com /news/articles/2018-01-25/uber-union-proposal-on-benefits-met-with-skepticism-from-labor.

Elliott, Christopher. "How Early Should You Really Arrive for Your Flight?" *USA Today*. Last modified February 20, 2017. https://www.usatoday.com/story/travel/advice/2017/02/19/how-early-to-arrive-before-flight/98036704/.

Ely, Bert. "Bad Rules Produce Bad Outcomes: Underlying Public-Policy Causes of the U.S. Financial Crisis." *Cato Journal* 29, no. 1 (2009): 93–114.

"Employer's Tax Guide to Fringe Benefits." *Internal Revenue Service* 15-B, no. 29744N (2018): 0–33. https://www.irs.gov/pub/irs-prior/p15b–2018.pdf.

"Employment by Major Industry Sector." *U.S. Bureau of Labor Statistics*. Last modified October 24, 2017. https://www.bls.gov/emp/tables/employment-by-major-industry-sector.htm.

"Employment Situation News Release." *U.S. Bureau of Labor Statistics*. Last modified October 5, 2018. https://www.bls.gov/news.release/archives/empsit_100520 18.htm.

Erikson, Clese, Karen Jones, and Casey Tilton. *2012 Physician Specialty Data Book*. Center for Workforce Studies, 2012, 7. https://www.aamc.org/download/313228/data/2012physicianspecialtydatabook.pdf.

Fan, Katherine. "Why Orlando Wants To Fire The TSA." *The Points Guy*. Last modified February 9, 2018. https://thepointsguy.com/2018/02/why-orlando-airport-wants-to-fire-the-tsa/.

Feeney, Matthew. "Is Ridesharing Safe?" *CATO Institute*. Last modified January 27, 2015. https://www.cato.org/publications/policy-analysis/ridesharing-safe.

Fleming, Susan. "Vehicle Safety Inspections." *U.S. Government Accountability Office*. Last modified August 25, 2015. https://www.gao.gov/products/GAO-15-705.

Folsom, Burton W. *The Myth of the Robber Barons: A New Look at the Rise of Big Business in America*. Virginia: Young Americas Foundation, 2007.

*Foreign Direct Investment, Net Inflows (BoP, current US$)*. The World Bank. https://data.worldbank.org/indicator/BX.KLT.DINV.CD.WD.

Frank, Burroughs. Personal interviews, September 2018.

*GDP (Current US$)*. The World Bank. Accessed September 5, 2018. https://data.worldbank.org/indicator/NY.GDP.MKTP.CD?end=2017&locations=US&start=1960&view=chart.

Gever, John. "ACR: A Tale of Vioxx, Opioids, and Falls." *Medpage Today*. Last modified November 12, 2010. https://www.medpagetoday.com/meetingcoverage/acr/23325?pop=0&ba=1&xid=tmd-md&hr=trendMD.

Gieringer, Dale H. "The Safety and Efficacy of New Drug Approval." *Cato Journal* 5, no. 1 (1985): 177–201. https://object.cato.org/sites/cato.org/files/serials/files/cato-journal/1985/5/cj5n1-10.pdf.

Ginsburg, Mitch. "How to Thwart a Gunman at 29,000 Feet, by the Only Pilot Who Ever Did." *The Times of Israel*. Last modified March 24, 2014. https://www.timesofisrael.com/how-to-defeat-airplane-terrorists-from-the-only-pilot-who-ever-foiled-a-skyjacking/.

Goldberg, Jeffrey. "The Things He Carried." *The Atlantic*. Last modified November, 2008. https://www.theatlantic.com/magazine/archive/2008/11/the-things-he-carried/307057/.

Goldman, Leah. "10 TSA Horror Stories of Pat-Downs Gone Wrong." *Business Insider.* Last modified November 22, 2010. https://www.businessinsider.com/tsa -security-horror-stories-2010–11.

Goldstein, Michael. "TSA Misses 70% of Fake Weapons But That's An Improvement." *Forbes Magazine.* Last modified November 9, 2017. https://www.forbes. com/sites/michaelgoldstein/2017/11/09/tsa-misses-70-of-fake-weapons-but-that s-an-improvement/#53bee20d2a38.

Goldstein, Michael. "Uber And Lyft Pound Taxis, Rental Cars In Business Travel Market." *Forbes.* Last modified February 22, 2018. https://www.forbes.com/sites/ michaelgoldstein/2018/02/22/uber-and-lyft-pound-taxis-rental-cars-in-business-tra vel-market/#4f77f98cb5e7.

Gonen, Yoav. "City Proposes Bill to Keep Log of Sexual Assaults in Taxis." *New York Post.* Last modified December 15, 2016. https://nypost.com/2016/12/15/city-proposes-bill-to-keep-log-of-sexual-assaults-in-taxis/.

Goodman, John C. *A Better Choice: Healthcare Solutions for America (Independent Studies in Political Economy).* Oakland: Independent Institute, 2015.

Gottlieb, Scott. "Statement from FDA Commissioner Scott Gottlieb, M.D., on the Signing of the Right to Try Act." *U.S. Food and Drug Administration.* Last modified May 30, 2018. https://www.fda.gov/newsevents/newsroom/pressannounceme nts/ucm609258.htm.

Greenwood, Brad N. and Sunil Wattal. "Show Me the Way to Go Home: An Empirical Investigation of Ride-Sharing and Alcohol Related Motor Vehicle Fatalities." *MIS Quarterly* 41, no. 1 (2017): 163–187. https://doi.org/10.25300/MISQ/2017/41.1.08.

Gwartney, James, Robert A. Lawson, Joshua C. Hall, Ryan Murphy, Robbie Butler, John Considine, Hugo J. Faria, Rosemarie Fike, Fred McMahon, Hugo M. Montesinos-Yufa, Dean Stansel, and Meg Tuszynski. "Economic Freedom of the World: 2016 Annual Report." *Fraser Institute.* Last modified September 15, 2016. https://www.fraserinstitute.org/studies/economic-freedom-of-the-world-2016-annual-report.

Hall, Jonathan and Alan B. Krueger. "An Analysis of the Labor Market for Uber's Driver-Partners in the United States." *The National Bureau of Economic Research* 71, no. 3 (2016): 705–732. https://doi.org/10.3386/w22843.

Hamblin, James. "The Disingenuousness of 'Right to Try'." *The Atlantic.* Last modified June 2, 2018. https://www.theatlantic.com/health/archive/2018/06/righ t-to-try/561770/.

Harlow, Caroline. "Education and Correctional Populations." *Bureau of Justice Statistics,* 2003. https://www.bjs.gov/index.cfm?ty=pbdetail&iid=814.

Harrington, Jason Edward. "Confessions of a Former TSA Officer." *The Week.* Last modified January 1, 2015. https://theweek.com/articles/441310/confessions-fo rmer-tsa-officer.

Harris, Gardiner. "F.D.A Official Admits 'Lapses' on Vioxx." *The New York Times.* Last modified March 2, 2005. https://www.nytimes.com/2005/03/02/politics/fda-of ficial-admits-lapses-on-vioxx.html.

*Health Insurance & Clinical Studies.* Seattle Cancer Care Alliance. Accessed November 30, 2018. https://www.seattlecca.org/patient-guide-clinical-trials/hea lth-insurance-and-clinical-trials.

Heimlich, John P. *Status of Air Travel in the USA*. Airlines for America, 2016. http://airlines.org/wp-content/uploads/2016/04/2016Survey.pdf.

Heisel, William. "Should Vioxx Still Be on the Market?" *Center for Health Journalism*. Last modified May 7, 2010. https://www.centerforhealthjournalism.org/blogs/should-vioxx-still-be-market.

Hemphill, Thomas A. "Extraordinary Pricing of Orphan Drugs: Is it a Socially Responsible Strategy for the U.S. Pharmaceutical Industry?" *Journal of Business Ethics* 94, no. 2 (2010): 225–242. https://link.springer.com/article/10.1007/s10551-009-0259-x.

Henderson, Diedtra and Christopher Rowland. "Once 'Too Slow,' FDA Approvals Called 'Too Fast'." *The Boston Globe*. Last modified April 10, 2005. http://archive.boston.com/news/nation/articles/2005/04/10/fda_criticized_as_too_quick_to_ok_drugs/.

Herlehy, Wm F. III and Tracy Ingalls-Ashbaugh. "Airline Employee Slowdowns and Sickouts as Unlawful Self Help: A Statistical Analysis." *Journal of Aviation/Aerospace* 3, no. 2 (1993): 0–11. https://commons.erau.edu/cgi/viewcontent.cgi?article=1090&context=jaaer.

Hernandez, Raymond. "Gypsy Cabs: A Hard, Chancy Life on the Side Streets of New York." *The New York Times*. Last modified September 24, 1992. https://www.nytimes.com/1992/09/24/nyregion/gypsy-cabs-a-hard-chancy-life-on-the-side-streets-of-new-york.html.

Herper, Matthew. "The Cost of Developing Drugs is Insane. That Paper That Says Otherwise Is Insanely Bad." *Forbes*. Last modified October 16, 2017. https://www.forbes.com/sites/matthewherper/2017/10/16/the-cost-of-developing-drugs-is-insane-a-paper-that-argued-otherwise-was-insanely-bad/#6b0659e52d45.

Hirshon, Lauren, Morgan Jones, Dana Levin, Kathryn McCarthy, Benjamin Morano, Sarah Simon, and Brooks Rainwater. *Cities, the Sharing Economy and What's Next*. National League of Cities, 2015. http://web.archive.org/web/20161108222255/http://www.nlc.org/Documents/Find%20City%20Solutions/City-Solutions-and-Applied-Research/Report%20-%20%20%20Cities%20the%20Sharing%20Economy%20and%20Whats%20Next%20final.pdf.

Hoffman, Liz, Greg Bensinger, and Maureen Farrell. "Uber Proposals Value Company at $120 Billion in a Possible IPO." *The Wall Street Journal*. Last modified October 16, 2018. https://www.wsj.com/articles/uber-proposals-value-company-at-120-billion-in-a-possible-ipo-1539690343.

"How Imatinib Transformed Leukemia Treatment and Cancer Research." *National Cancer Institute*. Last modified April 11, 2018. https://www.cancer.gov/research/progress/discovery/gleevec.

Huelskamp, Tim and Arianna Wilkerson. "Trump Keeps his Promise, Dying Patients Get a Second Chance at Life." *Washington Examiner*. Last modified June 4, 2018. https://www.washingtonexaminer.com/opinion/trump-keeps-promise-dying-patients-second-chance-at-life-right-to-try-act.

Huet, Ellen. "Uber, Lyft Cars Arrive Much Faster Than Taxis, Study Says." *Forbes*. Last modified September 8, 2014. https://www.forbes.com/sites/ellenhuet/2014/09/08/uber-lyft-cars-arrive-faster-than-taxis/#5ea0c45df2cb.

Hwang, Thomas J., Jonathan J. Darrow, and Aaron S. Kesselheim. "The FDA's Expedited Programs and Clinical Development Times for Novel Therapeutics, 2012–2016." *JAMA* 318, no. 21 (2017): 2137–2138. https://doi.org/10.1001/jama.2017.14896.

Hyde, Rachel R. "Uber–Safer Than a Regular Taxi?" *Investopedia.* Last modified October 19, 2018. https://www.investopedia.com/articles/professionals/102815/uber-safer-regular-taxi.asp.

Ijaz, Amna. "Security Theater Under President Trump." *Study Breaks.* Last modified March 28, 2017. https://studybreaks.com/news-politics/security-theater/.

Iliades, Chris. "How Safe Is the Food We Eat and Serve Our Families?" *Everyday Health.* Last modified June 15, 2018. https://www.everydayhealth.com/diet-nutrition-pictures/top-ten-food-contamination-culprits.aspx.

Inserra, David and Ceara Casterline. "Here's How Bad the TSA is Failing at Airport Security. It's Time for Privatization." *The Heritage Foundation.* Last modified November 20, 2017. https://www.heritage.org/transportation/commentary/heres-how-bad-the-tsa-failing-airport-security-its-time-privatization.

"Is an Uber Faster than an Ambulance?" *EMS1.* Last modified March 19, 2015. https://www.ems1.com/technology/articles/2139111-Trending-Is-an-Uber-faster-than-an-ambulance/.

Ivice, Paul. "Gator City Taxi Sued in 3 Deaths." *Jacksonville Business Journal.* Last modified July 21, 2003. https://www.bizjournals.com/jacksonville/stories/2003/07/21/story4.html.

Jaffe, Eric. "People in a Hurry Choose Uber Over Traditional Cabs." *CityLab.* Last modified August 29, 2014. https://www.citylab.com/life/2014/08/uber-has-an-enormous-wait-time-advantage-over-regular-taxis/379358/.

Jakubiak, Jeffrey M. "Maintaining Air Safety at Less Cost: A Plan for Replacing FAA Safety Regulations with Strict Liability." *Cornell Journal of Law and Public Policy* 6, no. 2 (1997). ISSN:0010-8847.

Jalbert, Jessica J., Louis L. Nguyen, and Marie D. Gerhard-Herman. "Outcomes After Carotid Artery Stenting in Medicare Beneficiaries, 2005–2009." *JAMA Neurol* 72, no. 3 (2015): 276–286. https://doi.org/10.1001/jamaneurol.2014.3638.

Jansen, Bart. "House Panel Blasts TSA Over Precheck Strategies." *USA Today.* Last modified February 27, 2018. https://www.usatoday.com/story/travel/flights/todayinthesky/2018/02/27/tsas-bomb-sniffing-dogs-allowing-travelers-precheck-raises-concerns-house-panel/376343002/.

Jensen, Michael C. and William H. Meckling. "Can the Corporation Survive?" *Financial Analysts Journal* 31, no. 1 (1978): 31–37. https://doi.org/10.2139/ssrn.244155.

Jones, Jeffrey M. and Thomas MaCurdy. *Welfare.* The Library of Economics and Liberty. Retrieved November 20, 2918. https://www.econlib.org/library/Enc/Welfare.html.

Josephson, Matthew. *Robber Barons.* Wilmington: Mariner Books, 1962.

Kaitin, K. I. and E. M. Healy. "The New Drug Approvals of 1996, 1997, and 1998: Drug Development Trends in the User Fee Era." *Drug Information Journal* 34, no. 1 (2000): 1–14. https://www.researchgate.net/publication/298813256_The_new_drug_approvals_of_1996_1997_and_1998_Drug_development_trends_in_the_user_fee_era.

Kao, Jennifer. *White Paper: Pharmaceutical Regulation and Off-Label Uses.* National Institute on Aging, 2016, 1–14. http://www.nber.org/aging/valmed/Wh itePaper-Kao9.2016.pdf.

Kazman, Sam. "Deadly Overcaution: FDA's Drug Approval Process." *Journal of Regulation and Social Costs* 1, no. 1 (1990): 35–54. http://cei.org/sites/default/ files/Sam%20Kazman%20-%20Deadly%20Overcatuion%20%20FDA%27s%20 Drug%20Approval%20Process.pdf.

Kazman, Sam. "Drug Approvals and Deadly Delays." *Journal of American Physicians and Surgeons* 15, no. 4 (2010): 101–103. http://www.jpands.org/vol15no4 /kazman.pdf.

Kennedy, Donald. "A Calm Look at 'Drug Lag'." *JAMA* 239, no. 5 (1978): 423–426. https://doi.org/10.1001/jama.1978.03280320039017.

Klein, Daniel B. and Alexander Tabarrok (a). *A History of Federal Regulation: 1902-Present.* FDA Review. Accessed October 12, 2018. http://www.fdareview .org/01_history.php#p01.

Klein, Daniel B. and Alexander Tabarrok (b). *Why the FDA Has an Incentive to Delay the Introduction of New Drugs.* FDA Review. Accessed October 16, 2018. http:// www.fdareview.org/06_incentives.php.

Klein, Daniel B. and Alexander Tabarrok (c). *Theory, Evidence and Examples of FDA Harm.* FDA Review. Accessed October 12, 2018. http://www.fdareview. org/05_harm.php.

Klein, Daniel B. and Alexander Tabarrok (d). *Quotations: Economists' Judgements about the FDA.* FDA Review. Accessed October 16, 2018. http://www.fdareview .org/12_quotations.php.

Klein, Daniel B. and Alexander Tabarrok (e). *Some Remarks about Medical Devices.* FDA Review. Accessed October 16, 2018. http://www.fdareview.org/08_devices.php.

Koc, Cagan and Ugur Yilmaz. "Why Uber Drivers Fear for Their Lives in Istanbul." *Bloomberg.* Last modified March 16, 2018. https://www.bloomberg.com/news/arti cles/2018-03-16/why-uber-drivers-fear-for-their-lives-in-istanbul.

Kolbert, Elizabeth. "NBC Settles Truck Crash Lawsuit, Saying Test Was 'Inappropriate'." *New York Times.* Last modified February 10, 1993. https://www.nytimes. com/1993/02/10/us/nbc-settles-truck-crash-lawsuit-saying-test-was-inappropriate. html.

Kramer, Mark. "The Perils of Counterinsurgency: Russia's War in Chechnya." *International Security* 29, no. 3 (2005): 5–63. https://doi.org/10.1162/01622880434 67450.

Krauskopf, Lewis. "Merck Agrees to Pay $4.85 billion in Vioxx Settlement." *Reuters.* Last modified November 9, 2007. https://www.reuters.com/article/us-merck-viox x-settlement/merck-agrees-to-pay-4-85-billion-in-vioxx-settlement-idUSL0929 726620071109.

Krauss, Michael I. "Loosening the FDA's Drug Certification Monopoly: Implications for Tort Law and Consumer Welfare." *George Mason Law Review* 4, no. 3 (1996): 457–483. http://georgemasonlawreview.org/archives/vol-4-no-3-spring-1996/.

Laband, David. "In Hugo's Path, a Man-Made Disaster." *Wall Street Journal*, 1989. http://academic.udayton.edu/Lawecon/Assignments/Contracts/In%20hugos%2 0path.pdf.

Lafrance, Adrienne and Rose Eveleth. "Are Taxis Safer Than Uber?" *The Atlantic*. Last modified March 3, 2015. https://www.theatlantic.com/technology/archive/201 5/03/are-taxis-safer-than-uber/386207/.

Lapidos, Juliet. "Does the TSA Ever Catch Terrorists?" *Slate Magazine*. Last modified November 18, 2010. https://slate.com/news-and-politics/2010/11/does-the-ts a-ever-catch-terrorists.html.

Lebergott, Stanley. "Labor Force and Employment, 1800–1960." *National Bureau of Employment Research*, 1966, 118. http://www.nber.org/chapters/c1567.pdf.

Lephardt, George P. and Joseph L. Bast. *The Economics of Taxicab Deregulation*. Heartland Institute Policy Study no. 3, 1985. https://www.heartland.org/publicati ons-resources/publications/the-economics-of-taxicab-deregulation.

Liddell, Nicholas. "So Where Does Uber's Value Come From Anyway?" *The Drum*. Last modified July 4, 2017. https://www.thedrum.com/opinion/2017/07/04/so -where-does-uber-s-value-come-anyway.

Lott, John R. "A Look at the Facts on Gun-Free Zones." *National Review*. Last modified October 20, 2015. https://www.nationalreview.com/2015/10/gun-free-zones-dont-save-lives-right-to-carry-laws-do/.

Marcus, Amy Dockser. "Frustrated ALS Patients Concoct Their Own Drug." *The Wall Street Journal*. Last modified April 15, 2012. https://www.wsj.com/articles/ SB10001424052702304818404577345953943484054.

Martín, Hugo. "Security Screening among Travelers' Top Annoyances, Survey Finds." *Los Angeles Times*. Last modified November 17, 2011. http://articles.lati mes.com/2011/nov/17/business/la-fi-tsa-survey-20111117.

Martin-Buck, Frank. *Driving Safety: An Empirical Analysis of Ridesharing's Impact on Drunk Driving and Alcohol-Related Crime*. Semantic Scholar, 2016. https:// pdfs.semanticscholar.org/3f1e/b273fcee888441147105882dd12ca811fd35.pdf?_ ga=2.18155449.1886715707.1550434077-2084686916.1550434077.

McFadden, Robert D. "Frances Oldham Kelsey, Who Saved U.S. Babies From Thalidomide, Dies at 101." *The New York Times*. Last modified August 7, 2015. https:// www.nytimes.com/2015/08/08/science/frances-oldham-kelsey-fda-doctor-who-exposed-danger-of-thalidomide-dies-at-101.html.

McKinley, Vern. "Sunrises without Sunsets Can Sunset Laws Reduce Regulation?" *Regulation* (1995): 57–64. https://object.cato.org/sites/cato.org/files/serials/files/r egulation/1995/10/v18n4-6.pdf.

Meng, Rufeng, Chengfeng Mao, and Romit Roy Choudhury. "Driving Analytics: Will it be OBDs or Smartphones?" *Zendrive*. https://s3.amazonaws.com/download.zendri ve.com/ResearchPapers/Zendrive+Whitepaper+-+Smartphone+Sensors+vs+OBD.pdf.

Meyer, Jared. "Uber-Positive: The Ride-Share Firm Expands Transportation Options in Low-Income New York." *Manhattan Institute for Policy Research*. Last modified September 7, 2015. https://www.manhattan-institute.org/html/uber-positive-ride-share-firm-expands-transportation-options-low-income-new-york-6703.html.

Miller, Henry. *To America's Health: A Proposal to Reform the Food and Drug Administration*. Stanford: Hoover Institution Press, 2000.

Miller, Henry and Gregory Conko. "The First Amendment Applies to the FDA Too." *Reason*. Last modified March 6, 2018. https://reason.com/archives/2018/03/06/t he-first-amendment-applies-to-the-fda-t.

Moore, Adrian T. and Ted Balaker. "Do Economists Reach a Conclusion on Taxi Deregulation?" *Econ Journal Watch* 3, no. 1 (2006): 109–132. https://econjwatch. org/File+download/103/2006-01-moorebalaker-reach_concl.pdf?mimetype=pdf.

*Mortality Risk Valuation.* EPA. https://www.epa.gov/environmental-economics/m ortality-risk-valuation.

Moskatel, Leon S. and David J. G. Slusky. *Did UberX Reduce Ambulance Volume?* University of Kansas, 2017. http://www2.ku.edu/~kuwpaper/2017Papers/20170 8.pdf.

Mueller, John E. and Mark G. Stewart. *Terror, Security, and Money: Balancing the Risks, Benefits, and Costs of Homeland Security.* New York: Oxford University Press, 2011.

Munzenrieder, Kyle. "Uber's Surge Prices Hit 9.9 Times the Normal Fare in Miami Beach During New Year's Eve." *Miami New Times.* Last modified January 4, 2016. https://www.miaminewtimes.com/news/ubers-surge-prices-hit-99-times-the-norm al-fare-in-miami-beach-during-new-years-eve-8148437.

*Myths vs. Facts About Clinical Studies.* Seattle Cancer Care Alliance. Accessed October 6, 2018. https://www.seattlecca.org/guide-clinical-trials/making-decision/ myths-vs-facts-about-clinical-studies.

"No Way to Treat a Criminal." *The Economist.* Last modified July 5, 2014. https://www. economist.com/leaders/2014/07/05/no-way-to-treat-a-criminal.

Nunn, Ryan. "The Future of Occupational Licensing Reform." *Brookings.* Last modified January 30, 2017. https://www.brookings.edu/opinions/the-future-of-occupa tional-licensing-reform/.

Odell, Kate Bachelder. "When Medical Innovation Meets Politics." *The Wall Street Journal.* Last modified August 24, 2018. https://www.wsj.com/articles/when-medical-innovation-meets-politics-1535147861.

O'Donnell, Christopher. "PTC Used Workers from Taxicab and Limo Firms to Nab Uber and Lyft Drivers." *Tampa Bay Times.* Last modified October 14, 2016. https:// www.tampabay.com/news/transportation/ptc-used-workers-from-taxicab-and-limo-firms-to-nab-uber-and-lyft-drivers/2297994.

Ogg, John. "This Is How Long You'll Wait at 40 Largest Airports." *The Wall Street Journal.* January 16, 2019.

Ohnsman, Alan. "Uber's Workplace Harassment Probe Results in At Least 20 Firings." *Forbes.* Last modified June 6, 2017. https://www.forbes.com/sites/alanoh nsman/2017/06/06/ubers-sexual-harassment-probe-results-in-at-least-20-firings/#3 16875d77960.

Olson, Walter. "It Didn't Start with the Dateline NBC." *National Review.* Last modified June 21, 1993. http://walterolson.com/articles/crashtests.html.

Palmaro, Aurore, Raphael Bissuel, Nicholas Renaud, Genevieve Durrieu, Brigitte Escourrou, Stephane Oustric, Jean L. Montastruc, and Maryse Lapeyre-Mestre. "Off-Label Prescribing in Pediatric Outpatients." *Pediatrics* 135, no. 1 (2015): 49–58. https://doi.org/10.1542/peds.2014-0764.

Peck, Jessica Lynn. *New York City Drunk Driving After Uber.* CUNY Academic Works, 2017. https://academicworks.cuny.edu/cgi/viewcontent.cgi?article=1 012&context=gc_econ_wp.

Peltzman, Sam. "An Evaluation of Consumer Protection Legislation: The 1962 Drug Amendments." *Journal of Political Economy* 81, no. 5 (1973): 1049–1091. https://www.jstor.org/stable/1830639?seq=1#metadata_info_tab_contents.

Pennacchi, George. "Narrow Banking." *Annual Review of Financial Economics* 4 (2012): 1–36. https://business.illinois.edu/gpennacc/GPNarrowBankARFE.pdf.

Perry, Mark J. "Thanks to a Private-public Taxi Cartel in NYC, the Value of a Taxi Medallion has Increased 5X Times Faster than the S&P500." *American Enterprise Institute.* Last modified April 6, 2014. http://www.aei.org/publication/thanks-to-a-private-public-taxi-cartel-in-nyc-the-value-of-a-taxi-medallion-has-increased-5x-times-faster-than-the-sp500/.

Perry, Mark J. "The Public Thinks the Average Company makes a 36% Profit Margin, Which is about 5X Too High." *American Enterprise Institute.* Last modified April 2, 2015. http://www.aei.org/publication/the-public-thinks-the-average-company-makes-a-36-profit-margin-which-is-about-5x-too-high/.

Philipson, Tomas J. and Eric Sun. *Is the Food and Drug Administration Safe and Effective?* National Bureau of Economic Research no. 13561, 2007. https://doi.org/10.3386/w13561.

Poitras, Marc and Daniel Sutter. "Policy Ineffectiveness or Offsetting Behavior? An Analysis of Vehicle Safety Inspections." *Southern Economic Journal* 68, no. 4 (2002): 922–934. https://www.jstor.org/stable/1061500?seq=1#page_scan_tab_contents.

Poole, Robert W., Jr. "Instead of Regulation: Alternatives to Federal Regulatory Agencies." *Southern Economic Journal* 49, no. 3 (1983): 207–227. https://doi.org/10.2307/1058750.

*Preventing Violence against Taxi and For-Hire Drivers.* OSHA, 2010. https://www.osha.gov/Publications/taxi-driver-violence-factsheet.pdf.

Pulham, Mark. "The Son of Sam." *Crime Magazine.* Last modified June 26, 2012. http://www.crimemagazine.com/son-sam.

*Quick Facts on Registered Nurses.* U.S. Department of Labor, Bureau of Labor Statistics. Accessed September 5, 2018. https://www.dol.gov/wb/factsheets/Qf-nursing.htm.

Ravallion, Martin and Menno Prasad Pradhan. *Demand for Public Safety.* World Bank Policy Research Working Paper no. 2043, 1999. SSRN: https://ssrn.com/abstract=604914.

Reilly, Katie. "Shoplifting and Other Fraud Cost Relaters Nearly $50 Billion Last Year." *Money.* Last modified June 22, 2017. http://money.com/money/4829684/shoplifting-fraud-retail-survey/.

Rolita, Lydia, Adele Spegman, Xiaoqin Tang, and Bruce N. Cronstein. "Greater Number of Narcotic Analgesic Prescriptions for Osteoarthritis Is Associated with Falls and Fractures in Elderly Adults." *Journal of the American Geriatrics Society* 61, no. 3 (2013): 335–340. https://doi.org/10.1111/jgs.12148.

Roosevelt, Franklin D. "Quotation Details." *The Quotations Page.* Last modified March 4, 1933. http://www.quotationspage.com/quote/3787.html.

Ross, Joseph S. and Harlan M. Krumholz. "Bringing Vioxx back to Market." *BMJ* 360 (2018). https://doi.org/10.1136/bmj.k242.

Rozumberkova, Martina. "The 'Right to Try Act': Another Compliance Requirement for Pharma and Biotech Companies." *Forbes*. Last modified June 11, 2018. https://www.forbes.com/sites/riskmap/2018/06/11/the-right-to-try-act-another-complian ce-requirement-for-pharma-and-biotech-companies/#151b0d4c2c2a.

"Salmonella." *Centers for Disease Control and Prevention*. Last modified February 21, 2019. https://www.cdc.gov/salmonella/index.html.

Samuelson, William and Richard Zeckhauser. "Status Quo Bias in Decision Making." *Journal of Risk and Uncertainty* no. 1 (1988): 7–59. https://sites.hks.harvard.edu/ fs/rzeckhau/status%20quo%20bias.pdf.

"Schiavo Criticizes FAA's 'Tombstone Mentality'." *The Washington Post*. https://www.washingtonpost.com/archive/business/1997/03/26/schiavo-criticizes-faas-to mbstone-mentality/dc79d429-b6bd-47ff-92345c77b1ac2154/?noredirect=on&u tm_term=.ab03510485d7.

Schleifer, Theodore. "Uber's Latest Valuation: $72 billion." *Recode*. Last modified February 9, 2018. https://www.recode.net/2018/2/9/16996834/uber-latest-valuati on-72-billion-waymo-lawsuit-settlement.

Schnee, Jerome E. "Regulation and Innovation: U.S. Pharmaceutical Indus-try." *California Management Review* 22, no. 1 (1979): 23–32. https://doi. org/10.2307%2F41164846.

Schneier, Bruce. "Why Are We Spending $7 Billion on TSA? (Opinion)." *CNN*. Last modified June 05, 2015. https://www.cnn.com/2015/06/05/opinions/schneier-t sa-security/index.html.

Shaw, David, Guido de Wert, Wybo Dondorp, David Townend, Gerard Bos, and Michael van Gelder. "Permitting Patients to Pay for Participation in Clinical Tri-als: The Advent of the P4 Trial." *Medicine, Health Care and Philosophy* 20, no. 2 (2017): 219–227. https://dx.doi.org/10.1007%2Fs11019-016-9741-2.

Shen, Lucinda. "Here's Where the $110 Billion in Wall Street Fines Went." *Fortune*. Last modified March 10, 2016. http://fortune.com/2016/03/10/bank-mortgage-f ines-wall-street/.

Shermer, Michael. "Why People Don't Trust Free Markets." *Michael Shermer*. Last modified January 29, 2008. https://michaelshermer.com/2008/01/why-people-dont -trust-free-markets/.

Shermer, Michael. "The Mind of the Market." *Michael Shermer*. Last modified Feb-ruary 2008. https://michaelshermer.com/2008/02/mind-of-the-market/.

Sinclair, Upton. *The Jungle*. Amazon Classic Edition, 2017.

Smallen, Dave. "2017 Traffic Data for U.S. Airlines and Foreign Airlines U.S. Flights." *Bureau of Transportation Statistics*. Last modified March 22, 2018. https://www.bts.gov/newsroom/2017-traffic-data-us-airlines-and-foreign-airlines-us-flights.

Smith, Aaron. "Shared, Collaborative and On Demand: The New Digital Economy; 2. On-demand: Ride-hailing Apps." *Pew Research Center: Internet & Technology*. Last modified May 19, 2016. http://www.pewinternet.org/2016/05/19/on-dema nd-ride-hailing-apps/.

Smith, Tony. "Are the Drug-regulatory Agencies Paper Villains?" *British Medical Journal* 281 (1980): 1333. Accessed October 9, 2018. https://doi.org/10.1136/bmj.281.6251.1333.

Snead, Jason. "Taxicab Medallion Systems: Time for a Change." *The Heritage Foundation*. Last modified December 10, 2015. https://www.heritage.org/transportation/report/taxicab-medallion-systems-time-change.

*Some Remarks about "Safety"*. FDA Review. Accessed October 12, 2018. http://www.fdareview.org/04_safety.php.

"State Nonfiscal Public Elementary/Secondary Education Survey Data: 1995–96 through 2013–14." *National Characteristics for Education Statistics*. Last modified February, 2016. https://nces.ed.gov/ccd/stnfis.asp.

Stigler, George J. "The Theory of Economic Regulation." *The Bell Journal of Economics and Management Science* 2, no. 1 (1971): 3–21. http://pirate.shu.edu/~rotthoku/Liberty/stigler_theory%20of%20econ%20regulation.pdf.

Stone, Brad. *The Upstarts: How Uber, Airbnb, and the Killer Companies of the New Silicon Valley Are Changing the World*. New York: Little, Brown and Company, 2017.

Sullivan, Thomas. "A Tough Road: Cost To Develop One New Drug is $2.6 Billion; Approval Rate for Drugs Entering Clinical Development is Less Than 12%." *Policy and Medicine*. Last modified May 6, 2018. https://www.policymed.com/2014/12/a-tough-road-cost-to-develop-one-new-drug-is-26-billion-approval-rate-for-drugs-entering-clinical-de.html.

Summers, Adam B. *Occupational Licensing: Ranking the States and Exploring Alternatives*. Reason Foundation, 2007. https://reason.org/wp-content/uploads/2007/08/762c8fe96431b6fa5e27ca64eaa1818b.pdf.

Sundararajan, Arun. *The Sharing Economy: The End of Employment and the Rise of Crowd-Based Capitalism*. Cambridge: MIT Press, 2016.

Sygnatur, Eric F. and Guy A. Toscano. *Work-related Homicides: The Facts*. Bureau of Labor Statistics, 2000. https://www.bls.gov/opub/mlr/cwc/work-related-homicides-the-facts.pdf.

Tabarrok, Alexander T. "Assessing the FDA via the Anomaly of Off-Label Drug Prescribing." *The Independent Review* 5, no. 1 (2000): 25–53. http://www.independent.org/pdf/tir/tir_05_1_tabarrok.pdf.

"Table B-3. Average Hourly and Weekly Earnings of All Employees on Private Nonfarm Payrolls by Industry Sector, Seasonally Adjusted." *U.S. Bureau of Labor Statistics*. Last modified February 1, 2019. https://www.bls.gov/news.release/empsit.t19.htm.

Taylor, John B. *Getting Off Track: How Government Actions and Interventions Caused, Prolonged, and Worsened the Financial Crisis*. Stanford: Hoover Institution Press, 2009.

*The Abigail Alliance for Better Access to Developmental Drugs*. The Abigail Alliance. https://www.abigail-alliance.org/.

"The Criminalisation of American Business." *The Economist*. Last modified August 28, 2014. https://www.economist.com/leaders/2014/08/28/the-criminalisation-of-american-business.

*The Drug Development and Approval Process*. FDA Review. Accessed October 12, 2018. http://www.fdareview.org/03_drug_development.php.

Thomas, Lacy Glenn. "Regulation and Firm Size: FDA Impacts on Innovation." *The Rand Journal of Economics* 21, no. 4 (1990): 497–517. https://doi.org/10.2307/2555465.

Thompson, Deanne. "News Releases." *John Wayne Airport, Orange County*. Last modified October 12, 2018. https://www.ocair.com/newsroom/news/default?nr=nr-2018-10-12&tr=no.

Thulin, Lila. "In 2018, Should We Take Ubers or Ambulances to the Hospital?" *Slate*. Last modified February 12, 2018. https://slate.com/technology/2018/02/when-should-you-uber-to-the-hospital-and-when-should-you-call-an-ambulance.html.

Tovanche, Juan Joel. "Dying to Wait: How the Abigail Court Got It Wrong." *Journal of Law and Health* 22, no. 53 (2009): 52–90. https://engagedscholarship.csuohio.edu/jlh/vol22/iss1/5/.

Triplett, Jack E. *The Measurement of Labor Cost*. Chicago: University of Chicago Press, 1983.

Trowbridge, Ronald L. and Steven Walker. "The FDA's Deadly Track Record." *The Wall Street Journal*. Last modified August 14, 2007. https://www.wsj.com/articles/SB118705547735996773.

Tversky, Amos and Daniel Kahneman. "Availability: A Heuristic for Judging Frequency and Probability." *Cognitive Psychology* 5 (1973): 207–232. https://msu.edu/~ema/803/Ch11-JDM/2/TverskyKahneman73.pdf.

United States Congress House. *Misconduct, Retaliation, and Obstruction at the Transportation Security Administration: Majority Staff Report, 115th Congress*. By Trey Gowdy, Chairman. Washington, DC: U.S. House of Representatives, 2018.

"Usual Weekly Earnings of Wage and Salary Workers Second Quarter 2018." *Bureau of Labor Statistics*. Last modified July 17, 2018. https://www.bls.gov/news.release/pdf/wkyeng.pdf.

Vega, Nicolas. "Uber Will Know If You're Drunk before You Even Get into the Car." *New York Post*. Last modified June 11, 2018. https://nypost.com/2018/06/11/uber-will-know-if-youre-drunk-before-you-even-get-into-the-car/.

Viscusi, Kip. *The Value of Life*. Harvard Law School, 2005. http://www.law.harvard.edu/programs/olin_center/papers/pdf/Viscusi_517.pdf.

Wardell, William M. "A Close Inspection of the 'Calm Look': Rhetorical Amblyopia and Selective Amnesia at the Food and Drug Administration." *JAMA* 239, no. 19 (1978): 2004–2011. https://doi.org/10.1001/jama.1978.03280460072023.

Warren, Tom. "Uber is Tracking its Drivers to See if They're Speeding or Braking Too Hard." *The Verge*. Last modified January 26, 2016. https://www.theverge.com/2016/1/26/10832314/uber-driver-tracking-gps.

Weaver, Paul H. *The Suicidal Cooperation*. New York: Touchstone, 1989.

Weimer, David L. "Safe and Available Drugs." In *Instead of Regulation: Alternative to Federal Regulatory Agencies*, edited by Robert Poole Jr. Lexington: D.C. Health, 1982.

Wellness, Berkeley. "Are These Claims Kosher?" *Berkeley Wellness*. Last modified January 14, 2017. http://www.berkeleywellness.com/healthy-eating/food-safety/article/are-these-claims-kosher.

Wildavsky, Aaron. *Searching for Safety*. New Brunswick: Transaction Publishers, 1988.

Williams, Walter E. *The State Against Blacks*. New York: McGraw-Hill Companies, 1984.

Yamanouchi, Kelly. "Survey: Airport Security Remains One of Biggest 'Pain Points' of Travel." *AJC*. Last modified October 24, 2017. https://www.myajc.com/blog/airport/survey-airport-security-remains-one-biggest-pain-points-travel/HpGKQQJdM8dE6za0RJAw7H/.

Yin, Wesley. "R&D Policy, Agency Costs and Innovation in Personalized Medicine." *Journal of Health Economics* 28, no. 5 (2009): 950–962. https://pdfs.semanticscholar.org/2cff/65143ec9a06903975e1e780a224347a39631.pdf.

Youshaei, Jon. "The Uberpreneur: How An Uber Driver Makes $252,000 A Year." *Forbes*. Last modified February 4, 2015. https://www.forbes.com/sites/jonyoushaei/2015/02/04/the-uberpreneur-how-an-uber-driver-makes-252000-a-year/#4a5e18424e8e.

# Index

# About the Author

**Thomas Tacker**, PhD, is professor of economics at Embry-Riddle Aeronautical University in Daytona Beach. He received his doctoral degree from the University of North Carolina, Chapel Hill. He has published numerous academic papers as well as a number of publications in the popular press. He won the *National Federation of Independent Businesses Award for Most Outstanding Paper on Entrepreneurship and Public Policy*. Professor Tacker has also won several teaching awards, including the *Leavey Award for Excellence in Private Enterprise Education*. In addition to his present position, over the years Professor Tacker has taught at the University of North Carolina at Chapel Hill, Wake Forrest University, North Carolina State University, Salem College, Rollins College, and the University of Central Florida. Much of the material in this book has been developed and shaped by numerous conversations with a wide variety of undergraduate, graduate, and professional students.

Made in United States
Orlando, FL
14 January 2024